Causation in Educational Research

Calls to understand 'what works' in education are being made the world over. We need to know not only 'what works' but under what conditions, how and why. Causation is central to this. Researchers, educationists, readers and users of research need to know the effects of causes and the causes of effects. This strongly practical book helps researchers and readers of research understand, plan and investigate causation in education. It guides readers through statistical matters, explaining them clearly and simply in words as well as numbers, and shows them how to investigate qualitative causal research in education.

After introducing deterministic and probabilistic causation, the book shows how these can be researched in different ways. It explains:

- how to determine causes from effects and how to link theory and practice in causal research
- how to plan and conduct causal research in education
- how to analyze, present and interpret causal data and the limits of causal understanding.

Containing worked examples from both qualitative and quantitative research, *Causation in Educational Research* provides a manual for practice, underpinned by a rigorous analysis of key issues from philosophy, sociology and psychology. It will appeal to new and established researchers, readers of educational research, social science students and academics.

Keith Morrison has worked in the UK and East Asia, formerly at the University of Durham, UK, and in Macau, as Vice-Rector. He is the author of thirteen books, including *Research Methods in Education* (6th edition) and *A Guide to Teaching Practice* (5th edition). He is the editor of the journal *Evaluation and Research in Education*.

Causation in Educational Research

Keith Morrison

Routledge
Taylor & Francis Group

LONDON AND NEW YORK

First published 2009
by Routledge
2 Park Square, Milton Park, Abingdon, Oxon OX14 4RN

Simultaneously published in the USA and Canada
by Routledge
270 Madison Ave, New York, NY 10016

Routledge is an imprint of the Taylor & Francis Group, an informa business

© 2009 Keith Morrison

Typeset in Garamond by
Book Now, London
Printed and bound in Great Britain by
TJ International Ltd, Padstow, Cornwall

British Library Cataloguing in Publication Data
A catalogue record for this book is available from the British Library

Library of Congress Cataloging in Publication Data
Morrison, Keith (Keith R. B.)
Causation in educational research / Keith Morrison.
        p. cm.
1. Education—Research. 2. Causation. I. Title.
LB1028.M665 2009
370.7′2—dc22   2008052127

ISBN13: 978–0–415–49648–3 (hbk)
ISBN13: 978–0–415–49649–0 (pbk)

ISBN10: 0–415–49648–9 (hbk)
ISBN10: 0–415–49649–7 (pbk)

For Fun Hei, who brings happiness

Contents

4   Approaching cause and effect   108

5   Determining the effects of causes   138

Figures

Tables

Preface

This book addresses causation for educational researchers. Calls for understanding 'what works' in education are being made the world over. We need to know not only 'what works' but also for whom, under what conditions, how and why, on what criteria, why they work in the way that they do, and why some interventions do not work. This places causation at centre stage. If educational practice is to advance then we need to know 'what causes what', what are the effects of causes, and what are the causes of effects. Why do things happen as they do?

The chapters here introduce and work with the fascinating debate on causation that has been running for hundreds of years. The study of causation is not straightforward. Causation is elusive; indeed, the further one goes into it, the more elusive it becomes. A causal explanation slips through your fingers just when you think you have found it. Simplistic ideas of 'what causes what' must be abandoned, and this is an important message that must be sounded loud and long to policy makers and researchers. John Locke's simple statement that 'a *cause* is that which makes any other thing, either simple idea, substance, or mode, begin to be; and an *effect* is that which had its beginning from some other thing' (Locke, 1997: 293) disguises the immense complexity of causation.

This book provides an introduction to causation, sets out key debates, and, above all, seeks to raise practical and theoretical matters, problems and their solutions in understanding causation. It is strongly practical in intent. If it makes researchers cautious of having any sense of certainty at all about causation, then this small volume will have done its work. We strive to understand causes and effects, but the task is not straightforward. At best we can make inferences and suggestions about causation, but that is all. We do not have the perfect knowledge required for causation to be established. This applies to those reading, using and doing research.

Writing this book has made me very sceptical of ever knowing 'what causes what', but it has made me want to try harder to find out, rather than to give up. Instead of the sometimes banal certainties of politicians, the careful researcher should have a large helping of modesty and humility in claiming that she or he might know the effects of causes or the causes of effects, and why things do or do not happen in the way that they do. In that spirit of modesty I hope that this book offers practical advice to researchers and those seeking to understand some limits of educational research and what can be said from it.

Keith Morrison
Macau

Acknowledgements

This book is dedicated to my wife, who has brought happiness in my life that I cannot express in words.

I owe an immeasurable debt to Professor Louis Cohen and our dear friend Lawrence Manion for having had faith in me many years ago to support my writing.

My thanks are due to Taylor and Francis Books UK for permission to use the following materials in this text: Cohen, L., Manion, L. and Morrison, K. R. B. (2007) *Research Methods in Education* (6th edition), pp. 264, 274–5.

Chapter 1

The world of cause and effect

The human mind is a wonderful analogue processor. It is the most sophisticated learning processor that we know. And it learns by telling stories for itself, stories of how things are, how they came to be, what is really happening, what will happen next, and why – in short, by thinking causally, filtering out the causally relevant from the causally irrelevant. Parents will know both the joy and the frustration of that period of their child's life when he or she endlessly asks 'why?'.

At the heart of learning and development lies causation: as Hume remarks in his work *An Inquiry Concerning Human Understanding*: 'on this are founded all our reasonings concerning matter of fact or existence' (Hume 1955: 87). Whether or not the world itself develops and emerges through cause and effect is largely immaterial; in order to avoid circularity, this book assumes that we think and we learn in part through cause and effect. Causation is both an ontological and an epistemological matter. This is unremarkable. However, how this happens is truly marvellous, for, as this book will argue, it involves a sophisticated process of evaluation and filtering, weighing up competing causal influences and judging exactly what each shows or promises. Whether we simply impose our way of thinking – in terms of cause and effect – on unrelated objects and events in order to understand them for ourselves, regardless of the fact that such cause and effect may or may not exist 'out there' in the objective world – i.e. that cause and effect is a theoretical construct used heuristically for humans to understand their world – is debatable. *Pace* Wittgenstein, the limits of our ways of thinking may define the limits of our world. The world may be disordered, unrelated and, in terms of cause and effect, insubstantial, but it's nearly all we have; it's all we can do in order to understand it.

Are we to believe Russell (1913: 1), who wrote that 'the law of causality, I believe, like much that passes muster among philosophers, is a relic of a bygone age, surviving, like the monarchy, only because it is erroneously supposed to do no harm', or Pearson (1892), who considered causation to be a mere 'fetish' that should be overtaken by measures of correlation, or Pinker (2007: 209), who reports some philosophers as saying that causation is as shoddy as the material used in Boston tunnels and should be kissed goodbye, or Gorard (2001), who writes that 'our notion of cause is little more than a superstition'? I think not. Maybe causation has little mileage for philosophers, but for social scientists it is a fundamental way of understanding our world, and we have to engage it. Indeed Pinker (2007: 219–20) shows how causation is deeply entrenched in our everyday language, in such phrases as causing, preventing, moving in spite of a hindrance, and keeping still despite being pushed.

There are several reasons why understanding and using causation are important (e.g. Lewis 1993; Salmon 1998: 3–10). For example, causation:

- helps us to explain events;
- helps us to get to the heart of a situation;
- helps us to understand why and how things happen;
- helps us to control our lives;
- helps us to manipulate our environment;
- helps us to predict events and outcomes;
- helps us to evaluate proposals and policies;
- helps us to establish 'what works';
- helps us to plan for improvements;
- can inform policy making;
- helps us to build knowledge cumulatively over time;
- helps us to control events to some extent;
- helps us to attribute responsibility and liability;
- is the way we think.

Understanding and using causation may not be straightforward. Indeed Glymour (1997: 202) argues that there is no settled definition of causation, but that it includes 'something subjunctive'. Causation is a multi-dimensional and contested phenomenon. Humeans would argue that *temporality* is a marker of causation: one event has to precede or proceed from another in time for causation to obtain. Hume provides a double definition of causation (see his work *A Treatise of Human Nature*; Hume 2000: 1.3.14: 35):[1]

> An object precedent and contiguous to another, and where all the objects resembling the former are plac'd in a like relation of priority and contiguity to those objects, that resemble the latter.

> An object precedent and contiguous to another, and so united with it in the imagination, that the idea of the one determines the mind to form the idea of the other, and the impression of the one to form a more lively idea of the other.

He adds to this in his *Inquiry*:

> An object followed by another, and where all the objects similar to the first are followed by objects similar to the second. Or, in other words, where, if the first object had not been, the second had never existed.
>
> (Hume 1955: 87)

The Humean model of priority and contiguity is represented in Figure 1.1. Note that the boxes of cause and effect are joined (the 'contiguity' requirement) and touch each other in time; there is no gap between the boxes and the arrow. Further, the cause only ever precedes the effect (the 'priority' requirement).

These are starting points only – indeed, they conceal more that they reveal – and this chapter will open up the definitions to greater scrutiny. Though Hume is concerned with regularities, other views also have to do with inferences and probabilities, and this opens the door to a range of issues in considering causation.

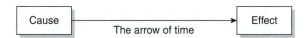

Figure 1.1 Priority and contiguity in cause and effect

A fundamental tenet from Hume's disarmingly simple yet profound analysis is that causation cannot be deduced by logic nor, indeed, can it be directly observed in experience (see also Fisher 1951; Holland 2004). Rather, it can only be inferred from the cumulative and repeated experience of one event following another (his 'constant conjunction' principle, in which the individual learns that if one event is followed by another repeatedly then it can be inferred that there is a probability that the two may be connected). This is questioned by Ducasse (1993), who argues that recurrence is not a necessary requirement of causation, that it is irrelevant whether a cause-and-effect event happens more than once, and that it only becomes relevant if one wishes to establish a causal *law* (Hume's 'regularity of succession'). Indeed Holland (1986: 950) suggests that Hume's analysis misses the effect that other contiguous causes may have on an effect.

Our knowledge of causation is inductive and the uncertainty and unpredictability of induction inhere in it. As a consequence, knowledge of causation is provisional, conjectural and refutable. It is learned from our memory – individual or collective – as well as perhaps being deduced from logic or observation (see also Salmon 1998: 15). Indeed, so strong is the inferential nature of causation that we can, at best, think in terms of probabilistic causation rather than laws of causation. This is a major issue that underpins much of this book.

We have to step back and ask 'What actually is a cause?' and 'What actually is an effect?': an event, a single action, a process, a linkage of events, a reason, a motive? One feature of causation is its attempt to link two independent, in principle unrelated events. 'Minimal independence' (Sosa and Tooley 1993: 7) is a fundamental requisite of causation, or, as Hume remarks, every object has to be considered 'in itself', without reference to the other, and 'all events seem entirely loose and separate. One event follows another, but we never can *observe* any tie between them. They seem *conjoined*, but never *connected*' (Hume 1995: 85). Does X cause Y, when X and Y are independent entities? Does small class teaching improve student performance? Does extra homework improve student motivation? The relationship is contingent, not analytic, i.e. the former, in itself, does not entail the latter, and vice versa; they are, in origin, unrelated. Indeed, in rehearsing the argument that the cause must be logically distinct from its effect, Davidson (2001: 13) argues that, if this is true, then it is to question whether reasons can actually be causes, since the reason for an action is not logically distinct from that action (see also Von Wright 1993).

One of the significant challenges to educationists and policy makers is to see 'what works'. Unfortunately it is a commonly heard complaint that many educational policies are introduced by political will rather than on the basis of evidence of whether they will actually bring about improvements. The move to evidence-based education has to be clear what constitutes evidence and what that evidence is actually telling us (Eisenhart 2005). In the world of medicine, a new drug might take ten years to develop, to undergo clinical trials, to meet the standards required by the appropriate authorities, and even then only between 1:2,000 and 1:10,000 drugs that have been tested are actually approved for human use. Now look at the world of education: policies and initiatives are introduced on the most slender of evidence, and a signal feature of many educational initiatives and interventions is their lack of a rigorous evidence base. There is an urgent need to understand causation in order to understand what works, for whom and under what conditions; what interventions are required; and what processes occur and with what effects. Understanding causation is vital here.

There have been several recent moves to ensure that educational policy making *is* informed by evidence rather than political will. For example, the Social, Psychological, Educational and Criminological Controlled Trials Register (SPECTR) has been established, with over 10,000 references (Milwain 1998; Milwain *et al.* 1999; Davies 1999; Evans *et al.* 2000), evidence is appearing in the literature (e.g. Davies 1999; Oakley 2000, Davies *et al.* 2000; Evans *et al.* 2000; Levačić and Glatter 2000), and an Evidence-Based Education Network has been established in the UK (http://www.cem.dur.ac.uk). The University of London's Institute of Education has established its 'EPPI-centre': the Evidence for Policy and Practice Information and Co-ordinating Centre (http://eppi.ioe.ac.uk/EPPIWeb/home.aspx), and it has already published very many research syntheses (e.g. Harlen 2004a; 2004b). The Campbell Collaboration (http://campbellcollaboration.org) and the What Works Clearinghouse (http://ies.ed.gov/ncee/wwc/) produce an evidence base for decision making. There is a groundswell of opinion to suggest the need for evidence to inform policy making (Davis 1995; Cohen *et al.* 2000: 394; Levačić and Glatter 2000; Ayres 2008). We should know whether something works, and why, before we put it into policy and practice.

There is a need to bring together the worlds of research, practice and theory. Goldthorpe (2007a: 8) berates social scientists for their inability to have developed laws and to have linked research with the development of cumulative theory, as has been done in the hard sciences. This book seeks to address this matter in part. It introduces and opens up an understanding of causation. It deliberately avoids the formulaic presentations that one reads in philosophical works and works on logic. That is not to demean these; on the contrary, they are essential in clarifying and applying concepts of causation. However, it places these into words, so that the novice reader can grasp their significance for the approach adopted here.

Causation – cause and effect – is no simple matter. If only it were, but it is not! This book indicates why causation is far from being as straightforward as policy makers might have us believe. It is complex, convoluted, multi-faceted and often opaque. What starts out as being a simple exercise – finding the effects of causes and finding the causes of effects – is often the optimism of ignorance. One can soon become stuck in a quagmire of uncertainty, multiplicity of considerations, and unsureness of the relations between causes and effects. The intention of this book is to indicate what some of these issues might be and how educational researchers, theorists and practitioners can address them. The book seeks to be practical, as much educational research is a practical matter. In this enterprise one important point is to understand the nature of causation; another is to examine difficulties in reaching certainty about causation; another is to ensure that all the relevant causal factors are introduced into an explanation of causation;

and yet another is to provide concrete advice to researchers to enable them to research causation and cause and effect, and to utilize their findings to inform decision making.

A final introductory note: readers will notice that the term 'causation' has been used, rather than, for example, 'causality'. This is deliberate; whilst both terms concern the relation of cause and effect, additionally 'causation' is an action term, denoting the act of causing or producing an effect. It expresses intention (Salmon 1998: 7). This is close to one express purpose of this book, which is to enable researchers to act in understanding and researching cause and effect.

Implications for researchers:

- Consider whether the research is seeking to establish causation, and, if so, why.
- Consider what evidence is required to demonstrate causation.
- Consider whether repeating the research is necessary in order to establish causation.
- Recognize that causation is never 100 per cent certain; it is conditional.
- Decide what constitutes a cause and what constitutes the effect.
- Decide what constitutes evidence of the cause and evidence of the effect.
- Decide the kind of research and the methodology of research that is necessary if causation is to be investigated.
- Decide whether you are investigating the cause of an effect, the effect of a cause, or both.
- Causation in the human sciences may be probabilistic rather than deterministic.

Chapter 2

Tools for understanding causation

This chapter traces in some key concepts in approaching and understanding causation, and, in doing so, indicates some of the historical antecedents of the discussion. As the chapter unfolds, it indicates an ever-widening scope of the concept of causation, beggaring naïve attempts to oversimplify it. At each stage of the discussion implications are drawn for educational researchers.

There are different kinds of causation, and the examples in this book instance deterministic causation and probabilistic causation. In deterministic causation, if such-and-such a cause obtains, then such-and-such an effect *certainly* follows. In probabilistic causation, if such-and-such a cause obtains, then (arguably, as discussed later) it raises the *likelihood* of such-and-such an effect, but does not guarantee it. Causation involves a change or transition (Belnap 2002: 4; Müller 2005). The examples in the book are vehicles for raising debates and concepts in understanding causation in educational research.

A worked example: the fight in the school playground

The problem of understanding and knowing what to include in understanding causation is not straightforward. Consider the following example.

Two teenage boys – David and John – are fighting in the school yard. The teacher separates them and then speaks to them both. David says that he had started the fight because John had insulted him, that he had returned an equally offensive insult, and the fight had ensued. Does the story remain there? Was the cause of the fight a couple of insults idly traded? Well, perhaps so or perhaps not. Maybe David and John had volatile personalities, such that any spark would cause a massive overreaction – i.e. maybe it was the personalities that caused the fight. Or say that David and John had had an argument a few days previously, which had ended by David saying that, if John ever spoke to him again, he would hit him. Does that constitute a cause of the present fight?

And why did David make this remark? Maybe there was a history of trouble between the two families that had pre-dated the particular events in question (the previous argument and the present fight). Maybe the combination of the family feuding and the volatile personalities involved, or maybe the family problems, mediated through the personalities involved, created an easily combustible mixture. Or maybe the fight was the culmination of an increasingly acrimonious feuding between the two boys, such that the final hurling of insults was the straw that broke the camel's back.

And why was there a history of trouble between the two families? Maybe both families were living in the same 'sink' estate of ghetto housing, in which 'problem families' were placed together by the local authority, perhaps because of a history of non-payment of housing rent, petty criminality, aggressive behaviour to authority figures and other members of the community, long-term unemployment and disrespect for other citizens. And why were such 'problem families' placed together in a single ghetto? The local authority, wishing not to have several neighbourhoods disturbed or vandalized, in order to restrict the effect of violent and disruptive families on law-abiding citizens who simply wanted to go about their business, and in order to 'contain' the potential criminal elements within the community and, hence, to be able to police the community more efficiently, had decided to house such disruptive elements together in a single estate, to contain the problem. Why had the local authority taken this decision?

On the one hand, in community and societal terms it was attempting to keep law and order, to restrict societal breakdown and to promote civilized behaviour. On the other hand, the local authority was poor, and it was attempting to ensure the greatest return on the money spent on the community and its policing. Why was the local authority so strapped for cash? Maybe it was because it had had to put money into providing additional incentives for teachers to work in its schools. And why was it so difficult to recruit teachers? Maybe it was because the media had orchestrated a high-profile campaign of negative publicity against government policy that, so the press had claimed, brought teachers massive pressure, responsibility and workload without due remuneration, respect and power, turning them into low-level technical operatives with little control over their working lives yet held accountable for matters over which they had no control and with which they did not agree – they had become the 'whipping boys' of a society going out of control.

So, what was the cause of the fight: the insult; the personalities; the argument; the aggressive inter-family feuding behaviour; the placing together of 'problem' families; the local authority's housing policy; the desire to promote and preserve decent community behaviour in the populace; the need to restrict and contain the outbreaks of unacceptable behaviour; the local authority's lack of money; the problem of balancing competing priorities; the government's education policy; the media? How *far back in time* does one have to go to establish causation (the temporal dimension: Hume's element of 'priority' as a fundamental feature of causation – the cause must precede the event) and over how many contexts (e.g. the spatial or environmental dimension – however defined) – *how far out* – does one have to go to establish causation? Indeed, *how far in* does one have to go to establish causation? Do more immediate conditions and causes override – screen off – earlier or more remote conditions (Salmon 1998: 43)? Is it necessary to go to the *causae causantes* (the originating causes) in order to understand the present situation (Belnap 2002; Müller 2005)? Discovering causation can recede *ad infinitum*. The notion of causation here can be represented diagrammatically as in Figure 2.1.

Understanding causation is problematical, as causes, causal processes and mechanisms are not easily observable, in fact may not be directly observable at all, which means that they are difficult, if not impossible, to ascertain fully or to measure at all (Holland 2004). The discovery of causes, causal processes and causal mechanisms is an exacting and tentative affair.

Cause and effect: the problem of inclusion

What are included and what excluded in the causes of an effect? If one includes everything, then establishing causation becomes unmanageable; if one excludes factors, then

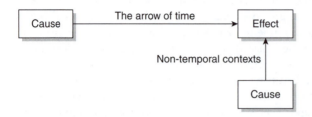

Figure 2.1 Temporal and non-temporal contexts of cause and effect

one is misrepresenting the nature of the causation through oversimplification and selectivity, though manageability becomes more straightforward. As Mill (2006: 332) remarks, to understand causation we have to include all the antecedent factors, i.e. the environment and all the conditions. A cause, he observes, 'is the sum total of the conditions positive and negative taken together … which being realized, the consequent invariably follows'.

Implications for researchers:

- Be prepared to look back in time and across a variety of contexts and conditions in establishing causation.
- Ensure inclusion of the relevant causes.
- Try to keep the number of causes to a manageable number, without omitting important ones.

Mill's view is not without its difficulties, however. Firstly, he is discussing regularity, a deterministic rather than a probabilistic view of causation. Secondly, Ducasse (1993) argues that, if the causal relation involves (a) the environment of an object, (b) some change in that environment, and (c) the resulting change in that environment, then it is impossible to include some change in the environment as part of a cause, because the cause itself consists of a change in that environment. If the cause of an effect involves a change in the environment, then it is impossible to use the environment as part of the cause without circularity.

Thirdly, Mill's view that all the antecedent conditions constitute causes, even if true, might become unwieldy in practice. One attempt to reduce this to manageable proportions is by identifying strong and weak causes, though it is not always clear which are strong and which are weak and how one measures strength – or, indeed, if 'strength' is important. Another attempt is made in the notion of *necessary* and *sufficient* conditions (e.g. Mackie 1993), and these are discussed below. Davidson (2001: 117) suggests that the more fully we can describe the *cause*, the greater is the possibility of demonstrating that it was *sufficient* to produce the effect; in addition, the more fully we can describe the *effect*, not only is there a greater possibility of demonstrating that the cause was *necessary*, but also the possibility of demonstrating that it was sufficient is reduced.

Implications for researchers:

- Identify the necessary and sufficient conditions and causes in the situation.
- Provide as full a set of details of conditions as possible.

What exactly is the cause? Can a macro-cause (e.g. the wider society) impact on the micro-situation (e.g. Durkheim's 'social facts' – 'any way of acting, whether fixed or not, capable of exerting over the individual an external constraint or which is general over the whole of a given society whilst having an existence of its own, independent of its individual manifestations' (1982: 59), where, in order to avoid reliance on psychological interpretations of social behaviour, one seeks social causes of individual behaviour)? Which are necessary and/or sufficient causes?

Further, returning to the example of the boys fighting, we have possible *reasons* for the fight, but are these causes? A reason might be a motive, but that may or may not be the same as a cause. This rehearses the ambiguity of the word 'why' as in 'Why were the boys fighting?'; it may refer to causes (e.g. historical and current antecedents), to reasons and to purposes (e.g. future intentions). Intentions may not be the same as causes; as Davidson (2001: 8) remarks, a person may go to church in order to please his mother, but behind this lies yet another cause or reason (e.g. Why does he wish to please his mother?). Maybe the reason behind the intention is actually the cause. Davidson (ibid.: 264) argues against the false equation of a motive with a reason in the context of establishing causation: I may have a motive to perform a certain act, but I may actually perform it for different reasons. For example, I may wish to set additional homework for a class of students in order for them to learn more science (the motive), but the reason I actually set them homework, in the event, was because it was a school requirement. Nonetheless, a motive may be a cause.

Ryan (1970: 117) distinguishes between reasons and causes in the criteria used to evaluate them. In the case of a reason one can say that it is good or bad, or somewhere in between. In the case of a cause the notion of 'good' or 'bad' seems inappropriate: something is or is not a cause; it brings about an effect, regardless of whether it is good or bad. There is a category difference between reasons and causes. A child in school may misbehave repeatedly in order to attract the teacher's attention; this is a cause, even though it is not a very good reason.

Implications for researchers:

- Consider whether the research is seeking to identify causes, reasons and/or motives.
- Recognize that reasons, motives and causes may be similar but also may be different.

Before we move on, it is useful to consider a little further the views of Mill (2006) in discovering evidence of causal relations. He indicates five main methods of such discovery:

Table 2.1 Attendance and non-attendance at lessons

		Chemistry lesson days	Non-chemistry lesson days
Attendance at school	High	No	Yes
	Low	Yes	No

(a) *Agreement*: 'If two or more instances of the phenomenon under investigation have only one circumstance in common, the circumstance in which alone all the instances agree, is the cause (or effect) of the given phenomenon' (Mill 2006: 390). For example, if we observe that two days in which students are absent from school are always the days on which chemistry lessons occur, we might infer that it is something about chemistry lessons that causes them to be absent, but if we observe that they are absent on other days as well then our causal inference is weakened. This is the method of correlation.

(b) *Difference*: 'If an instance in which the phenomenon under investigation occurs, and an instance in which it does not occur, have every circumstance in common except one, that one occurring in the former; the circumstance in which alone the two instances differ is the effect, or the cause, or an indisputable part of the cause, of the phenomenon' (ibid.: 391). For example, if we observe that on days when chemistry lessons occur then many students are absent, and that on days when no chemistry lessons occur they are present, then we might infer that chemistry lessons are the cause. However, there might be other reasons working here, for example, on the same days as those on which chemistry lessons occur there might also be physical education, and the lazy students decide to absent themselves on such days. In fact Mill is alluding to the experimental method in which control and experimental groups are matched on all variables except one. The isolation and control of all relevant variables, as will be discussed later, is probably unrealistic in much educational research, most of which conforms to non-experimental methodology.

(c) *Agreement and difference*: 'If two or more instances in which the phenomenon occurs have only one circumstance in common, while two or more instances in which it does not occur have nothing in common save the absence of the circumstance, the circumstance in which alone the two sets of instances differ, is the effect, or the cause, or an indispensable part of the cause, or the phenomenon' (ibid.: 396). This combines (a) and (b). So, for example, we could observe the attendance on chemistry days and on non-chemistry days as in Table 2.1.

Here we have a sample of chemistry lesson days (to see if attendance is low on such days) and non-chemistry lesson days (to see if attendance differs from chemistry lesson days in having high attendance). The research has four hypotheses:

  (i) Low attendance occurs on chemistry lesson days;
 (ii) High attendance occurs on non-chemistry lesson days;
(iii) There may be some chemistry days with high attendance;
(iv) There may be some non-chemistry days with low attendance.

What we have here is a statement of initial conditions (discussed in Chapters 2 and 3 here). We can see from the table that hypotheses (i) and (ii) are supported. The example is important, for it directs our attention to the need to make comparisons amongst different conditions (cf. Hage and Meeker 1988: 47); if one were to examine only chemistry lesson days or only non-chemistry lesson days, then we would have an incomplete test. Some of the hypotheses predict presence and some predict absence, so both conditions have to be included in the test.

(d) *Residue*: 'Subduct [remove] from any phenomenon such part as is known by previous inductions to be the effect of certain antecedents, and the residue of the phenomenon is the effect of the remaining antecedents' (Mill 2006: 398). Whilst (a) to (c) concerned the relationship between two variables (cause and effect), here Mill is referring to the issue of the possible effects of a third introduced variable, the control variable (discussed in Chapter 3 here). For example, we may suppose that the chemistry lesson deters students from attending school, but there may be a third variable, a number of sporting events on the television on the same day each week, that may be causing the effect.

(e) *Concomitant variation*: 'Whatever phenomenon varies in any manner whenever another phenomenon varies in some particular manner, is either a cause or an effect of that phenomenon or is connected with it through some fact of causation' (ibid.: 401). Mill is referring to correlational techniques here, those with large coefficients of correlation demonstrating greater correlation than those with lower correlation coefficients. Of course, correlation is not the same as causation, and this may be a problem with Mill's suggestion, except that constant conjunction in time (one event preceding another with great regularity) may infer causation (according to Hume). The strength of a correlation may or may not indicate its causal relation.

One can see resonances between Mill and his predecessor Hume, in that both are relying on induction to demonstrate causation.

Causes and conditions

The question of what to include and exclude in causation is problematic; there are many contributing causes, and the task is to identify which causes are important or relevant, and how to decide how to decide. Take the example of the case of somebody falling and breaking a hip whilst out walking. Maybe the fall was caused by a loss of equilibrium that, itself, was the result of a head injury years before. Maybe the road was icy and the earlier loss of equilibrium from the head injury played a part on this subsequent occasion. Maybe the person was wearing the wrong kind of shoes (e.g. with slippery soles); maybe there was no handrail to hold alongside the footpath; maybe there was a sudden gust of wind; maybe the person had a genetic disorder and was overweight, such that a simple overbalancing had a major effect; maybe the person was walking carelessly. Here the causes are not only several but are both genetic and environmental, and are not simultaneous – some are delayed from an earlier period and some are contemporary.

What we also see in this instance is an example of how the cause triggers the effect under a specific set of circumstances or conditions. As Mellor (1995: 69–70) suggests,

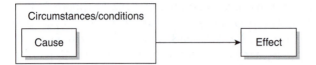

Figure 2.2 Circumstances, conditions and causation

for an effect to become the effect of a cause requires the presence of a specific combination of circumstances. For a car engine to work requires not only the spark, but the presence of an inflammable gas and air, i.e. specific circumstances or conditions. For a mountaineer to fall off a rock and die (ibid.) requires consideration of his weight, the brittleness of his bones, the distance he falls, the hardness of the substance on which he lands, which part of his body he lands on, whether he is wearing any protective clothing, whether he was roped up, the amount of adipose tissue on his body, and so on. In short, the cause takes place in a context of circumstances and conditions that, together, bring about the effect, and without which the effect would not occur: the car engine would not ignite if the mixture of gas and air were wrong; the mountaineer would not die if his fall was only 1 metre and he was roped up.

A cause takes place in the context of a set of specific circumstances/conditions that, together, bring about the effect: going from cause to effect involves a change or transition from one state to another (Belnap 2002: 7): in the example here this means from a non-fall to a fall, a non-engine start to a start, from life to death. A cause only causes an effect in these circumstances; in other circumstances it would not bring about the effect (Figure 2.2).

Indeed an effect is a consequence of a net or network of conditions, circumstances, intentionality and agency that interact in a myriad of ways, for example the context in which decisions are made about whether or not to go to university (Figure 2.3).

This argues powerfully for understanding the role of context in causal explanation (Maxwell 2004: 6–7) and for the combination of scattered events in bringing about an effect in space–time (Belnap 2002: 9), and even for questioning the simple linearity of cause and effect (see Chapters 3 and 7 of this book).

Causal chains and causal lines

What we see in the earlier example of David and John is a chain of events, the last one of which is the *trigger* to the fight. Is the trigger the same as the cause? Is the last event before the fight (the insult) the cause (Hume's principle of 'contiguity' – one event having to touch the next – the fundamental element of the causation)? Or can we say that an unbroken 'causal chain' – a set of events over time (a 'chain of causes which are contiguous among themselves' (2000: 1.3.2: 6)) which, as Hume remarks in the Abstract to his *Treatise* (para. 9), are 'connected together, either mediately or immediately' – offers a better explanation of the causation in this instance? Is it acceptable to include events as causes that had taken place some time, or a long time, previous to the present situation? Clearly so: birth follows nine months after conception!

Lieberson (1997: 379) suggests that, the longer the causal chain, the more difficult it is to unravel, and yet the timing of the point in the causal chain which the researcher investigates is important: if the independent and dependent variable are very close in a

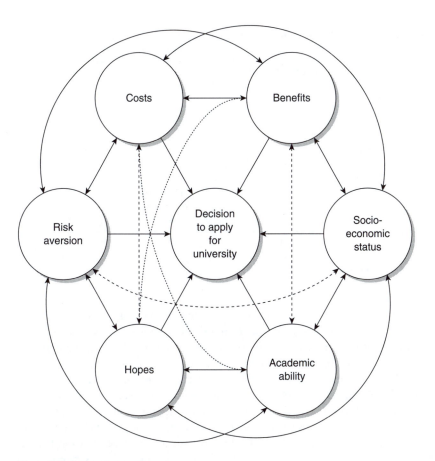

Figure 2.3 A net of causation

causal chain, then this might not yield much of interest; however, if there is a consider-able distance between the independent and dependent variable, then it might be more interesting for the researcher. Consider the example of adults joining the teaching profession. If one were to interview final-year teacher training students about their deci-sion to be teachers, this would yield fewer surprises than, for example, if one were to interview students at age 15 about possible intentions to become teachers. Greater com-plexity of causal chaining is likely in the latter case because the probability is less likely than in the former.

The chain of causation – a series of contiguous and constituent events that bring about an effect, linearly ordered (Salmon 1998: 209) – is an important feature of causa-tion, and it operates on the principle of *transitivity*: if A causes B and B causes C, then A causes C (e.g. Lewis 1993). It is important to recognize this, as, if we are trying to treat the cause of C and focus only on B, then we might be missing the true cause of C.

For example, let us imagine that the students in a school are making a lot of noise whilst moving round the building. The effect (C) – the students' noise – seems to be caused by their talking and movement (cause B). However, on closer examination it

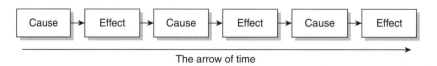

The arrow of time

Figure 2.4 A causal chain

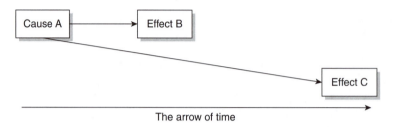

The arrow of time

Figure 2.5 Real and spurious causes

becomes clear that the problem lies behind this (cause A), for example: (a) the timetabling means that all the students move round the school at one single time, so there is congestion leading to talking; (b) there are only two ways in which the students can move round the school because of the arrangement of doors, corridors and classrooms, so there is congestion leading to talking; (c) the building materials and furnishings do not absorb sound well. Hence, even if the students were to be as quiet as mice (addressing cause B) there would still be a problem which was not solved. To solve the problem means addressing cause A rather than cause B, i.e. to go for the root cause rather than the symptom. One has to identify the most suitable part of the causal chain in which to intervene. (Of course, behind cause A in the example lie several other causes, but these are not explored in the example here.)

A causal chain can be represented diagrammatically (Figure 2.4). One has to be on guard against spurious causation here: A might cause B and then A might cause C, but B might not cause C. The issue is shown in Figure 2.5. In this case effect B is an *epiphenomenon*, not a genuine cause of C. Chapter 3 discusses the issue of controlling for the influence of a third, non-spurious variable.

The idea of a causal chain resonates with Russell's notion of 'causal lines'. Separable causal lines, he argues (1948: 487), allow for long-term persistence in events and processes, and he holds that, 'where there is a causal connection between two events that are not contiguous, there must be intermediate links in the causal chain such that each is contiguous'. A causal line, he avers (p. 333), is a temporal series of events so related that, if we know some of them, we can infer the others, and a causal line may demonstrate 'constancy of structure, or gradual changes ... but not sudden change of any magnitude' (p. 477). It may always be regarded, he asserts (p. 459), as 'the persistence of something'. A causal line may be traced over time provided that it does not change too greatly and that it persists separately from other things; it is string of causally connected events. Salmon (1998: 196) argues that Russell's causal lines fulfil Hume's requirements for causal relations to be established – contiguity, temporal priority and constant conjunction.

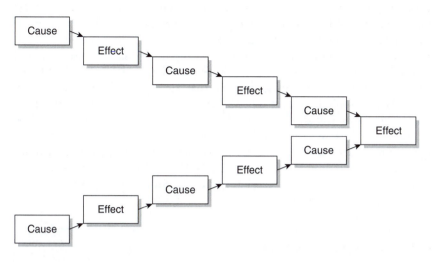

Figure 2.6 Causal lines producing the same effect

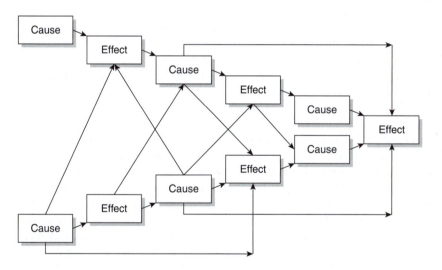

Figure 2.7 Interaction effects within causal lines

There can be more than one causal line that contributes to a single effect, for exam-ple in Figure 2.6. In fact the problem is compounded in that, in the real situation, the causal lines may not be separate, but there may be interaction effects both within and between the causal lines (Figure 2.7). We have to keep in mind that the empirically causal and the logically causal may not, in fact, coincide (Mellor 1995: 5).

Further, Salmon (1998: 224) suggests using the analogy of a 'rope' rather than a chain of causation, as this catches more completely the ongoing interconnections of all the elements together rather than only linearly, i.e. processes replace events. Bennett (1993) gives an example of the need to provide a complete chain of causation in the statement 'the April rain caused the forest fire'. That seems to be counter-intuitive. However, a full delineation of the causal chain reveals that there had been heavy rain in April, followed by many electrical storms in the ensuing two months such that, in June, a flash of lightning had occurred which caused the forest fire, and that, if there had been no heavy rain in April, in fact the fire would have started in May as conditions would have already been dry enough for a fire to start, and not in the later month of June. The point is that the heavy rain had delayed the forest fire, that it had caused the delay, not started the fire.

Returning to our earlier example of the fight, we could say that if the boys had not had the fight then they would not have been friends. Clearly this is counter-intuitive (and counterfactual), but, as will be seen later in this example, it is entirely plausible when the causal chain is complete.

Implications for researchers:

- Identify the circumstances and conditions in which the cause takes place.
- Identify causal chains, causal processes and causal lines.
- Be prepared to identify different causes, different causal chains and different causal lines that produce the same effect.
- Understanding the complexity of causes is increased the further back one goes in time before the event in question.
- Try to keep causal lines separate where possible.
- Recognize that causes interact with each other; it might be impossible to consider them separately.

Causal processes seem to be at work in the example of the playground fight. Indeed Salmon (1993a, 1993b, 1998: 224) regards causation as a set of continuous *processes* rather than as a relation between specific events. Events, even though they have a temporal dimension (Mellor 1995: 122) in a way that 'things' do not, are localized, whereas processes last much longer; as Salmon suggests, in a space–time diagram, an event would be represented as a point whereas a process would be represented as a line (akin to Russell's 'causal lines' above). Salmon is concerned to elucidate causation in terms of causal *production* and causal *propagation*. In a causal production, he avers (1993b), a cause produces a *direct* effect: hitting a nail pushes it into wood; the bolt of lightning ignites the forest. Causal propagation can be where an event or experience in one place or time influences what happens in another place or time: childhood experiences *influence* our adult lives; music reaches us through the electromagnetic waves from another place. Causal influence is *propagated* through causal processes (Salmon 1993b, 1998), whereas changes in such causal processes are *produced* through causal interactions (e.g. the interactions of ongoing events and processes).[1]

Implications for researchers:

- Identify causal production and causal influence (propagation).
- Causes produce effects, which become causes, and so on.

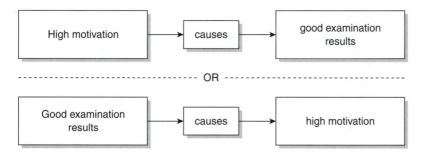

Figure 2.8 Directions of causation

The direction of causation

Turning back to our example of the playground fight, what we see in David's and John's situation is that causation has *direction*, even though sometimes this direction may be unclear. The insults caused the fight, not vice versa. This refers us to the frequently observed *asymmetry* of relations between cause and effect: the direction of causation may not be two-way or reversible (hence the importance of the temporal sequence of events (Rosenberg 1968: 11)). For example, let us say that females score more highly in language tests than males; one might infer that being female causes greater success in the language test than being male. However, one could not say that scoring more highly in the language test causes one to be female. Similarly Hage and Meeker (1988: 13) indicate that a child's success in school may be attributable to the level of his or her parents' education, but we could not say that the parents' level of education was attributable to the child's school achievements. As Kim (1993a: 25; 1993b) remarks, by bringing about the cause we bring about the effect, but it is untrue to say that by bringing about the effect we bring about the cause.

In many cases the direction of causation is clear. However, in other cases it may be less so. Let us take a further example, of teacher stress. A simple view might be that overwork causes teacher stress. However, it may be that teacher stress causes overwork: the stressed teacher, concerned not to seem to be at fault or underperforming, works too hard. Or take the relationship between motivation and examination success. One could suggest that motivation causes examination success – the more motivated one is, the more successful one is. On the other hand, it could be the examination success that causes the motivational level; high success may cause high motivation. Or take the relationship between liking the teacher and doing well at school. It may be that if the student likes the teacher then this causes the student to perform well; or it may be that if the student performs well then he or she likes the teacher. Stress may produce overeating, just as overeating may produce stress. The direction of causation may be unclear, as set out in Figure 2.8.

Implications for researchers:

- Consider the direction(s) of causation.
- Recognize that there may be more than one direction.
- Recognize that the direction of causation may be symmetrical and/or asymmetrical.

One sees the attempt to address the difficulty of understanding the direction of causation in educational research through the use of dependent and independent variables, but this does not always resolve the problem. For the purposes of the research the researcher may *stipulate* which are the dependent and independent variables, but this might misrepresent the real situation.

Returning to the playground fight between David and John: Can we really say that a simple trading of insults was the cause of the fight? Surely something as trivial as an insult, on its own, would hardly constitute sufficient grounds for a fight? So which are the major and which are the minor causes? What are the relative strengths of each cause? Which are more important and which are less important? Further, on their own the insults may not have been sufficient for the fight to have occurred; they were not the causes. They may have been reasons or conditions, but not causes. The causes may have lain elsewhere, for example in the cumulative development of other contributing factors over time. The insult was just the spark that lit the firestorm which had been brewing for some time. David and John had learned about their two feuding families over time by custom, habit and experience; there was almost an inevitability that they would fight at the slightest trigger, as this is the history of the problem between their two respective families. The final trigger is not the complete cause.

Implications for researchers:

- Ensure that you establish the actual causes rather than the presenting causes (e.g. the symptoms).
- Identify the strengths of the causes.
- Identify the triggers (the last cause in the chain) as well as the cumulative contributory causes.

This accords with two of Hume's elements of causation. Firstly there is 'constant conjunction' (two events are learned to be related if they repeatedly occur together): 'The idea of cause and effect is deriv'd from experience, which informs us, that such particular objects, in all past instances, have been constantly conjoin'd with each other' (Hume 2000: 1.3.6: 7) Secondly there is the view that experience, custom and habit alone create our experience of causation: 'a *stronger* conception, sometimes a more *lively*, a more *vivid*, a *firmer*, or a more *intense* conception' (Abstract to the *Treatise*, para. 22), 'a lively idea related to or associated with a present impression' (2000: 1.3.7: 5) rather than deduction and proof – as features of that learning. Causation is experienced rather than definitive or deducible; it is inductive: 'we give preference to that which has been found most usual' (Hume 1955: 71). As Hume writes: ''Tis therefore by experience only, that we can infer the existence of one object from that of another' (2000: 1.3.6: 2).

Implications for researchers:

- Recognize that causation may be a matter of inference rather than certainty.
- There are limits to inference.

In the Abstract to his *Treatise* Hume provides a neat example of the learned, the experienced, rather than the proven nature of causation–necessary connection. Taking the analogy from the game of billiards, popular at the time, Hume has an entirely new man – Adam – watching one billiard ball striking another. At first Adam cannot infer that the first ball striking the second causes the second to move. It is only by repeated observation of the 'constant conjunction' of these two events that he makes a causal inference that the first ball causes the movement of the second in the sense that he expects the second ball to move when struck by the first. He explains this in his later *Inquiry concerning Human Understanding*: 'From the first appearance of an object we never can conjecture what effect will result from it' (Hume 1955: 75). As he says: 'all reasonings concerning cause and effect are founded on experience' (Abstract to the *Treatise*: para. 13) and 'we are determined by custom alone to suppose the future conformable to the past. When I see a billiard ball moving towards another, my mind is immediately carried by habit to the usual effect' (para. 15). 'Tis not, therefore, reason, which is the guide to life, but custom' (para. 16), and 'our reason fails us in the discovery of the ultimate connexion of causes and effects' (2000: 1.3.6: 11). 'Experience only teaches us how one event constantly follows another, without instructing us in the secret connection which binds them together and renders them inseparable' (1955: 77). Of course, not every constant conjunction is causal; I can observe a constant conjunction between the rising of the sun and my eating breakfast, but the two are not causally related; the former is caused by the movement of the earth, whilst the latter is caused by hunger.

Implication for researchers:

- Recognize the limits of induction in treating causes and effects.
- Recognize that association, and regularity of association, though different from – and not – causation, may provide clues to causation.

Hume here is suggesting that 'necessary connexion' is no more than the connection imposed on two events by the human brain which thinks in terms of cause and effect, a mentalist conception wherein causes, like sensory awareness, lie in the mind rather than in the objects themselves: 'the repetition neither discovers nor causes any thing in the objects, but has an influence only on the mind . . . . consequently qualities of perception, not of objects, and are internally felt by the soul, and not perceiv'd externally in bodies' (2000: 1.3.14: 24). That Hume was aware of the possible outrage that this statement would cause is reflected in his comment

> What! the efficacy of causes lie in the determination of the mind! As if causes did not operate entirely independently of the mind, and wou'd not continue their operation, even tho' there was no mind existent to contemplate them, or reason concerning them. Thought may well depend on causes for its operation, but not causes on thought. (2000: 1.3.14: 26)

Implications for researchers:

- Causes may not be what we think they are; our minds may play tricks on us in believing a cause to be a cause when it is not.
- Causation concerns objective relations, not only subjective relations.

Necessary and sufficient conditions

In the example of David and John, the insult may have been an *insufficient* part of the fight in that, on its own, it was not enough to cause the fight, as its taking place required the previous history of the relationships between the two, their families and the local authority policy makers. However, the insult was *necessary* in the situation recorded, since without it there would have been no fight. The conditions themselves – the antecedents to the fight, including the trigger (the insult) – were themselves *unnecessary*, there being other conditions which could have led to the fight (one effect can have many different causes), but they were *sufficient* for the result under the circumstances. Necessary and sufficient conditions may explain causality (e.g. blowing a whistle may cause the dog to appear (a necessary condition), but deeper into the process are sound waves, operant conditioning and brain activity (Salmon 1998: 22).

Discussing necessary and sufficient criteria for causation is one way of reducing the overload of identifying all of Mill's recommended antecedent conditions. However, Mackie (1993) argues that necessary and sufficient conditions are those that obtain in a specific set of circumstances. His seminal work on the 'INUS' conditions involved in causation opens up the field of *necessary* and *sufficient* conditions for a cause to have an effect. He has an extended example of a house fire. The forensic experts indicate that it is caused by an electrical short-circuit. However, the situation is more complicated than this. For example, the short-circuit, on its own, is not a *necessary* condition for the fire, there being other possible ways of starting a house fire. Equally, the short-circuit is not a *sufficient* condition for the house fire, as, on its own, it need not have started a fire (e.g. if the short-circuit had not caused a spark, or if there was an automatic sprinkler system in the house, or if there was no flammable material in the house, or there was insufficient oxygen in the house to sustain the fire).

The point here is that, taken together, there was a complex set of conditions present that were *sufficient* for the fire to occur, triggered by the short-circuit, and, in these conditions, the short-circuit was *necessary* to set the house alight, or, as Mackie writes, the short-circuit which is the cause of the fire is an indispensable part of a complex sufficient, though not necessary, condition of the fire. Here 'the so-called cause is, and is known to be, an *insufficient* but *necessary* part of a condition which is itself *unnecessary* but *sufficient* for the result' (1993: 34). He terms this the INUS condition (an Insufficient but Necessary part of the condition which is Unnecessary but Sufficient to produce the effect).[2] (Here is not the place to raise criticisms of Mackie's project, but see Sosa and Tooley (1993) and Kim (1993b, 1993c).)

Mackie's work is important as it breaks with the determinism involved in terms such as 'always' and 'never' in discussing causation (Hage and Meeker 1988: 5), and this breaks with regarding 'necessary' conditions as being universal and omnipresent, replacing them with a discussion of the necessary conditions *in a particular situation*. It signals an important limit to deterministic causation, as deterministic causation indicates that effects follow if and only if ('iff') universal, specified causes are present and that, if they are present, the effect always follows. The issue is to identify and understand the significant condition or conditions (events or processes) that create the effects observed, asking 'What were the relevant sufficient conditions at the time to cause the effect?'[3]

Hage and Meeker (1988: 6) indicate further limitations to the deterministic view of necessary and sufficient conditions, in that they derive from formal logic: *if* such-and-such, *then* such-and-such. However, such a logical view of causation makes no mention of temporality, time sequence or conditions, preferring logical to temporal relations, and Hume's significant contribution to an understanding of causation is devolved, in part, on temporality and empirical demonstration. The difficulty with deterministic views of causation is their overemphasis on the *certainty* of prediction, of regularity, and in the empirical world this simply does not obtain (see the discussion in Chapter 3 of probabilistic causation). Mackie's work is an important marker in setting the conditionality and contextuality of causation.

Of course, there are occasions when such determinism is correct – the 'iff' condition ('if and only if'). For example, Salmon (1998: 40) indicates that paresis – a form of tertiary syphilis – *only* occurs in patients who have had primary and secondary syphilis. In the field of education, in some countries children may have to move from one form/grade level if they pass the appropriate examination, i.e. passing the examination *forces* the children to move to the next form/grade, and, let us imagine, you move to the next form/grade iff (if and only if) you pass the examination. So we would know, for example, that all and only the children in Form 5 were children who had passed the Form 4 examination. This is more than a condition, it is a cause. A condition is necessary but not sufficient as a cause: having food on the table is a condition of being able to eat, but it does not cause or force us to eat. In the field of education such examples of one-to-one correspondence or exclusive determinism are rare.

Implications for researchers:

- Identify the INUS conditions for the cause of the effects.
- Recognize that it may not be possible to identify all the INUS conditions.
- Recognize that the INUS conditions may vary from context to context and from case to case.

Real causes and real effects

Let us jump forward in time in our extended example of the boys fighting. Five years have passed, and in the interim David's family has moved away. The boys – now men – have not seen each other for four years, but happen to encounter each other in the street. At first they regard each other suspiciously and hearts start racing. Is another fight going to flare up, there having been five years of brooding to fuel the fire? No, David and John, as adults, greet each other, ask after each other's health, recall the silly occasion of their fight, agree to put it behind them, and part on very good terms. Is this an effect? If so, what is the cause? Of what is it an effect? It could not have happened without the fight, but the fight could not have happened without a preceding set of events. Can it be an effect after there has been such a time interval? When does an effect become an effect – at what point in time? When do we measure or ascertain the effect? Do we look for long-term effects (e.g. compensatory educational programmes that begin in very young children) or immediate effects? Can an effect be an effect if it is not contiguous with its cause, or if a continuous causal chain cannot be established?

Implications for researchers:

- Recognize that effects of causes may be delayed or take time to reveal themselves.
- Decide the time frame for the effect to reveal itself, and consider the suitability of that time frame.

During the five years since the fight David and John have grown up and reflected on the incident. Independently, each has realized that the fight was ridiculous, and each has promised himself that, were he to meet the other, then the first thing to happen would be a reconciliation and an agreement to be on friendly terms. So, when they meet up, it is hardly surprising that they greet each other and leave on friendly terms. But look what has happened here: an event in the future (the making-up) has had a backward-acting effect – the projected event has acted backwards in time; teleologically speaking, the unrealized, future goal has effected an action backwards in time. Or maybe it is that the decision concerning reconciliation was taken before the reconciliation, so temporal succession has not been breached. Nevertheless it raises the question of whether causation really requires temporal priority – cause *before* effect – that Hume accorded to it. We return to this point below. Suffice it to say here that it does.[4]

Let us say that David and John shake hands as soon as they meet. Shaking hands is a sign of friendship. At the point at which they shake hands they are friends; the two events (shaking hands and being friends) are coincident in time, simultaneous. Does Hume's causal priority – cause *before* effect – really stand? Kant provides a similar example of a heavy ball striking a cushion; the striking of the cushion by the ball causes a ball-shaped hollow in the cushion. Are the two simultaneous, or does the action of the ball temporally precede the shaping of the cushion? Mellor (1995: 220–3) shows persuasively that temporality is present.

Further, let us ponder a moment what is causing what – is it the shaking of hands that is causing the friendship, or is it the friendship that is causing the shaking of hands? Or, indeed, is it something else that is causing both the friendship and the shaking of hands, for example a human desire for conflict resolution? The friendship and the shaking of hands might simply be manifestations of a deeper factor – the desire for conflict resolution – in which case the two manifestations may be *supervenient* on, or entailed by, the base factor of conflict resolution. In this case the shaking of hands and the friendship covary but may not be causally related; correlation does not imply cause (discussed later). In another example, if I have large hands and large feet I would be hard pressed to prove that the size of my hands *caused* the size of my feet any more than I could prove that the size of my feet *caused* the size of my hands; they are epiphenomena, by-products of true causes (this raises the issue of 'screening off', discussed in Chapter 3). Maybe they are both manifestations of a deeper genetic feature of my make-up that causes me to have both large hands and large feet.

The issue of causation runs deeper. What we see in the reconciliatory greeting between David and John may not be the actual cause of the friendship, but simply a *description* of the cause. Davidson (2001: 150) remarks, in Humean voice, that 'it seems to be the "quality" or "circumstances" of an event that is the cause rather than the event itself, for the event itself is the same as others in some respects and different in other respects.' Davidson also argues for the need to separate the cause from the *description* of the cause (pp. 155–6). He gives the example of a match being struck, addressing the assertion that the match lit up because it was struck. This, he suggests, is not the case; the striking of the match is a description of a cause, but the cause may lie in a compound of factors (e.g. the presence of oxygen, the dryness of the match, the speed and firmness of the strike, the abrasiveness of the striking surface).

Implications for researchers:

- Consider whether temporal priority is necessary in establishing causation.
- Recognize that cause and effect may be simultaneous in certain circumstances.
- Do not confuse the description or presenting evidence of the cause for the cause itself.
- Recognize that causes may be compound: each cause on its own is insufficient to bring about the effect, but together they might do so.
- Recognize that there may be multiple causes of any effect, each of which could cause the effect.

If causation is problematic and conjectural, then a major task is to establish the correctness of the causation. A Popperian would suggest not only that we seek rival causes to explain effects, but that we subject possible causal explanations to the test of refutation: if a cause does not pass the refutation test then it must be rejected, and an alternative cause be suggested. Conjecture and refutation are partners in establishing causation. This is important not only *per se* but also because of its consequences.

Let us say that, in establishing the cause of the fight in the playground, we have two rival possible explanations of causes. One is that David and John were simply aggressive people who would take any opportunity to fight and so, when the opportunity arose – the simple insult – the causal mechanism was triggered (cause A). A rival explanation may lie in the housing policies of the local authority (cause B), placing 'problem families' together in the same housing estate. Depending on the causal explanation will be how the situation could be handled. The two causal hypotheses could lead to opposite ways of effective handling of the case, i.e. if cause A is accepted then individual counselling and anger management might be the treatment, whereas cause B might involve separating the families by moving them to different local authority estates. Here one treatment could frustrate the other and vice versa; one 'treatment' would be individual and the other social. If the first (cause A) is adopted then it could leave the problem to fester, as the families would continue to be in the same proximity, and would continue to annoy each other and cause yet more headaches for the local authority. If the second treatment (cause B) is adopted then it could lead to David and John being moved to separate housing estates, resulting in even further problems in the new housing estates to which they had moved, as the cause of the problem – the aggression of the two people – had not been addressed.

Implications for researchers:

- Consider rival explanations and hypotheses in establishing causation.
- Indicate what evidence and tests are necessary in order to falsify the hypothesis or explanation of causation offered.

Let us consider another example of this, in the field of medicine. Let us say that a particular medicinal preparation is being used on bandages to treat an open wound, but that this results on the wound becoming yet more infected. One explanation (cause A) may be that the medicinal compound on the bandage contains a chemical that immediately creates more infection in the patient through chemical change, so the more frequently the bandage is changed, the more infection is produced. An alternative explanation (cause B) might be that the medicinal compound on the bandage acts as a culture in which the already present bacteria in the wound could multiply. For cause A the solution might be infrequent changes of bandage, whilst for cause B the solution might be frequent changes of bandage. Epidemiological research shows that infrequent changes of bandage are more strongly associated with the increased infection than are frequent changes of bandage, hence cause B is taken to provide a better account of the causation. The issue here is that rival explanations of causation have to be tested.

Does cause always precede effect?

As mentioned above, a key feature of causation for Hume, as for many of his successors, is that causation has a temporal dimension: typically the cause precedes the event. Does causation require temporal precedence/sequence/priority/succession? Is causation temporal or simply interactional? Take, for example, the science laboratory at school. In the laboratory the students are investigating light shining through a prism. They shine the beam of light and, at the moment that it strikes the prism, it is separated into the colours of the spectrum. The breaking apart of the light into the rainbow of colours is simultaneous with − not precedent to − the light hitting the prism, yet it is clear that the cause of the splitting up of the beam of the light was the shining of the light. What we have here is more than a semantic difference between the verbs 'to cause', 'to determine', 'to depend' and 'to entail'; we have a substantive difference that challenges Hume. As Lewis (1993) remarks, an event may determine another without causing it.

Consider the example of a conditional offer to a student for a place at university: if she gains such-and-such a grade in public examinations then she will be accepted into the university. The day arrives that the results are published. She has passed the examinations at the required grade and so her place at university is secure. The two are simultaneous with one another − the gaining of the grades and the acceptance by the university. Consider the example, too, of a teacher who becomes a grandparent (A) *immediately* his daughter has a baby (B); the entry to grandparenthood is simultaneous with birth of the child.

Kim (1993a: 22–4) raises the issue that dependence and determination are not the same as cause. He gives the example of Socrates and his wife Xantippe: Xantippe simultaneously became a widow (A) when Socrates was executed (B). There was no temporal contiguity, precedence and sequence, the two events being coincident and simultaneous, nor was there any spatial contiguity, one event taking place in prison and the other elsewhere. The widowing of Xantippe was *entailed* by the execution of Socrates: the death of Socrates entailed the widowing of Xantippe. However, there is no symmetry of dependence: the death of Socrates determined the widowing of Xantippe but not vice versa.

Implications for researchers:

- Causes may be simultaneous with their effects.
- Determination and dependence may not be the same as causation.

The issue concerns the nature of *supervenience*. Supervenience, put simply, is where one cannot have an A-difference without having a B-difference, or, as Lewis remarks, 'we have supervenience when [and only when] there could not be difference of one sort without differences of another sort' (1986: 14). In supervenience, a set of properties, let us call them A, supervenes on (is determined by, is entailed by, depends on, covaries with) another set of properties, let us call them B, in the case that one cannot have any changes in these A-properties without having also having changes in their B-properties. There is, as McLaughlin (1995) remarks, 'dependent-variation'.

The student cannot be admitted to university (an A-property) without passing the examination (a B-property). The teacher cannot become a grandparent (an A-property) without the daughter having a baby (a B-property); A supervenes on B. Xantippe could not become a widow (an A-property) without Socrates dying (a B-property); A supervenes on B. The relationships are not causal, but nevertheless dependency, entailment and covariance exist. If Hume's requirement of temporal priority for causation to be present does not operate here, the two events being simultaneous, then the two events are not causally related (A is not caused by B). As Kim (1993a: 23) remarks, it is difficult to imagine a contingent empirical law that would support the causal relation between A and B.

In the three cases – (a) the admission to university; (b) grandparenthood and the birth of a grandchild; and (c) Socrates and Xantippe – the entailment relations are symmetrical: A entails B and B entails A. However, the *dependency* is not symmetrical: the admission to the university could have happened for reasons other than the gaining of the grades, the teacher could have become a grandparent without his daughter having a child (maybe the teacher had another daughter who had another child), i.e. the grandparenthood was not necessarily caused by the first daughter's baby. Similarly whether Socrates was executed did not depend on – was not causally determined by – whether Xantippe was a widow (he was executed for another reason: the alleged corruption of youths). If one were to try to trace in a causal chain, then the cause of Socrates' death was the drinking of hemlock, but the drinking of the hemlock cannot be said to cause the widowhood of Xantippe; the causal chain stops at the death of Socrates (Kim 1993a: 30). One can indicate how it was that Xantippe came to be a widow, but this does not necessarily constitute a *causal* explanation. Maybe the event – Xantippe's widowhood – had no cause, only entailment. McLaughlin (2005: 12) argues that, whilst supervenience may embrace dependence, in fact it does not actually *need* to; the supervenience of property A may not *depend* on property B, only covary with it; the size of my hands (A) may supervene on the size of my feet (B) but not depend on the size of my feet.

A supervenes on (is entailed by, depends on, is determined by, covaries with) B in that:

(a) A covaries with B (variations in A correlate with variations in B): covariance;
(b) B depends on A: dependence and entailment;
(c) A is not reducible to B.

Supervenience and entailment are closely related but are also different from each other. McLaughlin (2005: 6–7) sees both as being:

- *Reflexive* ('there cannot be an A-difference without there being a B-difference');
- *Transitive* ('if A-properties supervene on B-properties and B-properties supervene on C-properties, then A-properties supervene on C-properties');
- *Non-symmetric* (even though there are occasions, as noted above, where non-symmetry may be replaced by symmetry between the entailment of A and B and *vice versa*).

There are instances where supervenience and entailment differ. Consider, for example, the case of Jane and John. John is an only child, having no brothers or sisters, whilst Jane has one sister and no brother(s). Jane, therefore, is a sibling (an A-property) whilst John is not. Neither of them is a brother (a B-property). Though being a brother (B) entails being a sibling (A), being a sibling (A) does not entail being a brother (B). Being a sibling (A) does not supervene on being a brother (B), as in the case of Jane: two people can differ in respect of being a sibling (being either a brother or a sister) even though they may be exactly alike in respect of being a brother (cf. McLaughlin 2005: 7). Here the B-properties (being a brother) can entail the A-properties (being a sibling) even though A (being a sibling) does not supervene on B (being a brother).[5]

We have to separate (a) entailment, dependence and determination from (b) causation. They are similar to, but different from, one another. Supervenience may not necessarily *explain why* related factors are related, only that they are.

Implications for researchers:

- Consider whether the research is establishing causation or whether it is indicating entailment, dependency, determination, covariance and supervenience, and the implications for the research if it is not concerned with causation.
- Consider what are the base properties and the entailed properties in supervenience: what is supervenient on what.

Limitations of deterministic causation

The examples so far, particularly of the playground fight, and the discussions raised by the examples resonate with Hume's concepts of causation. Humean analysis is regularistic and deterministic: *if* such-and-such is the cause *then* such-and-such is the necessary effect, the consequence. If the necessary and sufficient conditions obtain then the effect follows. If the first billiard ball strikes the second billiard ball then the second billiard ball moves. This may be true in the physical world, where it is possible to identify and isolate causes and effects and universal laws. However, the human world is different from the purely physical world and its more deterministic, mechanistic situation; human intentions, conditions, motives, reasons, interactions and suchlike operate in ways that are not so susceptible to straightforward deterministic modelling (Maxwell 1996, 2004). Initial conditions do not negate human intentionality and responsibility. What constitutes the necessary and sufficient conditions for person A to perform an action may be different for person B, and the interactions of these conditions may be choreographed differently for each person. Just because one cause produces a particular effect once is no guarantee that it will produce it a second time. As the Chinese saying goes, we never jump into the same river twice; things change between the first and second time that we jump into the river. The circumstances in which the cause–effect relation are embedded may change.

Put simply, the certainty with which a cause may bring about an effect is not usually clear-cut, and a deterministic view of causation may be better replaced by a *probabilistic* view of causation in social sciences. Here *certainty* is replaced by *likelihood*. This may take the form of, for example, statistical likelihood, or the *prima facie* case in which the likelihood of effect B is greater if A were present than if A were not present (e.g. Suppes 1970, 1984; Lieberson 1997) (the counterfactual argument, discussed later). It is to probabilistic causation, and its associated analysis, that we turn in Chapter 3. Causation makes effects *more likely* rather than certain or less likely (though, as we will see later, this does not always hold true), or, as Mellor (1995: 68–70) argues, for there to be evidence that a cause is a cause of an effect, then that cause must raise the chances of its effects occurring; it must make them 'more probable than not' (ibid.: 69). The counterfactual argument (Kim 1993c; Lewis 1993) for causation states that if X had not happened then Y would not have happened.

Implications for researchers:

- Causation may be regularistic and deterministic in some circumstances, but is more likely to be probabilistic in understanding human behaviour.
- Probabilistic causation concerns the likelihood of a cause producing an effect, in comparison to what would have occurred if the cause had not been present.

Taking stock

The example of the fight in the school playground, and the associated discussion, has shown us that, in considering causation, several factors are concerned:

- Causes and effects are separate entities, contingent rather than analytic, and connections need to be established between them.
- Hume's rules for causation are:
  - *contiguity* (of space and time);
  - *priority/succession* (the cause precedes the effect);
  - *constant conjunction* (the coupling of one event and its successor beings found to recur repeatedly);
  - *necessary connection*.
- Necessary connection is learned from *experience*, habit and custom rather than deductive, logical, necessary proof.
- In deterministic causation 'the same cause always produces the same effect, and the same effect never arises but from the same cause' (Hume 2000: 1.3.15: 2).
- 'Where different objects produce the same effect, it must be by means of some quality, which we discover to be common among them' (ibid.: 1.3.15: 7).
- 'The difference in the effects of two resembling objects must proceed from that particular, in which they differ' (ibid.: 1.3.15: 8).
- Causes are known only by inference, conjecture and refutation.
- Causation is often probabilistic rather than absolute and deterministic.
- Some effects may be simultaneous with causes.
- Investigating causation involves identifying *necessary* and *sufficient* conditions.
- In studying causation it is useful to identify INUS conditions.
- Causes may vary in their relative strengths.
- The direction of causes may be clear, unclear or hypothesized.

- There is frequently an asymmetry in the direction of causation.
- It is more fitting to consider a chain of causation rather than a specific nexus of a single cause with a single event.
- There is a danger in isolating and focusing on singular causes separately from other contributing causes, contexts and conditions.
- It is fitting to regard causes as events or processes over time.
- Causal nets, conditions and interactions may provide better accounts of causation than linear determinism.
- It is sometimes unclear what actually constitutes a cause and what constitutes an effect.
- The context and conditions of an event are as important as the trigger of an effect.
- There is need to separate a reason from a cause.
- Some causes may be supervenient on other base factors.
- It is important to decide, in terms of temporality, what are relevant causes and what to include and exclude from studies of causation, e.g. how far back in time one needs to go in establishing causes, how far forward in time to go in establishing effects.
- It is important to decide, in spatial or environmental terms (however defined), how widely, narrowly and deeply to trawl in looking for causes and which to include and exclude, e.g. from the psychological to the social, from the micro to the macro, and to decide the direction and combination of such causes.
- It is important to identify which causes mediate, and are mediated by, other causes.
- The trigger of the effect may not be its sole cause.
- Causes often raise the likelihood of their effects.
- Causes often bring about changes or transitions.

The length of this list, started from a simple example of a fight in a school playground, may serve to quash any suggestion that causation is simple either to understand or even to demonstrate. This is not to suggest that establishing causation should not be attempted. There are regularities, there are likelihoods based on experience, and there are similarities between situations and people – indeed, the similarities may be stronger than the differences. This suggests that establishing probabilistic causation, whilst unstraightforward and daunting, may be possible.

Chapter 3

Probabilistic causation

This large chapter argues that probabilistic causation in proceeding in educational research is a more realistic approach to research than deterministic causation. We may not know for certain that a cause will always produce an effect; we have incomplete knowledge. Causal knowledge is inductive and inferential rather than deductive (Salmon 1998: 41) and, in causal knowledge, statistical generalization and probability replace certainty, whilst qualitative data can indicate *how* causation works. This chapter exposes several matters that arise in examining probabilistic causation, the effect of which is to challenge the acceptance of naïve causation in which policy makers may all too readily adopt research which purports to demonstrate that such-and-such is the effect of a cause, or that the cause can actually be identified. One of the purposes of the chapter is to indicate what researchers can do when they are working in this uncertain, probabilistic context. The 'probabilistic theory of causality' has been outlined by Suppes (1970).

Much of probabilistic causation lies in the realm of statistical treatments and probabilities (but not exclusively so), and so the chapter devotes a lot of attention to numerical analysis.[1] It presents many examples that provide readers with practical advice on different ways of investigating causation, including qualitative examples.

Smoking may cause lung cancer, but not always, and many non-smokers contract lung cancer. The relationship between cause and effect is not deterministic or regular, or, at least, not as routinely deterministic as Humeans would suggest. However, smoking may increase the likelihood of lung cancer, and it is this *probabilistic* view of causation to which we turn here. The cause raises the likelihood of an effect, though for any effect (e.g. lung cancer) there may be several causes. There are imperfect regularities. Causation is often subjunctive and probabilistic rather than deterministic. Some causes are necessary but not sufficient, whilst others are sufficient but not necessary (Mellor 1995: 13). As was argued in the last chapter, causes and effects take place in the context of specific circumstances and conditions, and it is these circumstances that cause the cause to have the effect, whereas in other circumstances it may not (e.g. ibid.: 16).

Implications for researchers:

- Causation is probabilistic and concerns the likelihood of an effect being produced by a cause and a cause being the cause of an effect.
- There may be exceptions to the probabilities.
- A 'cause' is an umbrella term for several causes.
- An 'effect' is an umbrella term for several effects.
- Causes may not be uniform or singular.
- Effects may not be uniform or singular.

Table 3.1 Scores on a mathematics test for control and experimental groups

	Average score overall	Average score of lowest third of students	Average score of middle third of students	Average score of highest third of students
Control group pre-test	50	20	50	80
Experimental group pre-test	50	20.3	48.7	81
Group 1 (10 schools)	55	23	54	88
Group 2 (10 schools)	46	17	44	76
Group 3 (10 schools)	49	21	48	79
Control group post-test	63	35	65	89
Experimental group post-test	62	33.7	45	89.3
Group 1 (10 schools)	62	30	60	96
Group 2 (10 schools)	55	25	55	85
Group 3 (10 schools)	69	46	74	87

Let us examine probabilistic causation through an example of small class teaching and its effects on students' mathematics performance. The example is probabilistic in that small class teaching does not guarantee students' raised mathematics performance (indeed it may lower it), and students' raised mathematics performance may not be due to small class teaching but to a range of other factors. However, the example indicates that small class teaching might increase the likelihood of students' raised mathematics performance, and this is probabilistic causation at work. The example is returned to in many parts of this chapter.

A worked example: small class teaching

A group of education policy makers decide that small class teaching should be introduced into its primary schools, *inter alia* in order to raise students' attainment in mathematics, so the policy is put into practice in 30 local primary schools, with some 600 teachers participating, i.e. the total population of teachers in the 30 participating schools, together with a further 30 schools, with some 600 teachers, acting as the control group in this experimental approach. The project runs for one school year, with pretests and post-tests of children's mathematics attainment in all the schools. In some schools the innovation corresponds to raised levels of average mathematics attainment in comparison with the control group; in others it seems to make no difference – the average scores of the control and experimental groups do not differ significantly statistically; in others the average mathematics attainment of the experimental group falls in comparison with that of the control groups. The scores on tests of mathematics attainment are presented in Table 3.1 (let us say that they are percentages).

This clearly is a simplified model, for heuristic purposes only. What are the researchers to conclude about causation? Did the innovation cause the several effects? Has it brought improvement, and, if so, to whom? Is the improvement uniform across the schools and the ability groups? Has it worked? It seems, for example, that, although there has not been an increased average performance over time between the control and the experimental groups (i.e. overall one might be tempted to say that the intervention has not worked), nevertheless the intervention seems to have made a very slight difference in the average performance (an improvement) between the control and the experimental group in respect of the high- ability students. Are we right to conclude that the results are caused by the intervention?

Even though the project operated on a highly simplistic model (an input–output 'black box' view of cause and effect), it still raises several points concerning our understanding of causation. Firstly, there is the question of what actually constitutes the cause, and here there are many contenders for inclusion. Superficially it might be a reduction to 25 students in each class in the experimental group, but that is simply the numerical independent variable and, in fact, could disguise the variation in the sizes of the experimental groups, say from 18 to 25 students. As any teacher will tell you, there is a huge difference between a class of 18 and a class of 19, let alone of 25. However, the INUS conditions of a causal statement (outlined earlier) require us to indicate the *insufficient* but *necessary* causes in the event, together with the *sufficient* but *unnecessary* conditions that obtained in the specific situations. Here the field suddenly opens up dramatically. For example, in School A the INUS conditions could be:

1 the class teacher's commitment to making the innovation work;
2 the move away from didactic teaching;
3 the provision of suitable resources for student-centred learning;
4 the pedagogic skills of the teacher for interactive teaching;
5 the number, range and kinds of student–teacher interactions;
6 the pressure from parents and the school for their children to perform well;
7 the willingness of the students to adopt the new teaching and learning approaches;
8 the ability of the students to adopt the new teaching and learning approaches;
9 the mathematical abilities of the students;
10 the relationships between the students and the teachers.

In School B the INUS conditions could comprise a different set of ten:

1 the visibility of the profile of the innovation of small class teaching in the school;
2 the familiarity of the student with being in a small class;
3 the enthusiasm of the teacher and students for interactive teaching;
4 the relationships between the teacher and the students;
5 the support from the parents for the innovation;
6 the incentives for the students to perform well in mathematics;
7 the motivations of the teacher;
8 the reaction of the teacher to an imposed, non-negotiated change;
9 the level of support from the senior staff of the school, particularly if things do not turn out well (i.e. risk avoidance);
10 the children's liking for mathematics.

In School C the INUS conditions could comprise yet another different set of ten:

1   the willingness of the students to be exposed to greater teacher scrutiny and inter-action;
2   the competitive nature of the classroom;
3   the inter-group and intra-group hostility between different students;
4   the familiarity of the students to being publicly accountable in class (i.e. exposure to others) for their mathematics working and thinking;
5   the arrangement of the desks and seats in the classroom (e.g. rows or groups);
6   the degree of formality of the mathematics lessons;
7   the pressure from an environment of frequent testing;
8   the ability of the teacher to handle differentiated teaching and tasks;
9   the ability of the students to handle differentiated teaching and tasks;
10   the distractions in the classroom.

These are only three out of the many schools and classes. These INUS conditions, highly incomplete and certainly not exhaustive, expose the difficulty of identifying what actually should constitute the 'causes' of the effects. Indeed the determination of what are necessary and sufficient conditions in human behaviour might be a never-ending occupation. Further, as can be seen, they vary from context to context. If we are to take Mill's suggestion to include all the antecedent conditions, then the list of factors will be unmanageably vast. But which ones should we include? Which ones, by their absence (counterfactually), are neither necessary nor sufficient, and how do we know? Which ones are necessary and sufficient, and how do we know? Which factors are minimally requisite and which are maximally relevant, and how do we know? It is difficult to ascertain the relevance or importance of excluded variables, which may have more causal significance than those that have been included. Indeed regression and multiple regression are incomplete, as they often exclude important variables (Scheines 1997: 188). Winnowing out potentially important variables in an attempt to establish simple causation in a regression analysis, or, indeed in any causal investigation, is a dangerous matter (Turner 1997: 42), as important variables might be overlooked, and therefore the researcher might discover false positives – i.e. false relationships and associations (e.g. in regression analysis) might be discovered which, if the correct variables had been included in the first place, would not have existed. Mackie's idea of INUS conditions is one way of paring down the number of causes to the essentials, but, in each situation (each school), not only could there be very many, but these will vary from school to school, and, even then, there is the problem of identifying what the factors are, let alone which are necessary and which are sufficient in human and social behaviour. The problem of overload is scarcely attenuated.

Implications for researchers:

- INUS conditions may vary from context to context and from group to group.
- Decisions on which variables to include and exclude affect the operation and analysis of causation.

Table 3.2 The strength of causal factors

Causal factors	Factor strength (1)	Factor strength (2)
1 The class teacher's commitment to making the innovation work	60%	80%
2 The move away from didactic teaching	30%	20%
3 The provision of suitable resources for student-centred learning	10%	30%
4 The pedagogic skills of the teacher for interactive teaching	80%	90%
5 The number, range and kinds of student–teacher interactions	50%	60%
6 The pressure from parents and the school for their children to perform well	90%	Removed from the list of factors
7 The willingness of the students to adopt the new teaching and learning approaches	60%	70%
8 The ability of the students to adopt the new teaching and learning approaches	50%	60%
9 The mathematical abilities of the students	20%	10%
10 The relationships between the students and the teachers	70%	80%

Further, one might be tempted to think that the matter could be addressed by examining the relative strengths of each of the factors, but that, too, is chimerical. For example, it may be impossible to calculate, measure or ascertain relative strength (even with, for example, beta coefficients in multiple regression, discussed later), as the problem is one of operationalization. Then there is the problem that in one classroom the *relative strength* of a factor may be high, whilst in another it may be very low, and in yet another the same factor may simply be absent.

Similarly a cause may be strong at one point in time but weaker at another point in time. Further, the absolute and relative strengths of the factors may be unstable, changing over time and context. For example, in School A ten conditions were identified as contributing causally to the students' performance in mathematics. Let us imagine that it were possible to measure the causal strength of these ten factors, and an index of that strength yielded the data in Table 3.2.

Now, at first glance in the column 'Factor strength (1)', we can see that parental pressure is the greatest contributing factor. However, let us imagine that not all of these factors actually obtain in a school; not all are present (the examples of Schools B and C suggest this possibility) or not all are included. In this circumstance the relative weights could change dramatically, as reported in the column 'Factor strength (2)'. This time the teacher's and students' commitment and abilities to handle interactive teaching and relationships have greater prominence. Eliminating one major factor ('the pressure from parents and the school for their children to perform well': factor 6) may strengthen or weaken the causal effects of the other factors, i.e. the factors and their strengths are unstable. Their strength is dependent, in part, on the presence of other causal factors. Indeed, strength is not a criterion of causation, and strong associations

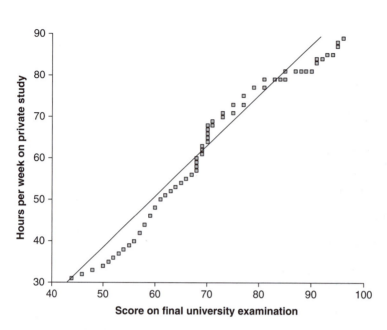

Figure 3.1 A scatterplot and regression line

are not necessarily more causal than weak associations. Calculating the relative strength of possible causes leads us to discussions of regression and multiple regression, and it is to these that the chapter now turns.

We can also notice that, in the much earlier example of small class teaching, the percentages are not zero sum; they do not total 100 per cent. Rather they are a 'positive sum' – there is no ceiling on the total percentage because there is no ceiling on the number of factors (the example included just ten factors for School A, but there could have been more). There is multiple, not single, causation. The performance in mathematics could be attributable repeatedly to many component causes.

Probability, prediction and regression

Simple regression analysis can let us predict the value of one variable when we know the value of another. For example, using fictitious data here, we might want to see the effect of hours of private study on students' scores in a final university examination. We find out the number of hours studied (the independent variable) and the marks in the final examination (the dependent variable). A scatter plot with the line of best fit and gridlines added (e.g. with SPSS) can be constructed (note the convention that the independent variable is the vertical axis and the dependent variable is the horizontal axis) (Figure 3.1).

Here one can predict from the data that, the more hours one studies privately, the higher is the examination score, and, indeed, one can read off the values of the dependent variable from the values of the independent variable. So, for example, someone

Table 3.3 The Adjusted R square (SPSS output)

Model Summary

Model	R	R Square	Adjusted R Square	Std. Error of the Estimate
1	.966[a]	.932	.932	3.000

a. Predictors: (Constant), Hours per week on private study

Table 3.4 Analysis of variance in a regression table (SPSS output)

ANOVA[b]

Model		Sum of Squares	df	Mean Square	F	Sig.
1	Regression	12154.483	1	12154.483	1350.089	.000[a]
	Residual	882.267	98	9.003		
	Total	13036.750	99			

a. Predictors: (Constant), Hours per week on private study

b. Dependent Variable: Score on final university examination

studying for 50 hours gains an examination score of 59 (rounded) and someone studying for 70 hours a week gains an examination score of 76 (rounded). (This separates
regression from correlations, as regression analysis gives exact values, whereas correlational analysis yields a coefficient of overall association.) The line of best fit is that line
which gives the closest fit to the variance in the data (i.e. data are either side of the
line), trying to have the same number of cases above and below the line and trying to
keep the cases as close to the line as possible. In the example here, one can see that there
is a very strong relationship between the number of hours and the score on the final
examination (the gradient of the slope is very steep). SPSS can also produce output to
indicate how much variance in the dependent variable is explained by the independent
variable (Table 3.3). The 'Adjusted R square' (adjusted to take account of the number
of independent variables and sample size) here is recorded at .932, that is, 93.2 per cent
of the total variance in the dependent variable is explained by the independent variable
(this is unusually high, and in the 'real world', i.e. with non-fictitious data, it would
probably be much lower).

SPSS also calculates the analysis of variance (ANOVA) here, and provides an indication of the level of statistical significance (Table 3.4). In the example the significance
level is $\rho = .000$, i.e. is highly statistically significant (stronger than .001).

Having such a robust significance level suggests that it is useful to continue with the
analysis, and this can be done with SPSS. SPSS calculates standardized coefficients, giving beta (ß) weightings. The beta weighting is 'the amount of standard deviation unit
of change in the dependent variable for each standard deviation unit of change in the
independent variable' (Cohen *et al.* 2007: 538). In the example here the standardized
beta weighting is .966, i.e. it is highly statistically significant ($\rho = .000$ in the 'Sig.'
column) (Table 3.5); this means that for every standard deviation unit change in the

Table 3.5 The beta coefficient (SPSS output)

Coefficients[a]

Model		Unstandardized Coefficients		Standardized Coefficients	t	Sig.
		B	Std. Error	Beta		
1	(Constant)	22.201	1.432		15.504	.000
	Hours per week on private study	.763	.021	.966	36.744	.000

a. Dependent Variable: Score on final university examination

Table 3.6 Adjusted R square for more than one predictor variable (SPSS output)

Model Summary

Model	R	R Square	Adjusted R Square	Std. Error of the Estimate
1	.969[a]	.939	.938	2.852

a. Predictors: (Constant), Motivation level, Hours per week on private study

independent variable ('hours per week on private study') there is .966 of a unit rise in the dependent variable ('score on final university examination') – i.e. there is nearly a one-to-one correspondence.

One has to be extremely cautious in using regression analysis, as regression is a predictor based on probability and data provided; it is not a measure of causation. Prediction and causation are not the same (Freedman 1997: 113–14). So, in the example here we could not say that 'hours per week on private study' *caused* the 'score on final university examination' to be what it is, only that there is a correspondence between the independent and dependent variable. It may be that a third variable (e.g. 'intelligence') or a fourth variable (e.g. motivation) caused both the 'hours per week on private study' and 'score on final university examination' (see the discussion of causal forks later in this chapter), i.e. that there was covariance between the two variables here in response to another cause. Nevertheless, regression analysis is widely used in data analysis for, and discussions of, causation.

Whilst simple regression is able to predict the value of one independent variable in relation to one dependent variable, multiple regression is useful in calculating the relative weighting of two or more independent variables on a dependent variable. Using the concept of the beta (β) weighting, defined above, multiple regression calculates how many standard deviation units are changed in the dependent variable for each standard deviation unit of change in each of the independent variables. For example, let us say that we wished to investigate the relative weighting of 'hours per week of private study' and 'motivation level' as independent variables acting on the dependent variable 'score on final university examination'. A multiple regression (e.g. using SPSS) can be calculated. In a fictitious example, let us say that data are computed as in Table 3.6.

This tells us that the Adjusted R square is .938, i.e. the amount of the dependent variable explained by the two independent variables is very high (93.8 per cent).

Table 3.7 Analysis of variance for more than one predictor variable (SPSS output)

ANOVA[b]

Model		Sum of Squares	df	Mean Square	F	Sig.
1	Regression	12247.676	2	6123.838	752.796	.000[a]
	Residual	789.074	97	8.135		
	Total	13036.750	99			

a. Predictors: (Constant), Motivation level, Hours per week on private study

b. Dependent Variable: Score on final university examination

Table 3.8 Beta coefficients with two variable predictors (SPSS output)

Coefficients[a]

Model		Unstandardized Coefficients		Standardized Coefficients	t	Sig.
		B	Std. Error	Beta		
1	(Constant)	22.577	1.366		16.531	.000
	Hours per week on private study	.714	.024	.904	29.286	.000
	Motivation level	.404	.119	.104	3.385	.001

a. Dependent Variable: Score on final university examination

Similarly, the analysis of variance (ANOVA) is highly statistically significant ($\rho = .000$) (Table 3.7), i.e. the relationship between the independent variable and the dependent variable is very strong.

Finally, the beta weightings (standardized coefficients) are presented (Table 3.8). These two beta weightings are calculated to show their strengths relative to each other; they are not independent of each other.

So, in the example here, the following can be observed.

- The independent variable 'hours per week of private study' has the strongest positive predictive power ($\beta = .904$) on the dependent variable 'score on final university examination', and this is statistically significant (the column 'Sig.' indicates that the level of significance, at .000, is stronger than .001).

- The independent variable 'motivation level' has strong positive predictive power ($\beta = .104$) on the dependent variable 'score on final university examination', and this is statistically significant (the column 'Sig.' indicates that the level of significance, at .001).

- Though both independent variables have a statistically significant weighting on the dependent variable, the beta weighting of the independent variable 'hours per week of private study' ($\beta = .904$) is much higher than that of the independent variable 'motivation level' ($\beta = .104$) on the dependent variable 'score on final university examination', i.e. 'hours per week on private study' is a stronger predictor of 'score on final university examination' than 'motivation level'.

So, the researcher can predict that, if the hours per week spent in private study were known, and if the motivation level of the student was known (here measured on a ten-point 'ratio level' data scale), then the likely score on the final university examination could be predicted. The formula would be:

'Score on final university examination' = (β × 'hours per week on private study') + (β × 'motivation level').

In the example, the β for 'hours per week on private study' is .904, and the β for 'motivation level' is .104. These are the relative weightings of the two independent variables. So, for example, for a student who spends 60 hours per week on private study and has a high motivation level (9) the formula becomes:

'Score on final university examination' = (.904 × 60) + (.104 × 9)
= 54.24 + .936 = 55.176

Multiple regression takes two or more variables and enables the researcher to calculate their relative weightings on a dependent variable. However, as with the simpler regression earlier, one has to be cautious: (a) prediction is not the same as explanation; (b) covariance may be due to the operation of another variable (e.g. an exogenous variable that precedes, and influences, the independent variables, causing them to covary with the dependent variable); (c) variables may interact with each other and may be inter-correlated (the issue of multicollinearity, and SPSS can calculate 'collinearity diagnostics' and remove variables that have strong collinearity/covariance), i.e. the model could be non-recursive (discussed later).

Multiple regression assumes that the participants have no relationship with each other, i.e. that they are independent of each other. It focuses on individuals rather than groups. However, in fact this may not be the case. For example children in family 1 may be similar to each other but different from children in family 2, and children in family 2 may be similar to each other but different from children in family 3, and so on. Schools A and B may be similar to each other but different from schools C and D, and schools C and D may be similar to each other but different from schools E, F and G, and so on, i.e. there are hierarchical clusters of participants – grouping effects.

Treating all the participants as independent, as is done in multiple regression, over-looks these similarities, and hence standard errors of regression coefficients are under-estimated which, in turn, leads to overstatement of statistical significance. Multi-level modelling recognizes such grouping effects and, as its name suggests, allows for different levels of grouping (by taking into consideration residual effects at each level in the hierarchical – grouping – structure, e.g. within-school effects and between-school effects, or within-family effects and between-family effects).

The Centre for Multilevel Modelling at the University of Bristol offers a wide range of information and materials on all aspects of multi-level modelling and statistical packages (e.g. MLwiN, HLM, SAS, SPSS), and the reader is advised to go to the following websites:

http://www.cmm.bristol.ac.uk/
http://www.cmm.bristol.ac.uk/learning-training/multilevel-models/index.shtml
http://www.cmm.bristol.ac.uk/team/mmsage.pdf
http://www.lrz-muenchen.de/~wlm/wlmmule.htm
http://statcomp.ats.ucla.edu/mlm/

In using regressions – simple or multiple – there are certain assumptions that have to be met (Cohen *et al.* 2007: 542), for example:

- random sampling;
- ratio data;
- the removal of outliers;
- the supposed linearity of the measures is justifiable;
- interaction effects of independent variables (in non-recursive models) are measured;
- the selection for the inclusion and exclusion of variables is justifiable;
- the dependent variable and the residuals (the distance of the cases from the line of best fit) is approximately normally distributed;
- the variance of each variable is consistent across the range of values for all other variables (or at least the next assumption is true);
- the independent variables are approximately normally distributed;
- collinearity/multicollinearity is avoided (i.e. there is no perfect linear relationship between one independent variable and another independent variable).

There are three important caveats in using regression techniques: (a) they assume linear relations between the independent and dependent variables (also discussed later in this chapter); (b) they concern prediction not causation; (c) they are only as robust as the variables included, and the inclusion or removal of one or more independent variables affects their relative weightings on the dependent variable. With these three major caveats in mind, regression techniques may be useful *guides* to possible causation.

Can one really calculate the relative strength of causes?

Though Salmon (1998: 213) is sceptical of the possibility of being able to measure the strength of a causal chain by statistics alone, he also adds that this does not mean that statistics are entirely unhelpful. Though the strength of a causal chain is not simply a function of the strength of its individual links (ibid.: 214), nevertheless individual probability values can help to define appropriate measures of causation.

Accepting this caveat, the calculation of the relative strength of causes can be approached through beta coefficients in multiple regression; this is useful but ephemeral. Beta coefficients indicate the *relative* strengths of given independent variables on a dependent variable at a particular moment in time. For example, let us consider the example of the possible causes of teacher stress (Garcia 2008). In the example, beta coefficients in the multiple regression were calculated for a range of causes of teacher stress, each cause having been derived from factor analysis of very many variables each. The SPSS output (edited here) is set out in Table 3.9.

Table 3.9 Beta coefficients of multiple variables (SPSS output)

Beta Coefficients

	Standardized Coefficients	Significance level
	Beta	
Teacher voice and support	.323	.000
Workload	.080	.000
Benefits and rewards of teaching	.205	.000
Managing students	.116	.000
Challenge and debate	.087	.000
Family pressures	.076	.000
Considering leaving teaching	.067	.000
Emotions and coping	.044	.000
Burnout	.157	.000
Balancing work, family and cultural expectations	.100	.000
Local culture	.071	.000
Stress from family	.058	.000
Stress reproducing stress	.164	.000
Control and relationships	.092	.000

Table 3.10 Altered weightings in beta coefficients (SPSS output)

Beta Coefficients

	Standardized Coefficients	Significance level
	Beta	
Teacher voice and support	.316	.000
Workload	.096	.000
Benefits and rewards of teaching	.219	.000
Managing students	.114	.000
Challenge and debate	.099	.000
Considering leaving teaching	.102	.000
Emotions and coping	.091	.000
Burnout	.156	.000
Local culture	.131	.000
Stress reproducing stress	.162	.000
Control and relationships	.130	.000

Here one can see the relative strengths (i.e. when one factor is considered in relation to the others included) of the possible causes of stress. In the example, it appears that 'teacher voice and support' exerts the strongest influence on the outcome (levels of stress) (beta of .323), followed by 'benefits and rewards' of teaching (beta of .205), then 'stress reproducing stress (beta of .164) (i.e. the feeling of stress causes yet more stress), followed by 'burnout' (beta of .157), 'managing students' (beta of .116), and so on down the list. However, if we remove those variables connected with family ('family

Table 3.11 Further altered weightings in beta coefficients (SPSS output)

Beta Coefficients

	Standardized Coefficients	Significance level
	Beta	
Principal behaviour	.270	.000
Clarity of jobs and goals	.087	.000
Teacher voice and support	.154	.000
Workload	.109	.000
Benefits and rewards of teaching	.124	.000
Managing students	.102	.000
Challenge and debate	.095	.000
Family pressures	.071	.000
Considering leaving teaching	.081	.000
Emotions and coping	.084	.000
Burnout	.129	.000
Balancing work, family and cultural expectations	.098	.000
Local culture	.088	.000
Stress from family	.067	.000
Stress reproducing stress	.150	.000
Control and relationships	.086	.000

pressures', 'balancing work, family and cultural expectations' and 'stress from family') then the relative strengths of the remaining factors alter (Table 3.10). In this revised situation, the factor 'teacher voice and support' has slightly less weight, 'benefits and rewards of teaching' has added strength, and 'control and relationships' takes on much greater strength.

On the other hand, if one adds in new causal variables ('principal behaviour' and 'clarity of jobs and goals'), then the relative strengths of the variables alter again Table 3.11). In Table 3.11, 'principal behaviour' greatly overrides the other factors, and the order of the relative strengths of the other factors alters.

These comments suggest that calculating beta coefficients of relative strengths may have some utility but that they may be limited, as:

(a) they are more concerned with correlational power than causal power – they do not explain cause, only assume it (and the assumption is based on a theory whose basis lies outside the correlation);
(b) they examine relative strengths of a given set of variables, and they typically do not explain the whole situation (i.e. the explained variance is never 100 per cent – the R square is probably never 1.0 in a multiple regression);
(c) they alter if variables are added or removed, i.e. they assume that all the variables included, and no others, are relevant;
(d) they may change over time and people.

It may be difficult to say with any certainty or sense of permanence what the strength of a causal factor may be in relation to other causes. Further, it is possible that the strength of a cause is revealed by examining its incidence in a wider population, rather than within an individual case relative to other factors, just as, in epidemiology, for example, the issue is how one can determine the strength of smoking as a causal factor in relation to lung cancer by examining statistics in a wide population to see the proportion of cases where smoking has a high and low presence in lung cancer, rather than examining its strength compared to other factors in an individual case. One can determine strength in relation to a population rather than in relation to other causes in a specific case.

Implications for researchers:

- Identifying the relative strengths of a cause concerns identifying not only their strengths relative to each other but their prevalence in the population.
- The relative strength of a cause is unstable, depending on the presence or absence of other causes in operation, the point in time at which the cause is active, and the populations in question.
- Calculating beta coefficients in multiple regression is useful for indicating relative strengths, but only for a given set of causes and at one point in time.

Linear and non-linear relations of cause and effect

So far we have considered only the *inter*-factor variation in strength. But suppose that the ten factors have *intra*-factor variations in strength, i.e. they are *continuous* variables (e.g. income, age, test scores) rather than, say, *nominal* variables (e.g. sex, race, school). In continuous variables it could be that the variables have further varying effects. For example, a little pressure may do us all good but a lot of pressure may be damaging; a little coffee may stimulate our concentration but a lot of coffee disturbs our concentration. A little dose of small class teaching may have a beneficial effect; a lot of it may be counter-productive, or it may benefit some groups (e.g. lower-attaining students) but not others. A little didactic teaching may be beneficial; a lot may be damaging. The relationship between a cause and its effect may not be linear; it may be curvilinear, non-linear, or impermanent/indeterminate and unpredictable (chaotic) (Figures 3.2 to 3.5).

Different values of each continuous variable may have different causal weight. Hence to treat a variable as a singular, homogeneous unit, exerting an unvarying effect, may be mistaken. If I have only a little money then I can do very little; if I have a lot of money I can do things at a much greater rate and with a much greater scope. Causation is often a matter of degree, and the degree varies; it is not singular or uniform for all cases, and its effects may be exponential rather than arithmetic.

Further, one cannot presuppose that there is only a single cause and a single effect; this may be over-reductionist. In the 'real world' there are multiple, simultaneous causes, many specific circumstances, and multiple effects. It is also unclear what the *interaction effects* may be between factors: taken separately they may cause little or few effects, but taken together – and in varying combinations – they may cause significant and many effects.

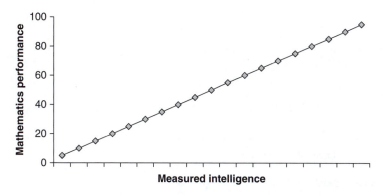

Figure 3.2 A linear relationship in a regression

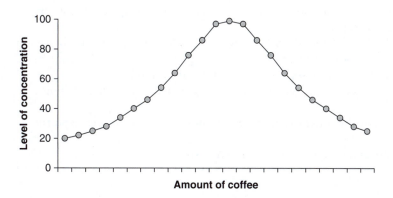

Figure 3.3 A curvilinear relationship in a regression

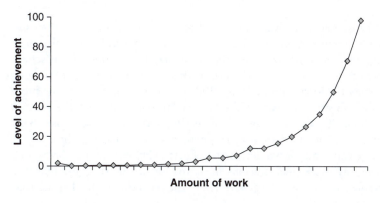

Figure 3.4 A non-linear relationship in a regression

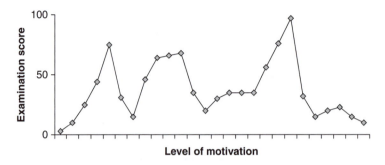

Figure 3.5 A chaotic and unpredictable relationship in a regression

---

Implications for researchers:

- Decide whether the variables are nominal (categorical) or continuous.
- If the variables are continuous then the effects of causes may vary according to the values in each variable.
- Consider whether the relationship between cause and effect may be linear, non-linear, curvilinear or chaotic.
- Relationships between causes and effect(s) may be unstable.
- Recognize the limits and dangers of seeking mono-causation and single effects.
- Examine the possible interactions between causes and their influence on the effect(s).
- Interactions may not be the same across contexts.

There is also the *time dimension* to be considered: not all of the causes may be operating all of the time; some may come earlier, some may appear later, some will mutate, some may reduce, some increase, some disappear, some reappear – i.e. the temporal context is unstable. At some points in time some of the factors may become redundant – i.e. neither sufficient nor necessary – whilst at other points in time they may be both sufficient and necessary.

Further, the same cause may not always produce the same effect. If a child swears at the teacher once, then the punishment may be light; a second time and the punishment may be much more severe; a third time and the child may be excluded from school ('three strikes and you're out'). There is evidence of this in the incidence of students repeating a year at school (Morrison and Ieong 2007): if a student fails one or more examinations then she repeats the year; if she fails them a second time then she is expelled from the school. This is the law of 'increasing returns'. Same cause, both greater and different effect, and the ratio may be geometric rather than arithmetic.

Conversely, the same cause may have decreasing effects. The teacher may bring in a new mode of teaching, say more presentations in drama form. The students may rise to it in the first instance, and it has a large effect. On the second and third times that the teacher employs it the novelty has worn off, and the effect is smaller and smaller. By the fourth time, boredom has replaced novelty, and the effect is to cause classroom disorder. This is the law of diminishing returns. Same cause, both less and different effect.

Implications for researchers:

- Recognize that causes and effects are not stable over time; they may appear, disappear and reappear over time.
- Not all of the causes of an effect may be operating at any one point in time.
- The same cause can have increasing and changing effects.
- The same cause may have reducing and changing effects.

Conditional probability

Let us say that in one class with small class teaching the teacher used highly didactic, formal teaching with marked social distance between himself and the students (Factor A), and this was deemed to be an inhibitor of the beneficial effects of small class teaching on students' attainment in mathematics: didactic teaching reduces mathematics performance. However the same highly didactic, formal class teaching (Factor A) significantly raises the amount of pressure placed on the students to achieve highly (Factor B), and this (Factor B) is known to be the *overriding* cause of any rise in students' performance in mathematics. For example, in small classes the teacher can monitor very closely the work of each child: high pressure raises mathematics performance. Now, it could be argued that Factor A – an ostensibly *inhibiting* factor for the benefits of small class teaching – actually causes *improvements* in mathematics performance in the small class teaching situation. This is known as 'Simpson's paradox'.

One can provide further examples of 'Simpson's paradox' outside and inside the field of education.

- In the case of the causal relationship between smoking (A), heart disease (B) and exercise (C), smoking (A) is highly correlated with exercise (C): smokers exercise much more than non-smokers. Though smoking causes heart disease, exercise actually is an even stronger preventative measure that one can take against heart disease. The corollary of this is that smoking prevents heart disease (Hitchcock 2002: 9).
- In the case of the causal relationship between taking contraceptive pills (A), thrombosis (B) and pregnancy (C), taking contraceptive pills (A) increases the chance of thrombosis, but pregnancy can also cause thrombosis, and taking contraceptive pills reduces the probability of pregnancy. Hence taking contraceptive pills may affect the probability of thrombosis, reducing or increasing it, depending on the relative strengths of each causal route (Hesslow 1976: 291). It may be that the likelihood of thrombosis from taking a contraceptive pill (the effect of A on C) is lower than the likelihood of thrombosis from the pregnancy (the effect of B on C, given A).

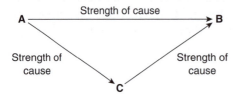

Figure 3.6 Direct and indirect effects of a cause

Let us take examples from education.

- Parental pressure (A) may increase a student's fear of failure (C), but parental pressure may also reduce a student's social life (B), and a student's social life may increase a fear of failure. In other words, the likelihood of the effect of A on C may be lower than the effect of B on C, given A.
- Greater examination pressure on students (A) increases their lack of self-confidence (C) but it also increases the student's hard work (B), and hard work reduces the student's lack of self-confidence. In other words, the likelihood of the effect of A on C may be lower than the effect of B on C, given A.
- A student having a vibrant social life (A) may increase the likelihood of her or his failure in academic examinations (C). But having a vibrant social life also reduces stress (B), and reducing stress reduces the likelihood of failure in academic examinations (C). In other words, the likelihood of the effect of A on C may be lower than the effect of B on C, given A.

A cause may raise the likelihood of an effect, but it may also lower that likelihood. Probability is conditional; it does not always guarantee the raising of the likelihood. The presence of other conditions affects the likelihood of an effect of a cause. A diagrammatic representation of these examples is shown in Figure 3.6. In formal terms, the conditional probability of B, given A and C, is formally defined in standard notation thus: $P(B|A) > P(B)$, where $P(B | A)$ is the probability of B, given A. However, in the two examples here it appears possible that $P(B | A) < P(B)$. What is required is to know the strength of the lines AB, AC and CB so that the relative strengths of each route (A to B) and (A to B via C) can be discovered.

What we observe here is that a cause may be inhibited, prevented, facilitated, enabled, increased, reduced and otherwise affected by the presence of other causes (cf. Pinker 2007: 219). If a cause is that which makes a difference, then it is not only its presence that must make a difference, but also its absence (Lewis 1993) (the counterfactual argument that if X had not happened then Y would not have happened); the presence of a cause may have caused the presence of its effects just as it absence may have caused the absence of its effects; this is perhaps an obvious point, but possibly a stronger argument than Hume's principle of 'constant conjunction' (Pinker 2007: 211). Constant conjunction can sanction correlation rather than causation, whereas *counterfactual* analysis requires causation to be present. Causation is *probabilistic* rather than deterministic or regularistic; it deals in likelihood rather than certainty. In notational terms we can say that A raises the probability of B, i.e. $P(B|A) > B | \text{not-A})$.

Implications for researchers:

- Some causes will have a positive or negative influence on other causes.
- Some causes may produce counter-intuitive effects, depending on the presence of other factors, hence it is important to identify the other factors operating in a situation.

If the issue of causation is beginning to appear intractable, then consider the further features of the earlier example of small class teaching (pp. 30 to 34). We have data on three schools, and these suggest that the causal conditions are largely indeterminate, or at the very least extremely unclear and open-ended in quantity, range, degree, influence and relative strength. They are specific to each school. We do not know what would happen if School A were subject to the conditions which obtain in School B and/or School C, or, indeed, in the control group. This rehearses the problem alluded to by Goldthorpe (2007a: 196), that the same people or, in this case, the same school cannot be in two groups simultaneously (Holland's 'Fundamental Problem of Causal Inference' (Holland 1986: 947), discussed in Chapter 5) – both the control group and the experimental group, both receiving and not receiving the innovation – so we cannot say with any certainty how School A would have performed in different conditions. So we have no way of attributing completely accurate causation because we cannot observe the same group in both conditions. We might have a group that *resembles* School A, with which School A can be compared, but resemblance, echoing the criticisms of Humean analysis of resemblance, is no substitute for certainty (*Treatise*: 1.3.8: 3). It will be argued later (Chapter 5) that randomization and matching are ways to address this problem.

Implications for researchers:

- Sampling is a critical issue in examining causation in control and experimental group methodologies (e.g. randomized controlled trials).
- Sampling yields approximations of effects rather than certainties, as two groups may be similar rather than identical.

Causes, events, states, processes and effects

Returning to the example, we have suggested that the causation involved in the small class teaching is not, in fact, a single event or process, nor is the outcome mono-causal. Rather it is a composite of multiple events, multiple conditions and multiple causes. To say with any certainty, then, that small class teaching improves mathematics performance may be to overstate considerably the claims that can legitimately be made about the causation involved or, indeed, its effects. Not only may there be multiple causes, each of which in itself is sufficient (see the discussion of overdetermination below), but there may also be compound causes (Scriven 1993) (we may need to have one cause (A) taken together with another (B) in order to produce the effect (C), with A and B individually insufficient to bring about C).

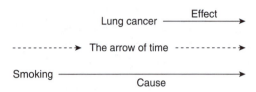

Figure 3.7 Temporal overlap of cause and effect

Causes may be events, processes or, indeed, states (Hage and Meeker 1988: 19). A 'state' variable, Hage and Meeker remark, has a degree of stability, sufficient for it to be measured, and which is situated at the 'beginning or end of a causal process'. They give examples of parents' or a child's level of education, which are sufficiently fixed for researchers to be able to measure them. State variables are like the nominal variables of demographic data or sampling characteristics, for example sex, level of education, place of birth or residence, attitudes, occupation, and so on. Whether, or to what extent, these exert a causal influence is challenged by Goldthorpe (2007a), discussed later.

Further, we have to ask at what point in time a factor ceases to be a cause and at what point in time an effect becomes an effect. Causation can be regarded as a *process* (the means or mechanisms that link A and B causally) and Salmon (1998: 16, 224, 286) argues powerfully that causal processes offer the connections between cause and effect that Hume sought. Kiser and Hechter (1998) argue for causation to be viewed in terms of processes and mechanisms, and that criteria of plausibility, reducing the time between cause and effect, and empirical testing are important in evaluating causal explanation. Causation takes place over time, and it may be that a temporal overlap exists between cause and effect – part of all of an effect may commence before part or all of the cause is fully over. If we say, for example, that smoking precedes lung cancer, then we can observe that not all incidences of smoking precede lung cancer, and smoking is an ongoing matter, not a single event: one may have lung cancer and continue smoking. It may be the final two years of a five-year period of smoking that triggers the onset of lung cancer. Temporality is not clear-cut, as Figure 3.7 indicates; notice that the cause continues after the effect has commenced.

The accuracy of the cut-off point between cause and effect may depend on the level of specificity in the definition of the cause and the effect. If the cause is reduced to unequivocal specifics and the same is done for the effect, then indeed no overlap may be found, one part of the cause being contiguous, but not overlapping, with the relevant effect, but in empirical practice this may be very difficult, impossible or unnecessary to ascertain. Whilst in principle cause and effect may be separate, contiguous and successionist, in practice, given the often general, subsumptive level of definitions of 'cause' and 'effect' (i.e. many events are contained under the umbrella of each), there may be practical overlaps in time.

It is also the case, as Goldthorpe (2007b: 268) remarks, that causes are not single events but may emerge over time. He gives the example of choices about future education that may take a period of weeks or months to be made, involving, for example, interactions between parents, students, teachers and peer groups.

Implications for researchers:

- Causation has to handle multiplicity of causes, processes and effects.
- Causes may be events, states or processes.
- Claims made for the cause of effects or the effects of causes generally should be cautious.
- An effect may commence before the cause has ended, i.e. whilst the cause continues.
- Different parts of a cause may occur whilst the different parts the effects are occurring.
- A cause is not necessarily a 'one-off' event, nor is an effect.
- A cause may emerge over time.

Returning to the example of small class teaching (pp. 30 to 34), it may be that the factor 'the pedagogic skills of the teacher for interactive teaching' is not a 'one-shot' affair, but, rather, that the skills develop, increase cumulatively – both quantitatively and qualitatively – over time. Is it fair to say, then, that (a) in the early stages of the development, the cause ('the pedagogic skills of the teacher for interactive teaching') may have a small effect (since they are relatively undeveloped) or, indeed, a large effect (because they are a novelty for the teacher and the students), or that (b) at a later point in time the same cause may have a larger effect (since the skills are more highly developed) or less effect (since the attrition of custom may have eroded their effect, or that they have been overtaken by other factors)? In either case the answer surely is 'no'. It is an empirical matter and a matter of probability.

Further, the earlier effects of the change in pedagogic skills may reveal themselves before the later sub-elements within the same factor ('the pedagogic skills of the teacher for interactive teaching') have appeared fully. Initially, for example, the effects of the causal factor may suppress mathematics performance, as the teacher is unskilled in the new techniques, the children are unprepared and unclear, and a period of confusion ensues. It is only later in the temporal sequence that the benefits may (or, indeed, may not) reveal themselves.

Not only may there be an overlap in timing between cause and effect but there is an issue of the timing of the evaluation of the effect. Too early an evaluation may find no effect; too late an evaluation, and the effect may have petered out (for example, some programmes of rehabilitation for drug offenders or criminals may have short-term benefits but, as recidivism rates tell us, these effects may be short-lived). In the example of small class teaching here, the arbitrary timing of the post-test (the end of the school year) could have been too soon or too late for the effect to have revealed itself. The issue is important, for it underlines the importance of establishing Hume's unbroken 'causal chain' of contiguous events and also of recognizing that it may take time for an effect to manifest itself. I might hate studying Latin in secondary school, considering it to be a worthless, dead language, only to find 30 years later that it is an invaluable aid to understanding the English language and its etymology.

> ## Implications for researchers:
>
> - Care has to be taken in deciding the point in time to evaluate the effects of a cause.
> - An effect at one point in time may different from the effect of the same cause at another point in time, or in another non-temporal context.

A cause may not reveal itself immediately. There may be an 'induction period' (the time taken to develop, for example, as in a disease), and the last point in the causal chain is not the entire cause, even though its induction time is zero in the sense that it is contiguous with the effect. We saw previously (p. 11) the example of the head injury early in life that, in later life, contributed to the person's fall on the icy sstreet. Similarly in epidemiology it is common for there to be an incubation or induction period of time in the development of a disease. Cancer may have a long induction period (i.e. take a long time to develop) and, indeed, a long 'latency' period (i.e. being present but undetected). In the example here, the small class teaching may have been having a developing but small effect but, because it was too small to be detected, may have been overlooked.

It has been assumed in the example of small class teaching that it is an innovation, and hence is designed to bring about change. That may not be an entirely appropriate assumption to make. A cause may bring about a change (Mellor 1995: 126), but it may also bring about a 'non-change' (Ducasse 1993; Pinker 2007: 220), keeping a situation stable when all around is changing, i.e. a non-change may still be causally relevant. For example, Hage and Meeker (1988: 15) indicate that causal influences may be at work in keeping a traditional society traditional in the face of changes all around, and that considerable energy may be expended by members of the society in preserving that tradition (e.g. in Amish communities). The difficulty that non-changes produce for an account of causation relates to the issue of the 'trigger' of change – the final event in the causal chain, at a time when the induction period is zero. In this case there is no trigger, only continuity. (It seems as though causation, in this case, is a counterfactual.) However, more fundamentally, the issue challenges the extent to which causation requires a trigger, and suggests that an effect may not require a causal trigger. For instance, in the small class teaching example, some of the schools may have been practising small class teaching already, in which case there is no change for pre-existing practice. The cause – small class teaching – may continue to produce its effect – small class teaching. Sosa and Tooley (1993: 18) suggest that there may be an entirely adequate causal explanation of why a pencil on a table continues to remain at rest, without having to employ any idea of change. Causation is causation is causation, regardless of triggers; triggers of change may be a special – if very frequent – instance of causation.

> ## Implications for researchers:
>
> - A cause may already have been in operation before it is realized or included.
> - An ongoing cause may exert an ongoing or delayed effect.
> - An effect of a cause may be a change or a non-change.
> - The absence of change does not necessarily indicate the absence of a causal process.

The issue of change and non-change runs deeper. It concerns: (a) inaction, absence and omission; (b) prevention; (c) overdetermination; (d) the discovery of latent causes and effects; (e) causal pre-emption; and (f) catalysed effects. With regard to inaction, absence and omission, the question is raised as to whether these constitute causation. For, in our example of small class teaching, we could say 'the teacher caused the poor mathematics performance by not using small class teaching'. Is this a cause? Is *not* doing something a cause? Beebee (2004) cites the example of 'I killed the plant by not watering it'. The problem is that no causal processes are in operation, so process theories of causation may be questioned. Dowe (2007: 13) reviews work that implies that these might indeed be cases of causation, the 'transfer of properties' being able to translate these negatives into positives; he then suggests that a more fitting term for these is 'quasi-causation'.

Quasi-causation

Quasi-causation extends to prevention. In our example of small class teaching, it may be that in one school the teacher used differentiated teaching (A) in a small class, but this did not raise the students' performance in mathematics (B) because the teacher was anxious about differentiated teaching (C). In this instance, A (differentiated teaching) occurred, but B (improved student performance in mathematics) was prevented from occurring because of the interaction of A with C (anxiety about differentiated teaching). A caused C – the differentiated teaching caused the teacher to be anxious about it – and if A had not occurred then the anxiety would have caused improved student performance in mathematics (for example C may have caused students and parents to work harder). Here, A and B are positive events or facts, and C is a variable over the events. Without A, C would have caused B. Whilst prevention may reach further, for example prevention by omission (e.g. omitting to water the plant may lead to its death), prevention of prevention, prevention of prevention of prevention (see Dowe 2007), this does not enhance or diminish its status as quasi-causation rather than fully fledged causation.

Implications for researchers:

- One causal factor may cancel out, prevent or offset another.
- Not doing something may become a cause or an effect.

Quasi-causation includes overdetermination. A familiar example is the issue of which bullet can be said to have killed a man, i.e. which causes his death (Horwich 1993), if two bullets simultaneously strike his head. Neither bullet is *necessary* for the death, so neither bullet is the cause of death; if bullet A did not kill him then bullet B did, and vice versa, though each bullet is *sufficient* for the death. Is it the case that neither bullet is the cause of the death, as, in respect of each, it could be that the other is the cause? (It is truer to say that 'either one bullet *or* the other' caused the death, rather than 'neither'; cf. Mellor 1995: 102.) What we have here is a case of 'causal overdetermination' – where a particular effect is the outcome of more than one causal chain, and each of those causal chains, in itself, would have been sufficient to have produced the effect. The man would have died even if one of the two bullets was not fired, and if bullet A did not cause the death it would be causally true to say that the man would have died. In our example of small class teaching, the lists of factors for each of the three schools in question could have overdetermined the effect – the rise in students' mathematics performance – indeed it may not have been necessary for all of the factors in each school to have been present in order to bring about the effect. One effect may have several causes/causal chains. Whilst this is commonplace, it is important to note, in order to refute the claims frequently made by protagonists of small class teaching, that its success is due to such-and-such a set of causes; if only it were that simple!

Implications for researchers:

- An effect may be overdetermined by the presence of more than one sufficient cause.
- One effect may have more than one cause.

In our example of small class teaching there are also latent causes and effects, causes and effects that may be unobserved because they are overshadowed or overruled by other causes and conditions. For example, it may be that a major factor driving the effectiveness of the small class teaching is the students' motivation for interaction in small groups, but this is either buried amongst a host of other factors or does not appear for want of being expressed and identified. It is present but not found. This is common in procedures of factor analysis and regression, where the amount of variance explained is calculated, and very seldom comes to 100 per cent, i.e. totality; factor analysis is designed to reveal underlying latent variables from a range of *given* variables. However, for our purposes here, it is important not only to identify possible latent factors but to ascertain what would have been the effects – what would be the situation – if these factors had not been present.

For example, I may have a headache, and I take a paracetamol, but my headache persists. I may say that the paracetamol has not worked, but this is untrue: it may have worked but the headache may have been so bad, or may have been increasing during the time of the working of the paracetamol, such that its effects are unnoticed. Put simply, the headache could have been even worse if I had not taken the paracetamol, but its benefits have been masked: the counterfactual argument. Morgan (1997: 61) argues that causes fit together in a range of different ways, sometimes being additive, sometimes cancelling each other out, sometimes being present but simply being lost in the face of more dominant causes, sometimes being prior causes, and sometimes being intervening causes.

Implications for researchers:

- Causes and effects may be latent and undiscovered, though present.
- Some causes and effects may be overshadowed and obscured by others.
- The continuation of an event does not mean that other causes were not having an effect on that event.

Or take the example of small class teaching: a major underlying causal factor influencing the mathematics performance may be the considerable time spent on small class teaching, but this has been overlooked in the identification of significant causes. It may be that without the presence of this cause the effectiveness of small class teaching may not be assured, but this cause is masked, or overshadowed, by the presence of a range of other factors. We have to consider the situation if this factor had *not* been present, i.e. the counterfactual situation. The argument is for meticulous consideration of all the variables involved.

In the same example, let us consider the effect on students' mathematics performance of one causal factor of 'the willingness of the students to adopt the new teaching and learning approaches'. In this instance we know the factor, but its effect has been superseded, overtaken by, say, 'the pedagogic skills of the teacher for interactive teaching'. We may have difficulty in ascertaining the effect of the cause 'the willingness of the students to adopt the new teaching and learning approaches' other than counterfactually, i.e. by examining the situation when this factor is *not* present. This brings us again to the problem outlined earlier, wherein the same group of students cannot both possess and not possess the factor in question (Goldthorpe 2007a: 196, 212) (Holland's (1986) 'fundamental problem of causal inference').

It has been suggested that one should not believe that probabilistic causation should operate simply on the principle that, the higher the probability, the stronger the causation, or that probability is demonstrated if the balance of likelihood is greater than 50 per cent. For example, in the case of small class teaching, it may be that in School A the probability of small class teaching improving students' mathematics performance may be higher than in School B, but this does not necessarily mean that the causation is stronger in School A; it might simply be that the obstructing or inhibiting factors in School A might be fewer or weaker than in School B. Not to consider the countervailing factors is to omit one side of the equation. We may cause something to happen not only by pressing the driving factors but by removing the obstacles.

The situation is less clear than a simple matter of the balance of probabilities or a simple equation. In fact the issue of 'causal pre-emption' suggests that a cause may actually lower, rather than increase, the probability of an effect. Consider this case (Hitchcock 2002), in which an assassin wishes to kill the king, so he puts poison into the king's drink, with a 30 per cent likelihood of death. The king drinks the poisoned cup and dies. The assassin had an associate, and the associate had agreed that, if the assassin's poison did not kill the king, then the associate would introduce an even stronger poison into the king's drink, with a 70 per cent likelihood of death. So, by introducing the initial poison into the king's drink, in net terms the assassin had actually lowered the chance of the king's death from 70 per cent to 30 per cent; the weaker cause pre-empted the stronger cause, and the assassin's work affected the likelihood of the king's death, firstly by only administering a weak poison and secondly by preventing the introduction of a stronger poison. The first cause has pre-empted the second. Clearly the temporal context of the situation is critical here. It may not always be true that causes necessarily make their effects more likely. (Of course, it may be argued that the action of the assassin in fact did increase the likelihood of the king's death, from zero to 30 per cent, i.e. there are three routes here, not two: (a) a 30 per cent chance of death; (b) a 70 per cent chance of death; and (c) no death.)

Consider this further example, from Sosa and Tooley (1993: 21). In this example there are two types of disease (A and B), and everyone catches either A or B; there are no exceptions. Disease A has a mortality probability of .1; disease B has a mortality probability of .8. If one catches disease A then one is immune to disease B and vice versa. A person contracts disease A and dies. Had the person not contracted disease A then he would have had a .8 probability of dying from disease B, i.e. higher than the probability of dying from disease A. In this case, too, 'it is not true that causes make their effects more likely' (ibid.); the causal pre-emption was to lower the likelihood rather than to raise it.

In our example of small class teaching, let us imagine that a student has been exposed to either a highly competitive environment (A) or a teacher who had no real expertise in interactive teaching (B). Now let us imagine that if the student is exposed to A then this suppresses her performance in mathematics by 20 percentage points, and if the student is exposed to B then this suppresses her mathematics performance by 40 percentage points. The student is exposed to A, and her performance drops by 20 percentage points, but had she been exposed to B then her mathematics performance would have had a probability of dropping even higher, i.e. the causal pre-emption lowered the likelihood of the effect (poor mathematics performance) rather than raised it.

Implications for researchers:

- The probability of an effect is not necessarily the greatest strength of its likelihood.
- A cause may lower the likelihood of an effect, as well as raise it.
- Causal pre-emption may lower the likelihood of an effect.

Finally there is the matter of whether a catalyst is the same as a cause. A catalyst may reduce the induction period. Consider the following. A person contracts a form of cancer through exposure to a particular carcinogen, and the induction period (the time taken for the disease to develop) is, say, 15 years. However, the disease is discovered and the process is treated through a drug (A) such that the induction period is reduced to five years. Is A a catalyst or a cause of the cancer? In this case drug A is both a catalyst *and* a cause; it causes the onset of the disease to occur ten years earlier than normal; it is a cause of the early onset of the disease and of the disease itself, as, without the drug, the disease would not have occurred at that point in time (temporality is part of the causation), and there is no guarantee that the person would have lived on between the fifth and the fifteenth year. The catalyst catalyses a causal mechanism and is considered to be a cause.

Implications for researchers:

- A catalyst may be considered to be a cause.
- A catalyst may catalyse a causal mechanism, not only a single event.

Table 3.12 Class size, students' scores and interactive teaching

Class size	Non-interactive teaching	Interactive teaching
Large class (>35 students)	20	25
Small class (≤35 students)	30	40

Calculating probabilities

Returning to the example of small class teaching and students' mathematics performance, what we have is an instance of *probabilistic causation*. How can we determine whether an event is a likely cause or how much the likelihood of an effect is raised by the presence of a particular cause? In short, how do we assess the probability of a cause bringing about an effect? A formulaic answer to this might be in terms of the conditional probability of B, given A, formally defined in standard notation (Hitchcock 2002: 7) as a ratio of probabilities, thus:

P(B | A) = P(A & B)/P(A)

where P(B | A) is the probability of B, given A. However, let us continue in words wherever possible, rather than in symbols and equations! What if there are several possible causes of an effect? How do we know which one is likely to raise the probability of an effect, given that they may occur in combination and given that a particular effect is the consequence of several causes?

One way is to make probabilistic inferences based on data. For example, let us imagine that research results in distributions in respect of high student scores in mathematics as shown in (Table 3.12). Amongst those who both use interactive teaching and are in small classes, what proportion of high scoring in mathematics is attributable to those small classes? The data tell us that the rate for such students is 40 cases. If these students were in large classes, we can infer that, there are 25 cases where students perform highly in mathematics. If this difference catches the causal role of small classes, then we could infer that, amongst those who are both in small classes and use interactive teaching, 15 out of the 40 cases (40–25), i.e. 37.5 per cent, are attributable to small classes. If we were to ask what proportion of students' high performance in mathematics was attributable to interactive teaching, then we could infer that 10 out of every 40 cases (40–30), i.e. 25 per cent, are attributable to interactive teaching. From amongst those who are both in small classes and exposed to interactive teaching, we can attribute 37.5 per cent of the cases to small classes and 25 per cent of the cases to interactive teaching.

A note of caution would add that these two causes do not represent the totality of causes of students' high performance in mathematics, as the high performance is not mono-causal – indeed several causes contribute to the high performance. The amount of high performance attributable to component causes has no upper limit, as there are so many component causes (and inter-variable variation and intra-variable variation feature here). Small class teaching may or may not be either a necessary or a sufficient condition for interactive learning, just as interactive teaching may take place with or without small classes, i.e. the findings may demonstrate correlation rather than causation. Indeed what we see here is numerical calculation rather than causal manipulation or demonstration. The meaning and theory of causation is lost to the arithmetic; the same procedure could be applied to any variables without causality having been built into the model or demonstrated (though see Scheines 1997 for discussion of an algorithm for moving from statistical data to inferences about causal structures). As Freedman (1997: 137) remarks, such calculations do not tell us anything about the world outside the computer or the computed statistic.

Indeed the same data might fit many models (Glymour 1997: 214). In this case, for example, the researcher may find that removing small class teaching or interactive teaching may have little or no effect on students' high mathematics scores. While there is a correlation to be found between small class teaching and high scores, and between interactive teaching and high scores, in fact the high mathematics scores are caused by a completely different factor or set of factors, i.e. the correlations are purely coincidental (cf. Freedman 1997a: 121). A net effect (the effect after controlling for variables) does not establish causation (Turner 1997: 31).

This point argues that such-and-such an independent variable may be likely to raise the probability of a result in an independent variable, without guaranteeing it, i.e. probabilistic rather than deterministic causation. Further, this raises the importance of seeking the *counterfactual* basis of causation (Lewis 1993); a cause is not a cause unless its counterfactual is true (Freedman 1997) (and the counterfactual has to be explored in research). The counterfactual element of causation addresses the conditional statement 'If X (the independent variable) had not occurred then Y (the dependent variable) would not have occurred'. This, it is argued (e.g. Lewis 1993; Menzies 2008), establishes causation very clearly. Indeed Menzies (2008: 4) contents that, where A and B are two distinct *actual* events, with A as the cause and B as the effect, A causally depends on B if and only if (iff), A were not to occur then B would not occur. Lewis (1993: 194) writes that 'we think of a cause as something that makes a difference, and the difference it makes must be a difference from what would have happened without it. Had it been absent, its effects – some of them at least, and usually all – would have been absent as well'.[2] In the example here, of (A) small class teaching, (B) interactive teaching and (C) high mathematics scores, (A) and (B) could only be considered to be causes, rather than correlates, of (C) if their absence would have caused the absence of (C).

Implications for researchers:

- It is possible to examine the relative strengths of causes on effects through a matrix construction.
- Matrix use is probabilistic rather than deterministic.
- Correlation may be easily mistaken for causation.
- Causation is established by demonstrating the counterfactual basis of a cause on an effect.
- Counterfactuals argue that an event may not have occurred if its cause had not occurred.
- Causation requires its counterfactual to be true.

Screening off and causal forks

Another method of ascertaining probabilistic causation is through a test situation, in which 'screening off' certain causes or conditions takes place. 'Screening off' is attributed to Reichenbach (1956), and involves holding fixed some factors so that the effects of other factors can be ascertained; it means making something 'statistically irrelevant' (Salmon 1993a). An example was given earlier of the relationship between smoking, exercise and heart disease, in which smoking was highly correlated with exercise: smokers exercised much more than non-smokers. Though smoking causes heart disease, exercise actually was an even stronger preventative measure against heart disease, i.e. smoking may actually cause less risk of heart disease in this instance. Now, let us suppose that we really wished to discover the relevance of smoking for heart disease; this would involve holding fixed the factor of exercise.

A neat example of screening off is reported by Harford (2008: 23). Here the research was to discover whether juvenile criminals responded to the threat of being sent to prison. In one American state where young criminals could be tried in the adult court at the age of 17, the research compared the difference in the behaviour of 15-year-olds and 17-year-olds. In another American state where young criminals could be tried in the adult court at the age of 19, the research compared the difference in the behaviour of 18-year-olds and 19-year-olds.

The research found that, in those states which handed down harsher sentences in the adult courts than in the juvenile courts, the difference in the behaviour of the young criminals was very noticeable – it dropped markedly when the young criminals reached the age of majority. However, in the states where juvenile courts were harsh in sentencing there was very little reduction in the criminal behaviour of these two age groups because the young people were already scared of contact with the criminal justice system.

One possible explanation of this was that harsher sentences reduced crime, because the criminals were actually locked up in prison, i.e. they were not available to commit the crime, what Harford (2008: 23) terms the 'incapacitation effect'. If you lock up a person for ten years then that person has no opportunity to commit a violent crime on the public during that period. However, the research 'screened out' this possible explanation of the difference found in crime rates and, instead, indicated that the better explanation was the deterrent effect of harsher sentencing.[3]

Salmon (1998: 45) suggests that some factors are much more relevant to a causal explanation than others; they render other factors irrelevant. Screening off, he avers, is a matter of 'causal proximity'. He gives the example of measles – a measles infection is related more closely to the spots and the fever than the spots and the fever are related to each other. In his other example, of a storm (ibid.: 218), atmospheric conditions are more closely related to the causes of a storm than is a fall in a barometric reading; it is possible to have a storm without a barometric reading but it is not possible to have a storm without certain atmospheric conditions prevailing – the necessary conditions. The barometric reading is a *spurious* cause of the storm, and is screened off from the storm by the actual atmospheric conditions which cause both the storm and the fall in the barometric reading (Salmon 1998: 218). Echoing Suppes (1970), Salmon argues that there is a *prima facie* case of causality (A causes B) if nothing screens off A from B.

Screening off means that, if correlations exist between two variables that are not causally connected, there is a prior variable or an event that can remove the correlations/

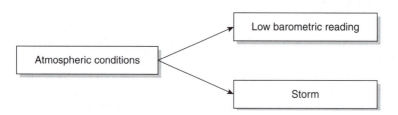

Figure 3.8 Correlation from a prior cause

associations. In the example of the storm and the barometric reading, the atmospheric conditions are the prior common cause for the correlation between the storm and the low barometric reading. The correlation between the storm and the low barometric reading is conditional on the prior event – the atmospheric conditions – and without this the two would not be related (cf. Müller 2005: 23–4). The situation can be represented diagrammatically (Figure 3.8).

In striving to understand causal processes that take account of different strengths, interactions, combinations and influences of causes, and embracing the issue of 'screening off' causes in order to determine the strengths of probable causes, Salmon (1993b) uses the concept of 'causal forks' from Reichenbach (1956). There are different kinds of causal fork.

In a 'conjunctive fork', two processes (A and B) may derive from the same background conditions (C), i.e. A and B have a common root cause and hence may be correlated, and the common cause (C) screens off the correlation between A and B: we could have A without having B and vice versa. Reichenbach's (1956) common cause principle states that if A and B are positively correlated, then C (the common cause of A and B) exists, effects A and B separately, and screens off A and B from each other, i.e. the common cause (C) makes each of the two effects (A and B), though related, 'statistically irrelevant to each other' (Salmon 1993a). In the example of small class teaching used earlier, we may suggest that student motivation (A) in one school and student performance (B) in a different, unconnected school increase and are positively correlated, both due to the common cause (C), small class teaching, and that, in relation to C, it is possible to consider A without considering B; they are capable of being screened off from each other (they are in different and unconnected schools). A and B may covary, but neither is causally related to the other; as the most elementary of social science research texts tell us, correlation is not the same as cause. Statistical association is not a necessary ingredient in establishing causation (Salmon 1993b): a storm is not caused by a fall in the barometric reading. I may have large hands (A) and large feet (B), but neither one causes the other, though both may be related to the common cause (C), e.g. a genetic predisposition to large hands and feet. The size of my hands (A) and the size of my feet (B) may be screened off from each other in considering their relationship to C; they may be considered in isolation, i.e. separately.

The conjunctive fork may be represented diagrammatically (Figure 3.9). Here the common cause (C) gives rise to the two separate effects (A and B), without there being any common effect that stems from A and B conjointly (Reichenbach 1956). For example, a public examination (C) may cause motivation in students in one school (A) and demotivation in students on another school (B), without A affecting B or vice versa. A and B are causally and statistically irrelevant to each other; C screens off A from B.

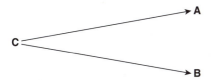

Figure 3.9 A conjunctive fork with two different effects

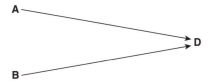

Figure 3.10 A conjunctive fork with a conjoint effect

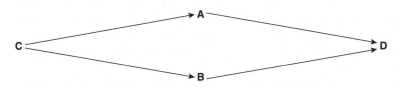

Figure 3.11 A closed conjunctive fork

In the conjunctive fork of Figure 3.10 there is no common cause, but two events, A and B, conjointly produce a common effect D. For example, a public examination (cause A) and parental pressure (cause B) might cause the student to work extra hard (D).

In the conjunctive fork of Figure 3.11, a combination of the previous two, there is a common cause C that produces the effects A and B, and these effects A and B causally produce the same effect D. A and B are both effects and causes in this causal chain. For example, a public examination (C) may cause motivation in students in one school (A) and demotivation in students in another school (B), with A and B contributing separately to an overall rise in the number of students meeting university entrance requirements (D).

In an 'interactive fork' (Salmon 1993b), an intersection between two causal processes (A and B) brings about a change to both, and, therefore, the correlation between A and B cannot be screened off by the common cause (C). For example, if I am playing snooker I might be aware that, in sinking the blue ball (process A), my cue ball will go into the pocket (process B); here there is a correlation between A and B, but the striking of the cue ball (common cause C) does not screen off such a correlation – we cannot have A without having B, and A causes B. In the example of small class teaching we may suggest that, for School C, 'the competitive nature of the classroom' (A) and 'the intergroup and intra-group hostility between different students' (B) constitute an

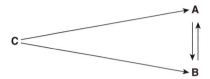

Figure 3.12 An interactive fork

Figure 3.13 Simple screening off of a cause and effect

interactive fork, in that they are positively correlated and that the common cause – small class teaching (C) – does not screen off A from B – we cannot have A without B and/or vice versa. In statistics this interaction effect could be determined through two-way ANOVA. The interactive fork may be represented diagrammatically (Figure 3.12). For example, a public examination (C) may cause positive motivation in students in one class in the school (A) and increased fear of failure in another class in the same school (B), but, being in the same school, the two groups of students interact with each other, i.e. A affects B and vice versa.

The difference between a conjunctive fork and an interactive fork lies in the screening off property; in a conjunctive fork screening off is possible, whereas in an interactive fork it is not. There is a causal interaction between A and B in an interactive fork, whereas no such causal interaction occurs in a conjunctive fork. In the conjunctive fork it would be possible to have A without B, whereas this would be impossible in the interactive fork (Salmon 1993b); in the former the existence of A is independent of B, and in the latter their existence depends on each other; they cannot exist independently.

Screening off goes further (Figure 3.13). In Figure 3.13 the values of C (the common cause) screen off the values of A from the values of B. For example, the desire not to let down the family (cause A) may affect the motivation to study for public examinations (cause C), and cause C may cause the outcome (B), e.g. gaining access to university. What one sees here is the importance of establishing the direction of causation and what actually causes what. One can take this further, to see that a chain of causation can become complex (Figure 3.14).

In Figure 3.14 the desire to escape the poverty trap (cause D) may bring increased motivation to study (cause C), which causes students in school A to study hard (A) and students in school B to take private tutorial lessons (B), without A affecting B and vice versa. Not only do we have D causing the common cause C which, in turn, causes A and B (i.e. through transitivity D causes A and B), but here C screens of the values of A from those of B, but this does not entail that the values of D screen off the values of A from those of B.

In Figure 3.15, the desire to escape the poverty trap (cause C) may bring increased motivation to study (cause D), which causes students in school A to study hard (A), and cause C might directly cause students in school B to take part-time employment in order to fund further higher education (B). Here, too, we see that the common cause C causes

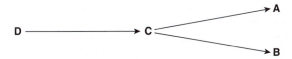

Figure 3.14 Complex screening off of cause and effect

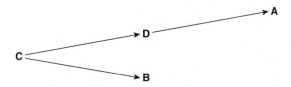

Figure 3.15 A common cause and screening off

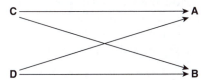

Figure 3.16 Screening off in multiple causes

B and D (with D causing A and, thereby, C causing A through transitivity), but here C screens off the values of A from B. But – unlike the previous case – this *does* entail that the values of D screen off the values of A from those of B. Hitchcock (2002: 18) remarks, in connection with these two preceding cases, that being a common cause of A and B is 'neither necessary nor sufficient for screening off the values of those variables'.

Finally there is the case of there being more than one common cause (Figure 3.16). In this example the desire to escape the poverty trap (cause C) may bring increased motivation to study (A) and also cause students to take part-time employment in order to fund higher education (B), whilst the pressure from parents (cause D) might have the same effects (A and B). In this sense A and B are 'overdetermined', in that they might have been produced by either C or D. Here C and D are common causes of A and B, but neither C nor D screens off the values of A and B. For example, if we were to hold the value of C constant and fixed, we would still expect A and B to be correlated because of the effect of D. Similarly, if we were to hold the value of D constant and fixed, we would still expect A and B to be correlated because of the effect of C.

Reichenbach also discusses the 'perfect fork', in which the interactive and conjunctive forks are indistinguishable from each other. As Salmon (1984) remarks, when there is no case where the processes do not produce the effects, then it is impossible to tell whether what is observed is a conjunctive or an interactive fork.[4]

To return to our example of small class teaching and its effects on students' mathematics performance, let us take three variables: (A) poor interactive teaching, (B) enjoyment of mathematics, and (C) poor mathematics performance. Poor interactive teaching may correlate with dislike of mathematics, i.e. students experiencing poor interactive teaching may dislike mathematics more than those who do not experience poor interactive teaching. Though poor interactive teaching may cause poor mathematics performance, dislike of mathematics may be an even stronger contributor to poor performance – i.e. poor interactive teaching, in the context of dislike of mathematics, may actually reduce the incidence of poor mathematics performance overall.

To simplify: if we wish to see the effect of A on B, in the presence of other causes (C), then we may need to hold C fixed (though Hitchcock (2002: 9) provides an instance of where this may not apply). If we wish to find out whether A causes B we need to know what happens if B is or is not present, whilst holding fixed other factors. We have to find inhibitors and preventers of A causing B, or other factors that, either on their own or in combination/interaction, may have a variable effect on B (mixed causes). But even if this is done, there is a myriad of ways in which one variable might depend on, or interact with, another, so to hold them fixed and constant may not always solve the problem – but it is a start. The matter is compounded when one takes continuous variables rather than simple binary, nominal or categorical variables (e.g. sex, social class, occupation); as discussed earlier, the relationships between causes and effects for continuous variables may not be linear. Put simply, the categorization of factors into preventers, inhibitors, facilitators and enablers may be frustrated because of the multiplicity of permutations. We may not be able to discover what causes what in any straightforward way or with any certainty.

The ecological fallacy

Whilst these preceding examples underline the importance of screening off and controlling for variables in order to ascertain causal influence more reliably and to identify the relationships between cause and effect more certainly, the examples also indicate the dangers of the 'ecological fallacy'. This is an error in which relationships that are found between aggregated data (e.g. mean scores) are assumed to apply to individuals, i.e. one infers an individual or particular characteristic from a generalization. It assumes that the individuals in a group exhibit the same features of the whole group taken together (a form of stereotyping).

For example, it could be hypothesized that the greater is the number of females in a class, the higher is the academic achievement of that class. This might be, for example (and these are stereotypes for heuristic purposes only here), because females, in comparison to males, are more highly motivated, are less disruptive, value academic education more, are less concerned to display anti-authority behaviours, and are less concerned to exhibit a disparaging attitude to school knowledge.

So, for example, let us consider the case of a secondary school. Class 1, with 32 students, has 24 (75 per cent) females and 8 (25 per cent) males, of whom 26 students (81.25 per cent of the class) gain 'Grade A' scores in the public examinations. In Class 2, again with 32 students, there are 50 per cent females and 50 per cent males, of whom only 18 students (56.25 per cent) gain 'Grade A' scores. The researcher concludes that her hypothesis holds: the greater the number of females in the class, the higher is the academic achievement.

However, on closer scrutiny of the data the following observations are made.

- In Class 1, 20 females gain fewer than 6 'Grade A' scores, whilst all 6 males gain 'Grade A' scores or higher.
- In Class 2, 8 females gain 'Grade A' scores, whilst 10 males gain 'Grade A' scores or higher.

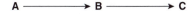

A ⟶ B ⟶ C

Figure 3.17 A recursive model of causation

From the aggregated data one might conclude that, the higher the number of females and the lower the number of males in the class, the greater will be the likelihood of the class scoring highly in public examinations. However, from the disaggregated data, the exact opposite might be true: the higher the number of males and the lower the number of females in the class, the greater is the likelihood of the class having higher scores in public examinations. This is the ecological fallacy – making incorrect inferences about individuals on the basis of aggregated data (it is also an example of the 'distorter' effect, discussed later).

The example here indicates that avoiding the ecological fallacy is possible if one controls for variables in the conduct of research. If one controls for variables/factors, then the likelihood of the ecological fallacy being committed is reduced. That said, in order to avoid the commission of the ecological fallacy, the importance of looking at *individual* behaviours within a group remains high.

Implications for researchers:

- In order to avoid the ecological fallacy it is important to control for variables and then, further, to investigate individual behaviours within groups and grouped data.
- Do not assume that the behaviour of a group is the same as the behaviour of the individuals within that group.
- Do not assume that the behaviour of the individual is the same as the behaviour found in aggregated data.

Recursive and non-recursive models

One can extend the earlier discussion of causal forks to include recursive and non-recursive models of causation. A recursive model appears in Figure 3.17. Here one can observe several features (Berry 1984):

(a) the variables are arranged in a linear sequence;
(b) the endogenous variables (those whose causes are represented in the model itself: A, B and C) are ordered such that the first (here it is A) is determined only by one or more exogenous variables (those variables that have values completely outside the model, i.e. that are excluded from the model);
(c) the endogenous variables other than the first (here they are B and C) are influenced only by the endogenous variable(s) preceding it and by any other exogenous variables (those excluded from the model);
(d) no endogenous variables are related reciprocally such that one influences the other and vice versa, i.e. the causation in the model is unidirectional;
(e) there are no indirect causal linkages between one endogenous variable and others that precede it in the causal model.

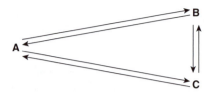

Figure 3.18 A non-recursive model of causation

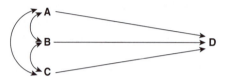

Figure 3.19 Reciprocal relations in a non-recursive model

It is unusual to find recursive models in educational research, as they tend to oversimplify the direction of variables and to overlook interaction effects. By contrast, and more frequent in educational and social research, are non-recursive models (Berry 1984), for example Figure 3.18. Here one can observe two features (Berry 1984):

(a)   each endogenous variable directly affects, and is affected by, all the other endogenous and exogenous variables in the model;
(b)   there is no clear unidirectional linear sequence of variables.

In some non-recursive models, non-reciprocal relations may obtain between one or more of the endogenous variables, for example Figure 3.19.

Examples of non-recursive models in education can be found in Berry (1984). Path analysis, structural equation modelling and regression techniques can be used to identify the strength of the relationship between causal lines in non-recursive models (see the later discussions of software and path analysis).

Hage and Meeker (1988) suggest that statistical procedures (e.g. path analysis, structural equation modelling) can be useful to identify the causal paths and the weights of the causal factors. In these the researcher hypothesizes the direction of causation and then tests the causal paths against the data, presuming a temporal sequence of events (the asymmetry of the direction of causation), and the researcher can also test for direct and indirect causal relations. They provide an example of this (1988: 25–30) in their reporting of research on 'peer influences on academic aspirations' (p. 25), in which the researchers hypothesized an increasing number of causal factors on students' aspirations. Starting with parental influences, they then add in the influence of 'best friends' and the 'best friend's' parents, then the boy's intelligence, then the boy's 'best friend's' intelligence, then the boy's occupational aspirations, then the boy's 'best friend's' occupational aspirations. The theoretical underpinning for the choice of variables could derive, in this instance, from theories of reference groups, peer relations in adolescents, motivation, social reinforcement, socialization influences, and suchlike.

What one can see in the modelling of causal relationships in non-recursive models is: (a) the hypothesized direction of causation; (b) the direct and indirect causal factors; (c) the interrelationships between the variables. It is only one small step to compute (e.g. through beta weightings or stepwise regression) the relative strength of these lines of causation (see also Halsey *et al.* (1980) for further examples). One sets up a model of the direct and indirect causal directions of variables and then tests the model with the data (see the discussion of path analysis later). Where these variables come from is an important point, the answer to which is often: relevant 'theory'. As Hage and Meeker argue (1988: 31), there is a need to identify and/or hypothesize the 'smoking gun' variables, that is, the states, events, processes or mechanisms that exert a causal influence on the phenomena under observation.

Implications for researchers:

- It is important to screen off causal processes in discovering true causation.
- Causal forks – conjunctive, interactive and perfect – are useful devices and useful modelling techniques for identifying causal lines, causal chains and causal processes.
- Causal forks – conjunctive, interactive and perfect – are useful devices for identifying causation through screening off the effects of some causes from other causes.
- Causal forks presume the temporal sequence of cause and effect.
- Statistical modelling and path analysis can test both hypotheses of causal paths and direct and indirect causal influences.
- The generation of explanatory hypotheses derives from relevant theoretical constructs.

How to control for different variables

Screening off the effects of variables requires controlling for variables. Controlling for a variable means holding it constant and unvarying so that one can see the true effects of other variables. For instance, we might be interested in examining the effects of gender on earnings, but these earnings are also affected by, for example, education level, type of work, qualifications, ethnicity, previous job experience, social behaviour and personality factors. If we wish to see the effects of gender then we have to control these other factors. This means that, in the case of gender for example, we would have to keep the males and females matched on the other variables, so that we could gain a true picture of the effects of gender rather than, say, education or job experience. Controlling for the effects of variables other than the one(s) in which we are interested can be achieved in several ways:

- randomization and random allocation of participants to control and experimental groups (in an experiment);
- isolating and controlling the effects of independent variables other than those in which we are interested, so that the two groups are matched on these other variables (matching subjects on other variables);

- ensuring that the two groups are matched on all important variables;
- having blind and double blind experiments;
- holding the values of other variables constant.

Controlling for a third variable

The importance of discovering and controlling for a third variable cannot be overstated. The familiar example is often cited of the relationship between the number of storks in an area and the birth rate: in Sweden a high birth rate was associated with the high number of storks in that area (Rosenberg 1968: 28). However, in fact both of these (the birth rate and the frequency of storks) were due to a third variable: the location. The high birth rate took place in a rural area and storks also lived in a rural area. Rosenberg also reports that, though there is a positive association between the number of firefighters at a fire and the amount of damage done by the fire, these are not causally related; both are due to a third factor: the size and intensity of the fire (ibid.).

Rosenberg (1968: 42–5) gives the example of research on the relationship between social class and parents' child-rearing behaviour, finding that working-class parents valued obedience in their children whereas middle-class parents valued children's self-control. When the research controlled for the degree of independence/supervision in a third variable – the parents' workplace – the social class influence halved. Those parents whose workplace emphasized supervision and obedience valued this in their children, whilst those parents whose workplace valued independence and self-control also valued this in their children. It was workplace practices rather than social class that exerted an important influence on child-rearing values. (Of course, 'social class' is a global concept which has many components, not least of which is the type of workplace in which one is employed and the kind of is employed one does, i.e. to use the crude concept of 'social class' is perhaps unhelpful.)

Introducing a third variable enables the researcher to understand the conditions and strength under which the relationship between two variables holds, what Rosenberg (1968: chap. 5) terms the 'conditional relationship'. This, he argues, is important in social science research, as, unlike in the physical sciences, social reality is conditional, and relationships are contextualized and dependent on the circumstances operating in a particular situation rather than there being universal laws. Social science combines the objective world of sociology with the subjective science of psychology (ibid.: 181). In some conditions there may be a relationship between two variables, whilst in other conditions that relationship may not hold, and it is important for educational research to discover what these conditions might be. The use of a third variable assists in this endeavour. Introducing a third variable, Rosenberg avers (ibid.: 194), enables a researcher to determine better the relationship between two variables, the conditions under which the relationship holds or does not hold.

Rosenberg (1968) provides a useful introduction to the importance and operations of a third variable. A third variable enables the relationship between two variables to be tested in several ways, e.g. for their strength, significance, meaningfulness and realism. He discusses four main kinds of third variable:

- an antecedent variable
- an intervening variable
- a suppressor variable
- a distorter variable.

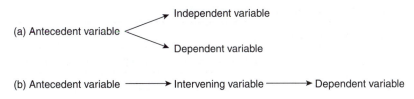

Figure 3.20 Antecedent and intervening variables

Antecedent and intervening variables

Rosenberg distinguishes between an 'extraneous' variable (one that is logically prior to the independent variable) and an independent variable (1968: 72); the third variable may be an 'antecedent' variable (coming before an independent variable) or an 'intervening' variable (coming between an antecedent variable and the dependent variable). He argues (ibid.: 55) that the difference between the antecedent and intervening variable is 'a logical and theoretical issue, not a statistical one', i.e. it is part of an assumed causal relationship and sequence that the researcher establishes. He also argues (ibid.: 55–6) that, with an exogenous, extraneous variable (e.g. a prior, antecedent variable), there need be no inherent link between the independent and dependent variable, whilst for an endogenous, intervening variable there should be an inherent connection between it and the prior and dependent variables.

If the third variable is a prior variable, then the prior variable operates on each independently and the independent variable is unrelated to the dependent variable, i.e. there is a symmetry between the independent and dependent variable. If the third variable is an intervening variable, then it relates to the prior and dependent variables. These two situations can be modelled as in Figure 3.20.

It is important for the researcher to determine 'what leads to what' in a causal sequence. Rosenberg (1968: 74) suggests that, if the third variable is an *intervening* variable, then, for it to be the causal variable, the relationship between the prior and the dependent variable should disappear when this third variable is controlled. However, if the third variable is a *prior* variable, then, for it to be a causal variable, the relationship between it and the dependent variable, should not disappear, but remain, when the intervening variable is controlled.

Rosenberg (1968: 68–9) provides three rules for determining whether a variable is an antecedent variable:

1   the antecedent, independent and dependent variables must be related;
2   when the researcher controls the antecedent variable, the relationship between the independent and the dependent variable should *not* disappear (i.e. the antecedent variable does not account for the relationship between the independent and dependent variable, but precedes that relationship in a causal sequence);
3   when the researcher controls the independent variable, the relationship between the antecedent and the dependent variable *should* disappear.

The suppressor variable

Another kind of third variable is the 'suppressor' variable (Rosenberg 1968: chap. 4): a variable which reduces, cancels out, conceals or weakens a true relationship between two

Table 3.13 Years of teaching and acceptance of dictatorial leadership

Acceptability of dictatorial principal behaviour

Item	*<10 years' teaching experience*	*≥10 years' teaching experience*
It's acceptable for a principal to be dictatorial	60%	58%

variables, i.e. which disguises a true relationship (ibid.: 85) (a false negative in which one accepts a null hypothesis when, in fact, the null hypothesis is false). For example, let us imagine that one were to examine the relationship between teachers' years of teaching experience and their acceptance of dictatorial leadership behaviour in school principals. Imagine that a survey has collected some numerical data (Table 3.13). It seems that there is no relationship between acceptability of dictatorial behaviour in principals and years of teaching experience. However, the introduction of a third variable – let us say managerial position in the school – indicates that the true relationship between the other two variables has been suppressed/concealed. When one controls for the third variable – managerial position in the school – the results appear very different, for example as in Table 3.14.

Within each category of level of managerial position in the school, it now becomes evident that there is a clear relationship between acceptability of dictatorial behaviour in principals and years of teaching experience, but that it varies according to the teachers' position in the managerial hierarchy, i.e. the original true relationship has been suppressed or concealed by the teachers' position in that hierarchy. Were it not for the higher managerial positions of some of the respondents, the results would indicate unacceptability of dictatorial behaviour, or, put the other way round, were it not for the lower managerial positions of some of the respondents, the results would show the acceptability of dictatorial behaviour. The point here is that, contrary to the original finding of no relationship between years of teaching and acceptability of dictatorial behaviour in principals, in fact there is a relationship, but this is concealed when the associated variable of position in the managerial hierarchy is not taken into account.

If one wished to show that a putative non-relationship is true (i.e. that there really is no relationship between the two variables), then one would have to demonstrate that the non-correlation between the two variables remains the same even when a third variable is used as a control. If one wishes to show that, in fact, a non-correlation is spurious (i.e. that there exists a real relationship between two variables) then one would need to prove that there exists a correlation between the two variables when one has controlled for the effect of a third variable.

The distorter variable

The fourth kind of Rosenberg's variables is the 'distorter' variable, which reveals itself where the correct interpretation of the data or of the relationships between two variables is exactly the reverse of what the original data suggest (1968: 94). For example, let us consider the case of the relationship between social advantage and formal,

Table 3.14 Controlling for a third variable

	Acceptability of dictatorial principal behaviour					
	Low-level manager		Middle manager		Senior manager	
Item	<10 years' teaching experience	≥10 years' teaching experience	<10 years' teaching experience	≥10 years' teaching experience	<10 years' teaching experience	≥10 years' teaching experience
It's acceptable for a principal to be dictatorial	19%	21%	26%	29%	35%	39%

Table 3.15 The effects of a distorter variable

Acceptability of formal, written public examinations

Formal, written public examinations	Socially advantaged	Socially disadvantaged
In favour	70%	35%
Against	30%	65%
Total per cent	100%	100%

Table 3.16 Controlling for the effects of a distorter variable

Acceptability of formal, written public examinations

	Traditionalist		Progressivist/child-centred	
Formal, written public examinations	Socially advantaged	Socially disadvantaged	Socially advantaged	Socially disadvantaged
In favour	65%	70%	35%	20%
Against	35%	30%	65%	80%
Total per cent	100%	100%	100%	100%

written public examinations. It is found that parents from socially advantaged backgrounds are more in favour of formal, written public examinations than those from socially disadvantaged backgrounds (see for example Table 3.15). The researcher interprets this as indicating that those from socially disadvantaged backgrounds are more in favour of other forms of assessment. However, let us assume that the study controlled for a third variable: educational philosophy, characterized as 'traditionalist' and 'progressivist/child-centred'. When the researcher examines the data after controlling for this third variable – educational philosophy – the results turn out to be very different (Table 3.16). The results here are almost the reverse of those in Table 3.15: the socially advantaged are more likely than socially disadvantaged parents to favour forms of assessment other than formal, written public examinations, and socially disadvantaged parents are more likely than socially advantaged parents to favour formal, written public examinations. The educational philosophies of each of the two groups have converted the positive relationship into a negative relationship. The investigation of distorter variables enables the researcher to avoid rejecting a true hypothesis and to avoid accepting a false hypothesis (ibid.: 100). Rosenberg (ibid.: 202–7) suggests that it is important to identify antecedent, intervening, suppressor and distorter variables.

Many statistical programmes (e.g. SPSS) enable controls to be made, i.e. holding constant particular factors. Consider the example of science test scores for males and females in Figure 3.21. Here the researchers are interested in the different results obtained by males and females. They match the groups in terms of size (252 males and 248 females) and compute the average score for males to be 75.6 per cent and for females to be 90.1 per cent, but they recognize that hours spent on homework may be exerting a confounding influence on the scores, so they decide to control for this. So they not only group the scores on the science test by males and females, but control for

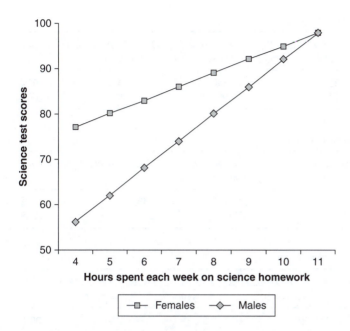

Figure 3.21 Regression for two different groups

hours spent on science homework (from 4 to 11 hours). They note that, indeed, the number of hours spent on homework is affecting the scores of both groups: the lower the number of hours spent, the greater is the difference between the results of females and males in respect of low scores, whereas the higher the number of hours spent, the smaller is the difference between the results of the females and males in respect of the higher score. Put simply, as hours spent increase, so the differences between males and females decrease. Controlling for hours spent on homework enables fairer comparisons to be made than simply examining average scores of males and females. This offers some causal explanation for differences found between the males and the females.

The issue here is fairly to compare like with like, and the examples below indicate how this might be approached. Controlling for variables is also possible through partial correlations and path analysis, and these are discussed below.

Example 1: Gender, earnings and educational attainment

Let us imagine that researchers wish to examine differences in earnings of young males and females and why, if such differences are found, these might occur. Initially the researchers establish that there is a difference, for example as in Table 3.17. They find a considerable discrepancy between the earnings of males and females, and they wonder if the employees' level of educational attainment may be a contributing factor to this, so they control for educational attainment. This means that they hold constant the levels of educational attainment and then compare males and females, as in Table 3.18.

It is clear that more males than females have low qualifications (fewer than five General certificate of Secondary Education (GCSE) passes) and vocational

Table 3.17 Differences in earnings at age 25

	Up to £18,000 per year	£18,001–£25,000 per year	£25,001–£35,000 per year	Over £35,000 per year	Total
Males	25%	35%	26%	14%	100%
Females	35%	37%	19%	9%	100%

Table 3.18 Qualifications of males and females

	Fewer than 5 GCSE passes	2 or more 'A' levels or equivalent	Post-18 vocational qualification	Undergraduate degree	Total
Males	17%	50%	9%	24%	100%
Females	12%	54%	5%	29%	100%

Table 3.19 Earnings and levels of qualification

	Up to £18,000 per year	£18,001–£25,000 per year	£25,001–£35,000 per year	Over £35,000 per year	Total
Fewer than 5 GCSE passes	69%	25%	5%	1%	100%
2 or more 'A' levels or equivalent	35%	37%	19%	9%	100%
Post-18 vocational qualification	38%	52%	8%	2%	100%
Undergraduate degree	27%	49%	22%	2%	100%

qualifications, and that more females than males have higher qualifications (Advanced Levels ('A' levels) and degrees). The researchers then investigate the relationship between earnings and levels of qualification, and these are presented in Table 3.19, where it can be seen that the trend is for higher qualifications to give greater earning power. Then the researchers divide this into males and females, as in Table 3.20 (rounded). Finally the researchers subtract the female percentages from the male percentages, and present the results, as in Table 3.21.

Hence, after controlling for educational attainment level, the researchers find that there are still inequalities in earnings. With low qualifications (fewer than five GCSE passes), more males than females are in high-paid jobs and more females than males are in low-paid jobs. The picture remains largely the same in respect of two or more 'A' levels or equivalent, though the difference is less marked for low-paid jobs and more marked for high-paid jobs. The picture also remains largely the same in respect of post-18 vocational qualifications and undergraduate degrees, though the difference is less marked for high-paid jobs (with reference to post-18 vocational qualifications) but markedly different (3.4 per cent) for jobs in the earning bracket £25,001–£35,000. Overall, the researchers conclude that, after controlling for level of educational attainment, there are marked differences between the earnings of males and females, to the advantage of males

Table 3.20 Earnings and qualifications by males and females

		Up to £18,000 per year	£18,001– £25,000 per year	£25,001– £25,000 per year	Over £35,000 per year	Total
Fewer than 5 GCSE passes	Male	28.7%	12.2%	2.9%	0.6%	44.4%
	Female	40.3%	12.8%	2.1%	0.4%	55.6%
2 or more 'A' levels or equivalent	Male	14.6%	18.0%	11.0%	5.5%	49.1%
	Female	20.4%	19.0%	8.0%	3.5%	50.9%
Post-18 vocational qualification	Male	15.8%	25.3%	4.6%	1.2%	46.9%
	Female	22.2%	26.7%	3.4%	0.8%	53.1%
Under- graduate degree	Male	11.2%	23.8%	12.7%	1.2%	48.9%
	Female	15.8%	25.2%	9.3%	0.8%	51.1%

Table 3.21 Differences in earnings by males and females, by different qualifications

	Up to £18,000 per year	£18,001– £25,000 per year	£25,001– £35,000 per year	Over £35,000 per year
Fewer than 5 GCSE passes	−11.6%	−0.6%	0.8%	0.2%
2 or more 'A' levels or equivalent	−5.8%	−1.0%	3.0%	2.0%
Post-18 vocational qualification	−6.4%	−1.4%	1.2%	0.4%
Undergraduate degree	−4.6%	−1.4%	3.4%	0.4%

Table 3.22 Teacher preferences of primary school boys and girls

	Boys	Girls	Total
Preference for a female teacher	160 (47.1%)	240 (80.0%)	400 (62.5% of total)
Preference for a male teacher	180 (52.9%)	60 (20.0%)	240 (37.5% of total)
Column total	340 (100%)	300 (100%)	640
Percentage of total	53.1%	46.9%	100%

at all levels of earnings; males earn more then females, even when controlling for levels of educational attainment.

Example 2: Males' and females' preferences for a male or female teacher

Let us say that we wish to investigate the preferences of primary school boys and girls to be taught by a teacher of their own sex (cf. Carrington *et al.* 2005), so we conduct an investigation that yields the crosstabulation in Table 3.22. Here we see that more boys

Table 3.23 Teacher preferences of younger and older primary school boys and girls

	Younger primary boys	Younger primary girls	Older primary boys	Older primary girls	Total
Preference for a female teacher	82 (48.5%)	118 (80.8%)	78 (45.6%)	122 (79.2%)	400 (62.5% of total)
Preference for a male teacher	87 (51.5%)	28 (19.2%)	93 (54.4%)	32 (20.8%)	240 (37.5% of total)
Column total	169 (100%)	146 (100%)	171 (100%)	154 (100%)	640
Percentage of total	26.4%	22.8%	26.7%	24.1%	100%

Table 3.24 Different teacher preferences of younger and older primary school children

	Younger primary boys	Younger primary girls	Older primary boys	Older primary girls	Total
Preference for a female teacher	120 (71.0%)	105 (71.9%)	91 (53.2%)	84 (54.5%)	400 (62.5% of total)
Preference for a male teacher	49 (28.9%)	41 (28.0%)	80 (46.8%)	70 (45.5%)	240 (37.5% of total)
Column total	169 (100%)	146 (100%)	171 (100%)	154 (100%)	640
Percentage of total	26.4%	22.8%	26.7%	24.1%	100%

prefer a male teacher (52.9%) than a female teacher and more girls prefer a female teacher (80.0%) than a male teacher. It seems that the variables are related, but we wish to discover whether this relationship might vary with a third factor: the age of the children. This third factor can be termed the control factor. To conduct the investigation we separate out the data according to this third variable – younger primary age children and older primary age children. We control for age, splitting the children into two groups, (a) younger primary and (b) older primary, and present the data as in Table 3.23.

When we look at this three-variable table – (a) sex of the primary children; (b) preference for a female or male teacher; and (c) age of the children – we see that the percentages in the partial tables (i.e. the younger children are one partial table and the older children are the other partial table) are extremely similar to those in the original table – i.e. age makes no appreciable difference to the relationship between sex and teacher preference; the differences in the cell percentages between the sexes of the children remains the same as in the original. The new three-variable table replicates the findings of the original two-variable table. Hence we conclude that age does not seem to be a causal variable affecting the relationship between the original two variables, i.e. the difference in the data may not be caused by age differences in the primary school children.

However, let us say that the results were different, as in the crosstabulation of Table 3.24. In this case, when we control for age we see that the differences between the younger primary boys and girls have almost completely disappeared (71.0 per cent matched to 71.9 per cent for 'preference for a female teacher' and 28.9 per cent and

Table 3.25 Do males score higher or lower marks in maths than females?

	Mathematics test score				
	≤60%	61%–70%	71%–80%	81%–90%	91%–100%
Males	7	31	44	57	113
	2.8%	12.3%	17.5%	22.6%	44.8%
Females	3	14	30	86	115
	1.2%	5.6%	12.1%	34.7%	45.6%

Table 3.26 Multiple regression for mathematics scores

Item	Standardized coefficient (Beta)	t-value	Significance level
1. How hard do you work for mathematics?	.572	16.739	.000
2. How many hours a week do you spend on your mathematics homework?	.246	7.135	.000
3. Intelligence Quotient (IQ)	.163	2.824	.043

28.0 per cent for 'preference for a male teacher'). When we look at the older primary boys and girls we see that the differences between the older primary boys and girls have almost completely disappeared (53.2 per cent matched to 54.5 per cent for 'preference for a female teacher' and 46.8 per cent and 45.5 per cent for 'preference for a male teacher'). We conclude that age is exerting an important causal influence on the voting and on the relationship between sex and teacher preference.

Example 3: Males' and females' mathematics scores

Let us take a common issue in education: differences in test score by males and females. Let us imagine that researchers wish to discover whether males score higher or lower marks in mathematics than females, and why this might be so. Initially they construct a matrix to present the mathematics scores, assuming that the maximum mark is 100 per cent, and present five grade levels: ≤60%, 61%–70%, 71%–80%, 81%–90% and 91%–100%. Then they insert the raw scores and percentages of males and females in each category (Table 3.25).

The percentages show that more males than females scored in the lower levels of the mark range (0–80% for marks), that considerably more females than males scored in the category 81%–90%, and that very slightly more females than males scored in the category 91%–100%. Why might this be? The researchers posit three possible causes of these effects: (a) how hard the students work on their mathematics; (b) how many hours a week they spend on mathematics homework; and (c) their IQ. They run a multiple regression to examine the possible weightings of these. With an Adjusted R square of .426, i.e. 42.6 per cent of variance explained (reasonably powerful), the analysis yields the data as in Table 3.26.

The three results demonstrate statistical significance below the .05 level,[5] and the beta weightings indicate that the factor with the strongest weighting is 'How hard do you work for mathematics?', followed by 'How many hours a week do you spend on your mathematics homework?' and then 'IQ'. The researchers wish to see how much of the difference between the scores of males and females is due to differences in these three factors, so they control for each of them. Controlling for a factor means looking at the results for a variable (in this case males and females) when other possible factors are held the same for that variable (e.g. males and females). In the case here it is in terms of:

(a) *how hard the students work on their mathematics*, comparing the scores of males and females when different levels of work are held constant, i.e. the researchers compare the scores of males and females at the level of 'working moderately hard', then at the level of 'working hard', and then at the level of 'working extremely hard';

(b) *how many hours a week they spend on mathematics homework*, i.e. the researchers compare the scores of males and females at the level of 'up to and including 5 hours a week', then at the level of '6 hours a week' then at the level of '7 hours a week', then at the level of '8 hours a week', then at the level of '9 hours a week', and finally at the level of '10 hours or more a week'.

(c) *intelligence quotient (IQ)*, comparing the scores of males and females at the level of 'IQ up to and including 90', then at the level of 'IQ from 91–110', then at the level of 'IQ from 111–125', and finally at the level of 'IQ at over 125'.

The researchers are holding constant each of these three factors in turn and then looking at the differences between the scores of the males and females each time. For each factor they have different values, i.e. three levels of working hard, six levels of time spent on homework, and four levels of IQ.

The Statistical Package for Social Sciences (SPSS) calculates these at the press of a button, by using the 'Crosstabs' function, entering the independent variable ('Sex') in the row, the dependent variable ('Mathematics test score') in the column, and the control variable ('IQ') in the 'Layer' box. The results present clearly the three matters of interest (sex, maths score and IQ level), as in Table 3.27. The same can be done for the other two factors ('hard work' and 'time spent on homework').

Let us say that all the crosstabulations have been computed. The results are collated into a single table, e.g. Table 3.28. From the rather formidable Table 3.28 one can present a single table of the comparative results by subtracting the female scores from the male scores (or, indeed the male from the female scores), as in Table 3.29.

There are three questions here:

1 Do males and females with the same level(s) of work score the same marks in mathematics?
2 Do males and females with the same amount(s) of homework score the same marks in mathematics?
3 Do males and females with the same level(s) of IQ score the same marks in mathematics?

• Looking at the 'Working moderately hard' category, the researchers see large differences in the 61–70 per cent and 81–90 per cent test score categories.
• Looking at the 'Working hard' category, the researchers see large differences in the 61–70 per cent, 71–80 per cent, and 81–90 per cent test score categories.
• Looking at the 'Working extremely hard' category, the researchers see no large differences in the test score categories.

Table 3.27 Crosstabulation of sex, mathematics and IQ (SPSS output)

Sex * Mathematics test score * IQ Crosstabulation

				Mathematics test score					
				60	70	80	90	100	Total
IQ up to 90	Sex	male	Count	2	5	4	4	0	15
			% within Sex	13.3%	33.3%	26.7%	26.7%	.0%	100.0%
		female	Count	1	3	1	12	2	19
			% within Sex	5.3%	15.8%	5.3%	63.2%	10.5%	100.0%
	Total		Count	3	8	5	16	2	34
			% within Sex	8.8%	23.5%	14.7%	47.1%	5.9%	100.0%
IQ 91-110	Sex	male	Count	2	13	16	21	41	93
			% within Sex	2.2%	14.0%	17.2%	22.6%	44.1%	100.0%
		female	Count	2	5	16	38	40	101
			% within Sex	2.0%	5.0%	15.8%	37.6%	39.6%	100.0%
	Total		Count	4	18	32	59	81	194
			% within Sex	2.1%	9.3%	16.5%	30.4%	41.8%	100.0%
IQ 111-125	Sex	male	Count	1	8	16	25	56	106
			% within Sex	.9%	7.5%	15.1%	23.6%	52.8%	100.0%
		female	Count	0	1	11	32	40	84
			% within Sex	.0%	1.2%	13.1%	38.1%	47.6%	100.0%
	Total		Count	1	9	27	57	96	190
			% within Sex	.5%	4.7%	14.2%	30.0%	50.5%	100.0%
IQ over 125	Sex	male	Count	2	5	8	7	16	38
			% within Sex	5.3%	13.2%	21.1%	18.4%	42.1%	100.0%
		female	Count	0	5	2	4	33	44
			% within Sex	.0%	11.4%	4.5%	9.1%	75.0%	100.0%
	Total		Count	2	10	10	11	49	82
			% within Sex	2.4%	12.2%	12.2%	13.4%	59.8%	100.0%

From this the researchers deduce that, generally speaking, when the amount of work is held constant, that there are still major differences in the scores of males and females in the 61–90 per cent category, but not in the 60 per cent and below and 91 per cent and over categories. So the answer to question 1 is generally 'no', i.e. the amount of effort put in by males and females is associated with their test scores, apart from if they both work 'extremely hard'.

- Looking at the 'Maths homework ≤5 hours a week' category, the researchers see no large differences in the test score categories (the 100 per cent difference is due to a single case, and hence can be discounted).
- Looking at the 'Maths homework 6 hours a week' category, the researchers see large differences at all levels but one (6 hours) in the test score categories, with males overrepresented in the lower mark range (up to 80 per cent) and females overrepresented in the higher mark range (81–100 per cent).
- Looking at the 'Maths homework 7 hours a week' category, the researchers see large differences at all levels, with males overrepresented in the 71–80 per cent category, and the females overrepresented in all the other mark ranges.
- Looking at the 'Maths homework 8 hours a week' category, the researchers see large differences at all levels apart from the up to 60 per cent mark category, with males

Table 3.28 Do males score higher or lower marks in maths than females, and why?

	Maths test score				
	≤60%	61%–70%	71%–80%	81%–90%	91%–100%
Males work moderately hard	3 15.8%	12 63.2%	2 10.5%	1 5.3%	1 5.3%
Females work moderately hard	2 14.3%	7 50.0%	1 7.1%	3 21.4%	1 7.1%
Males work hard	3 6.8%	15 34.1%	13 29.5%	5 11.4%	8 18.2%
Females work hard	1 2.8%	6 16.7%	4 11.1%	19 52.8%	6 16.7%
Males work extremely hard	1 0.5%	4 2.1%	29 15.3%	51 27.0%	104 55.0%
Females work extremely hard		1 0.5%	25 12.6%	64 32.3%	108 54.5%
Male maths homework ≤5 hours a week					
Female maths homework ≤5 hours a week					1 100%
Male maths homework 6 hours a week		1 16.7%	3 50.0%	1 16.7%	1 16.7%
Female maths homework 6 hours a week			1 12.5%	5 50.0%	3 37.5%
Male maths homework 7 hours a week		1 6.7%	5 33.3%	4 26.7%	5 33.3%
Female maths homework 7 hours a week	1 7.7%	2 15.4%	3 23.1%	5 38.5%	2 15.4%
Male maths homework 8 hours a week	5 5.9%	19 22.4%	14 16.5%	25 29.4%	22 25.9%
Female maths homework 8 hours a week	2 2.5%	4 4.9%	12 14.8%	49 60.5%	14 17.3%

Table 3.28 (Continued)

	≤60%	61%–70%	71%–80%	81%–90%	91%–100%
			Maths test score		
Male maths homework 9 hours a week	1 1.0%	8 8.1%	19 19.2%	24 24.2%	47 37.5%
Female maths homework 9 hours a week		7 8.1%	10 11.6%	24 27.9%	45 53.3%
Male maths homework ≥10 hours a week	1 2.1%	2 4.3%	3 6.4%	3 6.4%	38 80.9%
Female maths homework ≥10 hours a week		1 1.7%	4 6.8%	4 6.8%	50 84.7%
Male IQ up to 90s	2 13.3%	5 33.3%	4 26.7%	4 26.7%	0 0%
Female IQ up to 90	1 5.3%	3 15.8%	1 5.3%	12 63.2%	2 10.5%
Male IQ 91–110	2 2%	13 14.0%	16 17.2%	21 22.6%	41 44.1%
Female IQ 91–110	2 2.0%	5 5.0%	16 15.8%	38 37.6%	40 39.6%
Male IQ 111–125	1 0.9%	8 7.5%	16 15.1%	25 23.6%	56 52.8%
Female IQ 111–125		1 1.2%	11 13.1%	32 38.1%	40 47.6%
Male IQ >125	2 5.3%	5 13.2%	8 21.1%	7 18.4%	16 42.1%
Female IQ >125		5 11.4%	2 4.5%	4 9.1%	33 75.0%

overrepresented in the lower ranges (up to 80 per cent) and in the highest category (91–100 per cent), and the females overrepresented in the 81–90 per cent category.
- Looking at the 'Maths homework 9 hours a week' category, the researchers see few differences at the lowest two levels (up to 70 per cent), males overrepresented in the mid-range category (71–80 per cent), and the females overrepresented in the highest two categories (81–100 per cent mark range).
- Looking at the 'Maths homework 10 hours a week and more' category, the researchers see few differences at all levels.

Table 3.29 Comparative results of factors influencing mathematics scores

Percentage difference (males–females)	Maths test score				
	≤60%	61%–70%	71%–80%	81%–90%	91%–100%
Overall difference between males and females	1.6	6.7	5.4	−12.1	−0.8
Working moderately hard	1.5	13.2	3.4	−16.1	−1.8
Working hard	4.0	17.4	18.4	−41.4	1.5
Working extremely hard	0.5	1.6	2.7	−5.3	0.5
Maths homework ≤5 hours a week					−100 (1 case)
Maths homework 6 hours a week		16.7	37.5	−33.3	−20.8
Maths homework 7 hours a week	−7.7	−8.7	10.2	−11.8	17.9
Maths homework 8 hours a week	3.4	17.5	1.7	−31.1	8.6
Maths homework 9 hours a week	1.0	0.0	7.6	−3.7	−15.8
Maths homework ≥10 hours a week	2.1	2.6	−0.2	−0.4	−3.8
IQ up to 90	8.0	17.5	21.4	−36.5	−10.5
IQ 91–110	0.2	9.0	1.4	−15.0	4.5
IQ 111–125	0.9	6.3	2	−14.5	5.2
IQ >125	5.3	1.8	16.9	9.3	−32.9

The researchers deduce that, generally speaking, when the amount of homework is held constant, there is little difference between males and females at the very lowest and very highest number of hours spent on homework, but in the 6–9 hours per week spent on homework, females tend to be overrepresented in the higher mark ranges and males overrepresented in the lower mark ranges, with the exception of males spending 8 hours a week on homework (where they were overrepresented in the highest mark category (91–100 per cent). It seems that, for the range of 6–9 hours a week on homework, this is generally associated with females scoring more highly on the mathematics test score. So the answer to question 2 ('Do males and females with the same amount(s) of homework score the same marks in mathematics ?') is generally 'no', apart from at the lowest and highest extremes of amount of homework.

- Looking at the 'IQ up to 90' category, the researchers see considerable differences at all levels of the mark range, with males overrepresented in the lower-range categories (up to 80 per cent), and the females overrepresented in the highest two categories (81–100 per cent mark range).
- Looking at the 'IQ 91–110' and the 'IQ 111–125' categories, the researchers see few differences at the lowest level and at the level (71–80 per cent), and considerable differences at all the other levels of the mark range, with males overrepresented in all mark range categories with the exception of 81–90 per cent (in which females are overrepresented).

- Looking at the 'IQ over 125' category, the researchers see few differences at the lower levels (up to 70 per cent), and considerable differences at all the other levels of the mark range, with males overrepresented in all mark range categories with the exception of 91–100 per cent (in which females are overrepresented).

The researchers deduce that, generally speaking, when the variable 'IQ' is held constant, there are few differences between males and females at the very lowest mark category (with the exception of the lowest level of IQ) and considerable differences at the other levels, particularly in respect of the highest two mark categories (81–100 per cent), where very low and very high IQ females are overrepresented.

So the answer to question 3 ('Do males and females with the same level(s) of IQ score the same marks in mathematics?') is generally 'no', with the few exceptions noted above.

Hence the researchers deduce that differences in the mathematics scores of males and females are due, in part, to how hard they work, the amount of time spent on homework and IQ.

When controlling for variables, holding them constant enables truer causality and the weight of different causal variables to be ascertained with greater reliability than if these variables are either excluded or not held constant. Indeed, introducing a control variable enables researchers to identify spurious relationships: if one introduces a control variable which is causally prior to both the independent and dependent variables (Hage and Meeker 1988: 59) and the relationship between the independent and dependent variable disappears, then one has discovered the spurious relationship.

Hage and Meeker (1988: 59–60) also offer useful advice for investigating the presence and influence of indirect variables. They recommend hypothesizing the independent and dependent variables and then suggesting what the process may be by which the independent variable affects the dependent variable. They then propose finding a measurable variable that is an indicator of this process, and introducing it as a control variable (that is, dividing the sample into different groups based on how they score on the control variable) and seeing if the original relationship is changed. The control variable here is an *intervening* variable, coming between the independent and the dependent variable in the time sequence, and the researcher believes that there is a plausible reason to think that it mediates the effects of the independent variable on the dependent variable.

Implications for researchers:

- In order to discover relative strengths of causes it may be necessary to screen off causes from each other.
- In order to discover relative strengths of causes it may be necessary to hold some causes fixed in a test situation.
- It is important to control for variables in order to assess more fairly and accurately the effects of causes.
- One can control for a third variable by fixing it at an unchanging level, so that it is unable (i.e. not free) to vary.
- Controlling for a third variable can help researchers to identify spurious relationships.

Example 4: Juvenile smoking, exercise and heart disease

Let us take a further fictitious example of determining the effects of causes, where screening off includes holding variables constant (placing controls on the data analysis). Let us say that schools are trying to address a health crisis in society, putatively caused by juvenile smoking, lack of exercise and effects of these on future heart disease. We wish to find the relationship of different amounts of smoking and exercise on future heart disease. The constants held fixed here are the numbers of smokers and non-smokers (the numbers are equalized at 700 of each). This indicates that: (a) four times as many smokers as non-smokers contract heart disease in the future; (b) in the smoking population the ratio of 4:3 will contract heart disease; (c) in the non-smoking school population, six times as many students will not contract heart disease than will contract heart disease. This enables the effects of other variables to be manipulated, as the number of smokers and non-smokers has been matched (fixed); in this example the variables that are manipulated are: (a) the number of cigarettes smoked each day (none, 10 and 30); (b) the amount of exercise taken each week (none, 30 minutes, 60 minutes). From here the relative likelihood of heart disease in respect of smoking and exercise, from nothing to different levels of each, can be calculated. The data are presented in Table 3.30.

What can we tell from this table? How much effect do different levels of exercise have on future heart disease, when different amounts of cigarettes are smoked? The results indicate the following.

- For non-smokers who take no exercise there is a 7.1 per cent chance (50 out of 700) of their contracting heart disease.
- For non-smokers who exercise for 30 minutes there is a 4.3 per cent (30 out of 700) chance of their contracting heart disease.
- For non-smokers who exercise for 60 minutes there is a 2.9 per cent (20 out of 700) chance of their contracting heart disease.
- For smokers of 10 cigarettes a day and who take no exercise there is a 10 per cent chance (70 out of 700) of their contracting heart disease;
- For smokers of 10 cigarettes a day and who exercise for 30 minutes there is an 8.6 per cent (60 out of 700) chance of their contracting heart disease.
- For smokers of 10 cigarettes a day and who exercise for 60 minutes there is a 7.1 per cent (50 out of 700) chance of their contracting heart disease.
- For smokers of 30 cigarettes a day and who take no exercise there is a 12.9 per cent (90 out of 700) chance of their contracting heart disease.
- For smokers of 30 cigarettes a day and who exercise for 30 minutes there is a 12.1 per cent (85 out of 700) chance of their contracting heart disease.
- For smokers of 30 cigarettes a day and who exercise for 60 minutes there is a 7.9 per cent (55 out of 700) chance of their contracting heart disease.

We can see, then, that, perhaps as expected:

- not smoking is much healthier than smoking, and that the health of non-smokers is increased by exercise;
- the effect of a small amount of smoking (10 cigarettes a day) is to increase the likelihood of heart disease by a maximum of 2.9 per cent (10 per cent minus 7.1 per cent), but that this reduces with exercise, so that, if a 10-a-day smoker takes

Table 3.30 Smoking, heart disease and exercise

	Non-smokers	Non-smoker and no exercise	Non-smoker and 30 minutes exercise	Non-smoker and 60 minutes exercise	Smoker (10 a day) and no exercise	Smoker (10 a day) and 30 minutes exercise	Smoker (10 a day) and 60 minutes exercise	Smoker (30 a day) and no exercise	Smoker (30 a day) and 30 minutes exercise	Smoker (30 a day) and 60 minutes exercise	Total smokers
Future heart disease	100 (14.3%)	50 (7.1%)	30 (4.3%)	20 (2.9%)	70 (10%)	60 (8.6%)	50 (7.1%)	90 (12.9%)	85 (12.1%)	55 (7.9%)	400 (57.1%)
No future heart disease	600 (85.7%)	290 (51.5%)	270 (3.9%)	60 (8.6%)	60 (8.6%)	50 (7.1%)	40 (5.7%)	75 (1.1%)	40 (5.7%)	25 (3.6%)	300 (42.9%)
Total	700 (100%)	340 (48.6%)	300 (42.9)	80 (11.4%)	130 (18.6%)	110 (15.7%)	90 (12.9%)	165 (23.6%)	125 (17.6%)	80 (11.4%)	700 (100%)

60 minutes of exercise then his or her likelihood of contracting heart disease is the same as that of a non-smoker who takes no exercise (7.1 per cent);

- the effect of a large amount of smoking (30 cigarettes a day) is to increase the likelihood of heart disease by a maximum of 5.8 per cent (12.9 per cent minus 7.1 per cent), but that this reduces with exercise, so that, if a 30-a-day smoker takes 60 minutes of exercise then his or her likelihood of contracting heart disease is 7.9 per cent;
- for non-smokers, the effects of exercise can reduce the likelihood by a minimum of 2.8 per cent (7.1 per cent minus 4.3 per cent) and a maximum of 4.2 per cent (7.1 per cent minus 2.9 per cent);
- for light smokers, the effects of exercise can reduce the likelihood of heart disease by a minimum of 1.4 per cent (10.0 per cent minus 8.6 per cent) (if the smokers take 30 minutes of exercise) and a maximum of 2.9 per cent (10.0 per cent minus 7.1 per cent (if the smokers take 60 minutes of exercise);
- for heavy smokers, the effects of exercise can reduce the likelihood of heart disease by a minimum of .8 per cent (12.9 per cent minus 12.1 per cent) (if the smokers take 30 minutes of exercise) and a maximum of 5.0 per cent (12.9 per cent minus 7.9 per cent) (if the smokers take 60 minutes of exercise);
- screening out the effects of exercise, smoking increase the likelihood of heart disease by a minimum of 2.9 per cent (10.0 per cent minus 7.1 per cent) (for a 10-a-day smoker) and a maximum of 5.8 per cent (12.9 per cent minus 7.1 per cent) for a 30-a-day smoker);
- screening out the effects of smoking, exercise decreases the likelihood of heart disease by a minimum of 2.8 per cent (7.1 per cent minus 4.3 per cent) for a 30-minute exerciser and a maximum of 4.2 per cent (7.1 per cent minus 2.9 per cent) for a 60-minute exerciser.

Screening out/controlling can enable us to make powerful inferences. In the above example, we can see:

(a) the effects of smoking on heart disease, when exercise is screened out/controlled;
(b) the effects of exercise on heart disease, when smoking is screened out/controlled;
(c) the different effects on heart disease of different levels of smoking and different levels of exercise when combined.

One can deduce from this that the overall effects of smoking on future heart disease are stronger in increasing the likelihood of heart disease (2.9 per cent, i.e. 5.8 per cent minus 2.9 per cent) than are the overall effects of exercise in reducing future heart disease (1.4 per cent, i.e. 4.2 per cent minus 2.8 per cent) – i.e. the effects of smoking on future heart disease are stronger than the effects of exercise. This can be powerful if we wish to ask questions such as:

- If smoking is held constant at such-and-such a level, what are the effects of exercise on future heart disease?
- If exercise is held constant at such-and-such a level, what are the effects of smoking on future heart disease?
- What are the overall relative strengths of the effects of smoking and exercise on future heart disease?
- What are the effects of different levels of smoking and different levels of exercise on future heart disease?

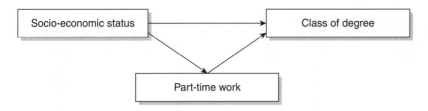

Figure 3.22 Construction of a causal model

In this example smoking has been screened off from exercise and vice versa, so that we can see the effects of each on future heart disease. Further, we can see their combined effects at different levels.

These four examples indicate the importance of controlling for variables in order for causation to be determined more rigorously. As Rosenberg (1968: 37) remarks, if a relationship still holds after controls have been applied to the variable(s) in question, then the confidence that the relationship is real is strengthened.

Implications for researchers:

- Using numerical research may demonstrate the likelihood of one event influencing another rather than proving causation.
- The likelihood of finding causation may increase by controlling variables.

Example 5: Controlling with categorical bivariate data

Data can be crosstabulated, and many of the data may be nominal (categorical) variables rather than continuous variables. How can one determine causality with categorical (non-metric) variables, e.g. sex, ethnic group, occupation, socio-economic status, kind of school, class of students (Primary 1, Secondary 2, etc.), i.e. nominal data or variables? Crosstabulations can assist here (Hellevik 1988). For example, let us consider the case of three variables: the case of undergraduate students who are working part-time during their period of study, and let us take three variables: say socio-economic status, part-time work and class of degree (e.g. first, upper second, lower second, etc). We are interested to see if socio-economic status and part-time work affect students' final degree classification. We construct a causal model based on theoretical assumptions, that the independent variables 'socio-economic status' and 'part-time work' have an effect on the dependent variable 'class of degree'. (The construction of a causal model is rooted in relevant theory and, itself, may be contestable.) The causal path is from socio-economic status to part-time work to degree classification, as in Figure 3.22.

The causal pathway suggests that socio-economic status itself affects the class of degree (a direct effect), and also that it affects whether an undergraduate student takes a part-time job, and this, in turn (through the principle of transitivity), affects the class of degree (an indirect effect of socio-economic status). Let us say that, for the ease of clarity in the example, we categorize students thus:

Table 3.31 Socio-economic status, part-time work and class of degree

Socio-economic status	Part-time work	Class of degree	Frequency
High	Yes	High	70
High	Yes	Low	50
High	No	High	85
High	No	Low	45
Low	Yes	High	40
Low	Yes	Low	65
Low	No	High	55
Low	No	Low	60
		Total	470

Table 3.32 Probability of gaining a certain class of degree

Class of degree	Absolute frequency	Percentages	Proportions
High	250	53	.53
Low	220	47	.47
Total	470	100	1.00

- socio-economic status: two groups (high and low);
- part-time work: a 'yes/no' variable ('yes' = works part-time, and 'no' = does not work part-time);
- class of degree: 'high/low' (high = first or upper second; low = lower second, third or pass).

That this massively oversimplifies the situation is acknowledged, but for heuristic clarity let us proceed on this basis. This means that there are several possible permutations, and Table 3.31 not only indicates these but inserts some frequencies, for the sake of the worked example. A high-class degree is obtained by 250 people (53 per cent of the sample (rounded), a .53 proportion), and a low-class degree is obtained by 220 people (47 per cent of the sample (rounded), a .47 proportion). Proportions are obtained by dividing the percentage by 100, and they indicate the probability that a person will have the characteristic in question (in this case a high- or a low-class degree). Probabilities vary from 0 to 1, with 0 indicating the certainty that the characteristic will *not* be found, and 1 indicating the certainty that the characteristic *will* be found. So, in the case here, if no high degrees had been awarded then the probability would have been 0, and if only high degrees had been awarded then the probability would have been 1. We can present the proportions in Table 3.32.

Let us imagine that we are interested in finding the relationship between socio-economic status and class of degree. Does the probability of gaining a high-class degree differ by socio-economic status? To address this we can use the data from Table 3.31 to construct a further table (Table 3.33). Here the dependent variable (class of degree) is the row variable and the independent variable (socio-economic status) is the column variable. The proportions are calculated thus: $(155/250) = .62$; $(95/250) = .38$; $(95/220) = .43$; $(125/220) = .57$. Looking at Table 3.33 one can observe that:

Table 3.33 Socio-economic status and class of degree

| Class of degree | Absolute frequencies | | | Proportions | | |
| | Socio-economic status | | | Socio-economic status | | |
	High	Low	Total	High	Low	Differences
High	155	95	250	.62	.43	.19
Low	95	125	220	.38	.57	−.19
Total	250	220	470	1.00	1.00	0.00

Table 3.34 Part-time work and class of degree

| Class of degree | Absolute frequencies | | | Proportions | | |
| | Part-time work | | | Part-time work | | |
	Yes	No	Total	Yes	No	Differences
High	110	140	250	.49	.57	−.8
Low	115	105	220	.51	.43	.8
Total	225	245	470	1.00	1.00	0.00

- a higher proportion of students with a high socio-economic status obtained a higher class degree (the difference in proportions is .19);
- a higher proportion of students with a low socio-economic status obtained a lower class degree (the difference in proportions is −.19).

We might also wish to investigate the relationship between students taking part-time work and their final class of degree. Does the probability of gaining a high-class degree differ by whether students take part-time work during their studies (Table 3.34)? Here the dependent variable (class of degree) is the row variable and the independent variable (part-time work) is the column variable. The proportions are calculated thus: (110/225) = .49; (115/225) = .51; (140/245) = .57; (105/245) = .43. Looking at Table 3.34 one can observe that:

- a higher proportion of students who were *not* taking part-time work than students who were taking part-time work obtained a higher class degree (the difference in proportions is −.8);
- a higher proportion of students who were taking part-time work than students who were not taking part-time work obtained a lower class degree (the difference in proportions is .8).

When we compare the difference between the class of degree by socio-economic status and by taking/not-taking part-time work, we find that the differences are greater for socio-economic status than for taking/not taking part time work (.19 and .8 respectively), i.e. the probability of obtaining a higher degree seems greater in relation to socio-economic status than in relation to working or not working part-time.

Table 3.35 A trivariate crosstabulation

Socio-economic status	Absolute frequencies				Proportions			
	High		Low		High		Low	
Part-time work	Yes	No	Yes	No	Yes	No	Yses	No
High class degree	70	85	40	55	.58	.65	.38	.48
Low class degree	50	45	65	60	.42	.35	.62	.52
Total	120	130	105	115	1.00	1.00	1.00	1.00

Example 6: Controlling with categorical trivariate data

The example of socio-economic status and working/not working part-time is of *bivariate* tables (two variables only). However, Figure 3.22 indicated that the two independent variables might, themselves, be associated, i.e. that the degree classification is related to the interaction of the two independent variables. It may be that socio-economic status interacts with working part-time to influence the class of degree. How can we address this? This moves us from a *bivariate* analysis to a *multivariate* analysis (many variables), in this case a *trivariate* analysis (three variables). The issue here is the extent to which the independent variables contribute to the variance between the several groups. To calculate the association between socio-economic status and class of degree we have to calculate the differences in proportions between those who are working and those who are not working, i.e. to render the variable 'working status' (working or not working part-time) the control variable. To keep 'working status' as a control variable requires us to hold it constant every time we calculate the association between socio-economic status and class of degree. This can be presented as in Table 3.35.

Here the dependent variable (class of degree) is the row variable and the independent variables (socio-economic status and part-time work) are the column variables. The proportions are calculated thus: $(70/120) = .58$; $(50/120) = .42$; $(85/130) = .65$; $(45/130) = .35$; $(40/105) = .38$; $(65/105) = .62$; $(55/115) = .48$; $(60/115) = .52$. Looking at Table 3.35 one can observe that:

(a) the most fortunate students are those with a high socio-economic status who are not working: the proportion gaining a high class degree is .65;
(b) the next most fortunate students are those with a high socio-economic status who are working: the proportion gaining a high degree is .58;
(c) the most unfortunate students are those with a low socio-economic status who are working: the proportion gaining a low class degree is .62;
(d) the next most unfortunate students are those with a low socio-economic status who are not working: the proportion gaining a low class degree is .52;
(e) amongst students who *are* working part-time, those with a high socio-economic status have a probability of .20 (.58–.38) of obtaining a high-class degree, compared with students with a low socio-economic status;
(f) amongst students who are *not* working, those with a high socio-economic status have a probability of .17 (.65–.48) of obtaining a high-class degree compared with students with a low socio-economic status;

Table 3.36 Likelihood of obtaining a high-class degree

	Socio-economic status		
	High	Low	Differences (partial associations for socio-economic status)
Working part-time	.58	.38	.20
Not working part-time	.65	.48	.17
Difference (partial associations for working/not working part-time)	−.07	−.10	

Table 3.37 Likelihood of obtaining a low-class degree

	Socio-economic status		
	High	Low	Differences (partial associations for socio-economic status)
Working part-time	.42	.62	−.20
Not working part-time	.35	.52	−.17
Difference (partial associations for working/not working part-time)	.07	.10	

(g) amongst students who *are* working part-time, those with a high socio-economic status have a probability of −.20 (.42−.62) of obtaining a low-class degree, compared with students with a low socio-economic status;

(h) amongst students who are *not* working, those with a high socio-economic status have a probability of −.17 (.35−.52) of obtaining a high-class degree compared with students with a low socio-economic status.

In (e) to (h) above, the *partial* associations between socio-economic status and class of degree have been calculated, controlling for working status (working part-time or not working part-time); the independent variable of part-time working has been controlled. These are *partial* associations because the proportions relate to part of the matrix rather than to the whole matrix, i.e. the values on the control variable have been controlled (cf. Hellevik 1988: 8). A partial correlation is that correlation which refers to two variables in a multi-variable matrix, rather than all the variables in it.

In order to summarize the likelihood of obtaining a high- or low-class degree from the data presented, one can extract the proportions from Table 3.35 for the sake of clarity, as in Tables 3.36 and 3.37. One can observe that the size of the partial associations varies according to which independent variable is held constant (the row differences and the column differences are not the same), i.e. that there is an *interaction effect* between the two independent variables. If one observed that the size of the partial associations was the same, i.e. the proportions were the same regardless of which independent variable was held constant, then one could assume that there was no interaction effect between the two.

In the worked example, it was observed that the independent variable 'part-time work' not only affected the dependent variable ('class of degree') but, itself, was affected by the prior variable of 'socio-economic status', i.e. part-time work and class of degree are affected by socio-economic status. Students with high socio-economic status gain more high-class degrees than students with low socio-economic status and, conversely, students with low socio-economic degrees gain more low-class degrees than students with high socio-economic status. As high socio-economic status seems to increase the likelihood of a high-class degree and low socio-economic status seems to increase the likelihood of a low-class degree, it appears that socio-economic status contributes to the differences of class of degree. Hence part of the association between part-time working and class of degree is generated by the variable 'socio-economic status' rather than being a causal effect of part-time working on class of degree. There is a *spurious effect* at work here (Hellevik 1988: 11), where the association between part-time work and class of degree is due to the prior variable 'socio-economic status', i.e. that association between part-time working and class of degree is partly a result of the direct effect of the former on the latter, but is also partly a result of a spurious effect created by the prior variable of socio-economic status.

Hellevik (1988: 11–19) indicates that the spurious effect is the 'difference between gross association and causal effect' (p. 19), and he suggests how it can be investigated. Gross association, he avers, is that association 'directly attributable to the independent variable itself, and association resulting from both variables being related to other variables' (p. 12). He contrasts this with 'net association' (ibid.), which is the effect of the independent variable when the other (e.g. a prior or third) variable has no influence, i.e. is controlled (kept constant), as discussed above. Net association is that association found after controlling other variables. As was demonstrated above, the task is to calculate the net association, i.e. how much influence on the dependent variable (class of degree) is exerted by the independent variable 'part-time working' independent of the prior variable 'socio-economic status', or, as Hellevik remarks (ibid.), to ascertain how much the control variable contributes to the gross association between the independent and dependent variable.

The preceding analysis indicated how to control for the effect of a prior variable ('socio-economic status') in investigating the association betweens part-time work and class of degree. The task now becomes to ascertain the size of the net association. As can be seen in the trivariate tables, the partial association between the independent variable 'socio-economic status' and the dependent variable 'class of degree' was not uniform; the proportions varied by each of the two classes (values) of socio-economic status (high status and low status) and class of degree (high class and low class). Similarly the partial association between the independent variable 'part-time work' and the dependent variable 'class of degree' was not uniform; the proportions varied by each of the two values ('working part-time' and 'not working part time') and class of degree (high class and low class). In trying to calculate the direct effect of socio-economic status on class of degree by controlling for part-time work, a stronger effect of socio-economic status was found for students who *did not* work part-time and a weaker effect was found for students who *did* work part-time.

What we have here are measures of association and proportions of associations which, when used to compare relative strengths of independent variables, can suggest causation. Clearly one has to be cautious in equating correlation with cause; correlation does not imply causation. Causation may imply correlation but not vice versa. As Freedman (1997: 155) suggests, correlational research may suggest causal inferences, but only with limited guarantees.

The example here has used simple, dichotomous variables: high/low; working/not working; high class of degree/low class of degree. These can yield simple 2 × 2 crosstabulations and both bivariate and trivariate analysis. However, the analysis can be used with larger tables (many values per variable) and for multivariate analysis. That said, the greater the number of rows and columns, the more cumbersome the analysis becomes. This is where multivariate analysis using computer software (e.g. SPSS) pays great dividends.

Finally here, a cautionary note has to be struck; it is relatively easy to introduce a range of variables (for example, sex and social class are routinely used in much social science). Whilst these may be important, they might also *not* be important. The decision of which variables to include has to be made on the grounds of relevance, i.e. it is a logical rather than a statistical matter (Rosenberg 1968: 38). In the worked example here, socio-economic status and part-time working were deemed to be relevant to class of degree. There are many occasions where novice researchers include variables that are simply irrelevant but which are included because they believe that they ought to be included for the sake of tradition or convention.

Implications for researchers:

- Controlling for variables can be undertaken with nominal data through crosstabulations.
- Controlling for variables may indicate the likelihood of causation.
- Controlling for mediating and prior variables has to take account of interaction effects between variables.
- Bivariate and trivariate analysis can assist in identifying causation.
- Regression and correlational analysis, in particular partial correlations and multiple regression, can assist in identifying causation and the relative strengths of independent variables.
- Software is available to compute the relative strengths of direct and indirect influences on dependent variables.
- Crosstabulated data can be looked at in trivariate and multivariate analysis in order to determine the influence of prior and intervening variables on a dependent variable.
- Crosstabulations can be calculated for nominal data and partial correlations calculated to control for the effects of one or more independent variables.
- Controlling for variables must ensure that the controlled variables are logically relevant to the matter in hand.
- It is important for the researcher to determine whether a variable is a prior or an intervening variable, to determine the causal sequencing of independent variables and to understand which variables need to be controlled.

One can observe that, as we move from a bivariate to a trivariate table (and, indeed, to a multivariate table), the number of sub-groups increases significantly, rendering analysis very cumbersome. Similarly, whilst calculations such as those in the preceding examples can be performed manually, in fact it is highly laborious. Computer software is available to do this easily. For example, from simple data on correlations and

Table 3.38 Grouping data on socio-economic status, part-time work and level of degree

Variable		Value		
Socio-economic status	High:	485 (48.5%)	Low:	515 (51.5%)
Part-time work	Yes:	447 (44.7%)	No:	553 (55.3%)
Class of degree	High:	463 (46.3%)	Low:	537 (53.7%)

multiple regression (e.g. from SPSS or some other statistical software, the free down-loadable program Medgraph (http://www.vicoria.ac.nz/psyc/staff/pauljose/files/medgraph/medgraph.php) plots out the direct and indirect influences of an independent and mediating variable and presents the data graphically, using Excel. Data on correlations and multiple regressions are entered into the Medgraph program, which automatically generates the graph and enters the coefficients. Medgraph comes with full, easy-to-follow instructions.

Other software which can be used is AMOS (in SPSS) and LISREL, and these have the advantage of being able to work with more than one mediating variable (Medgraph only works with one independent variable and one mediating variable). Such software programs run path analysis (discussed below). Medgraph and similar programs are useful in that they separate out prior from intervening variables. Prior variables come before other independent variables in a causal model and influence the intervening variables, whilst intervening variables come between prior variables and the dependent variable, influenced by the former and influencing the latter.

Example 7: Partial correlations using SPSS

SPSS is also widely used to facilitate data analysis and presentation for crosstabulated data and multivariate analysis. Let us imagine that we have 1,000 students in a survey, and that we group them according to socio-economic status (high/low); part-time work (yes/no) and class of degree (high/low) (Table 3.38). A cross-tabulation, controlled for socio-economic status, indicates the distributions of the categories, set out by part-time work and socio-economic status as the row variables (using SPSS to control for socio-economic status, as set out earlier (p. 88)), and with the class of degree as the column variable (Table 3.39).

We wish to explore the relationship between part-time working and class of degree, controlling for socio-economic status. Using SPSS software, partial correlations can be calculated straightforwardly. Partial correlations enable the researcher to control for a third variable, i.e. to see the correlation between two variables of interest once the effects of a third variable have been removed, hence rendering more accurate the relationship between the two variables of interest. As Turner (1997: 33) remarks, partialling can rule out special or specific relationships that do not hold true when variables have been controlled. In our example we may be interested in investigating the effect of part-time working on class of degree, controlling for the effects of socio-economic status. SPSS enables us to do this at the touch of a button: go to 'Analyze', then 'Correlations', then 'Partial Correlation' (entering variables to be correlated in the 'Variables' box and the variables to be controlled in the box

Table 3.39 Part-time work and class of degree, controlled for socio-economic status (SPSS output)

Part-time Work by Class of Degree, Controlled for Socio-economic Status (SES)

SES				High class of degree	Low class of degree	Total
High	Part-time work	Working part-time	Frequency	75	57	132
			% within Part-time work	56.8%	43.2%	100.0%
		Not working part-time	Frequency	246	107	353
			% within Part-time work	69.7%	30.3%	100.0%
	Total		Frequency	321	164	485
			% within Part-time work	66.2%	33.8%	100.0%
Low	Part-time work	Working part-time	Frequency	96	219	315
			% within Part-time work	30.5%	69.5%	100.0%
		Not working part-time	Frequency	46	154	200
			% within Part-time work	23.0%	77.0%	100.0%
	Total		Frequency	142	373	515
			% within Part-time work	27.6%	72.4%	100.0%

marked 'Controlling for'; opening the 'Options' box on this screen, one has then to tick the 'zero-order correlations' box, as this gives original correlations, i.e. those prior to controlling for variables. Returning to the original screen and clicking on the 'OK' button produces output on partial correlations (Figure 3.23).

The SPSS output in Figure 3.23 indicates that, in the second of the tables, the correlation coefficients have been controlled for socio-economic status (marked as 'Controlling for . . SES'). The top row for each variable presents the correlation coefficient; the middle row indicates the numbers of people who responded; and the bottom row presents the level of statistical significance ($\rho = .000$). Here the results indicate that there is a very little partial correlation between part-time working and class of degree ($r = -.0150$, degrees of freedom $= 997$, $\rho = .636$), but that this is not statistically significant, i.e. there is no significant correlation between part-time work and class of degree, when controlled for socio-economic status. However, when we examine the correlation coefficient for socio-economic status, in the first table there was a very different correlation coefficient ($r = -.1451$), and this was highly statistically significant ($\rho = .000$). This suggests to us that controlling for socio-economic status has a very considerable effect on the strength of the relationship between the variables 'part-time work' and 'class of degree'. Had the two coefficients here been close, then one could have suggested that controlling for socio-economic status had very little effect on the strength of the relationship.

This time let us imagine that we wish to explore the relationship between socio-economic status and class of degree, controlling for part-time working (Figure 3.24). The SPSS output indicates that the correlation coefficients have been controlled for part-time work (marked as 'Controlling for . . Work'). Here the results indicate that there is a very strong partial correlation between socio-economic status and class of degree ($r = .3629$, degrees of freedom $= 997$, $\rho = .000$), i.e. that this is statistically significant. When we examine the correlation coefficient for socio-economic status, in the first table we see that the correlation coefficient ($r = .3870$) is very similar to the correlation

```
- - - PARTIAL CORRELATION COEFFICIENTS - - -

Zero Order Partials

                     WORK        DEGREE          SES

WORK               1.0000        -.1451        -.3413
                   (    0)       (  998)       (  998)
                   P= .          P= .000       P= .000

DEGREE             -.1451        1.0000         .3870
                   (  998)       (    0)       (  998)
                   P= .000       P= .          P= .000

SES                -.3413         .3870        1.0000
                   (  998)       (  998)       (    0)
                   P= .000       P= .000       P= .

(Coefficient / (D.F.) / 2-tailed Significance)

" . " is printed if a coefficient cannot be computed


- - - PARTIAL CORRELATION COEFFICIENTS - - -

Controlling for..    SES

                     WORK        DEGREE

WORK               1.0000        -.0150
                   (    0)       (  997)
                   P= .          P= .636

DEGREE             -.0150        1.0000
                   (  997)       (    0)
                   P= .636       P= .

(Coefficient / (D.F.) / 2-tailed Significance)

" . " is printed if a coefficient cannot be computed
```

Figure 3.23 SPSS output from partial correlation, controlling for socio-economic status (size reduced from the original)

coefficient found when the variable 'part-time work' has been controlled (the coefficient before being controlled being .3870 and the coefficient after being controlled being .3629). This suggests that controlling for part-time work status has very little effect on the strength of the relationship between the variables 'socio-economic status' and 'class of degree'. Partial correlation enables relationships to be calculated after controlling for one or more variables.

```
- - - P A R T I A L   C O R R E L A T I O N   C O E F F I C I E N T S  - - -

Zero Order Partials

                DEGREE            SES            WORK

DEGREE          1.0000           .3870          -.1451
            (      0)        (    998)        (    998)
            P= .             P= .000         P= .000

SES              .3870          1.0000          -.3413
            (    998)        (      0)        (    998)
            P= .000          P= .            P= .000

WORK            -.1451          -.3413          1.0000
            (    998)        (    998)        (      0)
            P= .000          P= .000          P= .

(Coefficient / (D.F.) / 2-tailed Significance)

"  .  " is printed if a coefficient cannot be computed


- - - P A R T I A L   C O R R E L A T I O N   C O E F F I C I E N T S  - - -

Controlling for..    WORK

                DEGREE            SES

DEGREE          1.0000           .3629
            (      0)        (    997)
            P= .             P= .000

SES              .3629          1.0000
            (    997)        (      0)
            P= .000          P= .

(Coefficient / (D.F.) / 2-tailed Significance)

"  .  " is printed if a coefficient cannot be computed
```

Figure 3.24 SPSS output for partial correlations, controlling for part-time work (size reduced from the original)

Implications for researchers:

- Computer software can be used in the calculation of partial correlations and controlling for the effects of one or more independent variables.
- Controlling for variables by partial correlations enables spurious and real effects to be measured.

Path analysis

Path analysis is a statistical method that enables a researcher to determine how well a multivariate set of non-experimental data fits well with a particular causal model that has been set up in advance by the researcher (i.e. an *a priori* model). It is a particular kind of multiple regression analysis that enables the researcher to see the relative weightings of independent variables on each other and on a dependent variable, to establish pathways of causation, and to determine the direct and indirect effects of independent variables on a dependent variable (e.g. Heise 1969; Land 1969; Blalock 1971). The researcher constructs what she or he thinks will be the causal pathway between independent variables and between independent and dependent variables (i.e. constructs a causal model), often based on literature and theory, and then tests this to see how well it fits with the data.

In constructing path analysis, computer software is virtually essential. Programs such as AMOS (in SPSS) and LISREL are two commonly used examples. Let us imagine that we are doing further work on the example of degree classification introduced above, but this time, instead of using only two independent variables, we are using three:

- socio-economic status
- part-time working
- level of motivation for academic study.

These three variables are purported to have an effect on the class of degree that a student gains (the dependent variable). The researcher believes that, in this non-recursive model (discussed earlier), socioeconomic status determines part-time working, level of motivation for academic study and the dependent variable 'class of degree'. The variable 'socio-economic status' is deemed to be an exogenous variable (caused by variables that are *not* included in the causal model), whilst the variables 'part-time working' and 'level of motivation for academic study' are deemed to be endogenous variables (those caused by variables that *are* included in the model) as well as being affected by exogenous variables. The researcher constructs a model using AMOS, as in Figure 3.25.

In the model (Figure 3.25) the dependent variable is 'class of degree' and there are directional causal arrows leading both to this and to and from the three independent variables. One can see that the model assumes that the variables 'part-time work' and 'level of motivation for academic study' influence each other and that 'socio-economic status' precedes the other independent variables rather than being caused by them (the asymmetry of causation mentioned in Chapter 2). In the model there are also three variables in circles, termed 'e1', 'e2' and 'e3'; these three additional variables are the error factors, i.e. additional extraneous/exogenous factors which may also be influencing the three variables in question, and AMOS adjusts the results for these factors. (AMOS will draw this model and let the researcher manipulate its layout.)

AMOS then calculates the regression coefficient of each causal relationship and places then on the model, as presented in Figure 3.26 (using the 'standardized estimates' in AMOS). Here one can see that:

(a) 'Socio-economic' status exerts a direct powerful influence on class of degree (.18), and that this is higher than the direct influence of either 'part-time work' (−.01) or 'level of motivation for academic study' (.04);

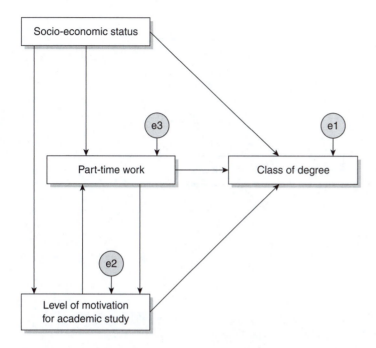

Figure 3.25 Path analysis modelling with AMOS (AMOS output)

(b) 'Socio-economic status' exerts a powerful direct influence on 'level of motivation for academic study' (.52), and this is higher than the influence of 'socio-economic status' on 'class of degree' (.18);

(c) 'Socio-economic status' exerts a powerful direct and negative influence on 'part-time work' (−.21), i.e. the higher the socio-economic status, the lesser is the amount of part-time work undertaken;

(d) 'Part-time work' exerts a powerful direct influence on 'level of motivation for academic study' (1.37), and this is higher than the influence of 'socio-economic status' on 'level of motivation for academic study' (.52);

(e) 'Level of motivation for academic study' exerts a powerful negative direct influence on 'part-time work' (−1.45), i.e. the higher is the level of motivation for academic study, the lesser is the amount of part-time work undertaken;

(f) 'Level of motivation for academic study' exerts a slightly more powerful influence on 'class of degree' (.04) than does 'part-time work' (−.01);

(g) 'Part-time work' exerts a negative influence on the class of degree (−.01), i.e. the more one works part-time, the lower is the class of degree obtained.

AMOS also yields a battery of statistics about the 'goodness of fit' of the model to the data, most of which is beyond the scope of this book; suffice it to say here that the chi-square statistic must *not* be statistically significant (i.e. $p > .05$), i.e. to indicate that the model does not differ statistically significantly from the data (i.e. the model is faithful to the data), and the goodness of fit index (the Normed Fit Index (NFI) and the Comparative Fit Index (CFI)) should be .9 or higher.

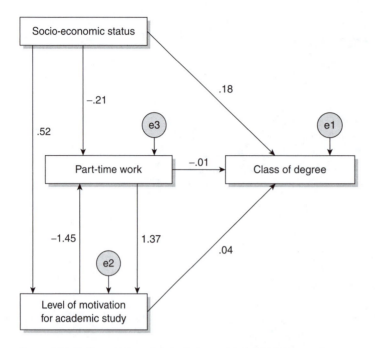

Figure 3.26 Path analysis with calculations added (AMOS output)

Path analysis assumes that the *direction* of causation in the variables can be identified (Duncan 1969), that the data are at the interval level, that the relations are linear, that the data meet the usual criteria for regression analysis, and that the model's parsimony (inclusion of few variables) is fair (Heise 1969: 68–9; Blalock 1971). Whilst path analysis is a powerful tool in the armoury of causal modelling, it is only as good as the causal assumptions that underpin it, and, as mentioned later in this chapter, it does not prove causation unequivocally; rather it tests a model based only on *assumed* causal directions and influences. That said, its utility lies in its ability to test models of causal directions, to establish relative weightings of variables, to look at direct and indirect effects of independent variables, and to handle several independent variables simultaneously.

Implications for researchers:

- Path analysis using software packages such as AMOS or LISREL can be used to test causal modelling.
- Path analysis enables the relative strength of exogenous and endogenous independent variables to be calculated.
- Path analysis enables the relative direct and indirect strengths of independent variables to be calculated.
- Path analysis does not prove causation; it only tests an a *priori* putative causal model set up by the researcher.

Statistics and causation

This chapter has mentioned several statistical procedures for understanding causation. At the same time it has been careful to suggest that statistics will not prove causation, and that to believe that they will is to engage in circular thinking. Rather, it is the theoretical underpinnings and assumptions that embody causation, and the role of statistics might support, challenge, extend and refine these underpinnings and assumptions. Behind the statistics lie theories and models, and it is in the construct validity of these that causation lies. Statistics on their own do not prove causation. As Rosenberg (1968: 200) suggests, data do not prove a theory; they only support, challenge, or refine a theory developed by the researcher.

The history of statistical approaches to causation (e.g. Porter 1986) attests to the equivocal role of statistics in attributing causation. In the earliest days the thinking was that tabular analysis and graphs would demonstrate causation; this was superseded by crosstabulations, then correlational and regression analysis, which, in turn, were was superseded by factor analysis, which, in turn, was superseded by path analysis, LISREL and AMOS software and causal modelling, which, in turn, were superseded by structural equation modeling, logistic regression, logit analysis, multi-level models, autoregressive and cross-lagged models (these latter are beyond the scope of this book, though they are based on regression analysis). Indeed statistics, at best, might yield only powerful measures of correlation and association rather than causation; they do not establish causation (cf. Gorard 2001: 12), only perhaps Hume's 'constant conjunction'. They might only yield data on the conditions in which causation is located and in which it operates. Early research on school effectiveness placed considerable store on associations rather than causal relations between independent and dependent variables (cf. ibid.). For example, whilst Mortimore *et al.* (1988) could find associations between a set of characteristics and effective schools, these were not causal, only powerfully correlational, even with controls applied.

Clogg and Haritou (1997), Hedström (2005) and Goldthorpe (2007a) tellingly remark that statistics do not hold the answer to the mechanisms of causation, and it is the mechanisms rather than numbers that should concern researchers. Here qualitative data come into their own, and the examples that follow, and those in Chapters 5 and 6, attest to this.

Example 8: Qualitative research on a science innovation in schools

Qualitative research is ideal for identifying the processes and mechanisms of causation. In-depth description, narrative accounts, ethnographies, case studies and a range of qualitative methods are essential ingredients in understanding causation (e.g. Maxwell 1996, 2004; Eisenhart 2005: 253). Qualitative research may argue that, since it seeks naturalism (Cohen *et al.* 2007), it is not only impossible but undesirable to control variables, causes and effects, yet word-based data in response to semi-structured interviews and observations might pattern themselves within or across sites (e.g. Miles and Huberman 1984).

This example takes a qualitative study of change in science teaching (cf. Morrison *et al.* 1989). Let us imagine that a group of schools has been involved in moving away from a content- and facts-based emphasis in their science curricula and towards a process-, experimental- and observation-based approach, and that this is in response not only to external pressure for change from government initiatives in science teaching but also to felt need within the science departments concerned. The heads of the science departments have been attending a course on a process-based approach to science teaching, and they then bring this to their science colleagues, who examine the current practices in their departments, write new curricula, prepare new materials, trial the new curricula, seek to identify positive and negative outcomes, and assess students' attainment.

Let us further imagine that an evaluator is appointed to chart the nature, implementation, effectiveness and outcomes of the innovation in the several schools. The evaluator is seeking to understand the main causal drivers of the innovation, the facilitating and inhibiting factors for the innovation and their relative strengths, the rates of change at different stages of the innovation and the reasons for these differences of speed, and the effectiveness of the new science curricula in improving student attainment.

The evaluator gathers qualitative data from semi-structured interviews and observations with the science staff at the schools. Looking at the data she observes commonalities across the schools in terms of:

- the stages of the innovation, from planning to preparation to implementation;
- the rates of change at different stages of the innovation;
- the facilitating and inhibiting factors at each stage of the innovation.

She decides to organize the data by the stage of change and the rate of change. Since she is using qualitative data she constructs a cross-site chart (see Miles and Huberman 1984) to map the commonalities at each stage of the innovation and in terms of the rate of change at each of these stages. The results are presented in Figures 3.27 and 3.28. Running through the first of the figures is the sequence of the unfolding of the innovation ('chronological sequence'), arranged into stages of change, within which are also the rates of change. When these stages and rates of change are set out, the cross-site analysis reveals not only the presence of the same inhibiting and facilitating factors but their causal influences and effects, the direction of those influences, the factors that they affect, and the relative strengths of those facilitating and inhibiting and factors (marked as a series of '+' signs in the causal chart (Figure 3.28)). Though Figure 3.27 may appear rather formidable, nevertheless it enables the researchers to understand the effects of different factors within qualitative data, and it establishes causal chains. Figure 3.28 distils out from this first chart the key facilitating and inhibiting factors in the innovation. Whilst, for some, this might smack of an unacceptable positivism and might violate the principles of qualitative data, one perhaps should not think that qualitative data are all of the same type and can only be treated in a limited number of ways (indeed the origins of content analysis, so favoured by qualitative researchers, lies in frequencies generated by word counts in newspaper articles).

Implications for researchers:

- It is possible to organize qualitative data by factors.
- Organizing by factors in qualitative data can reveal their relative causal strengths.
- Constructing causal and cross-site charts can indicate the nature, strength and directions of causation in qualitative research.

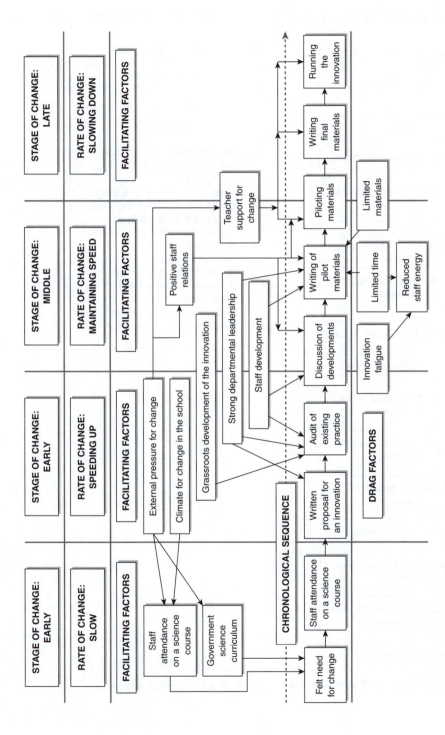

Figure 3.27 Cross-site analysis of qualitative data

CAUSES		KEY:	

FACTORS FACILITATING CHANGE

Support of science staff	+		= Noticeable but not strong factor
Staff relations	++	+	= Quite a strong factor
Climate of change in the schools		++	= Very strong factor
External pressure for change	++		
Grassroots development strategy	+		
Confining innovation to manageable numbers of staff			
Awareness of need for change			

EFFECTS

1 Slowing down rate of change
2 Setting innovation in a broad perspective
3 Seeing innovation in a longer and more realistic time frame
4 Change of leadership
5 Slow preparation of curriculum materials
6 Limited uptake
7 Increased staff turnover
8 Promotion of new head of department
9 Increased funding for innovation
10 Trialling of new materials

FACTORS IMPEDING CHANGE

Nature of the innovation	+
Personal aspects of the innovation	+
External resource support for change	++
External pressure for change	++
Innovation fatigue	+
Limited commitment and goodwill	
Dissipation of science staff to other departments	+
Time to develop curricula	++

Figure 3.28 Factors facilitating and impeding change in qualitative data analysis

Example 9: Investigating causation in ethnographic research

How causation works is a major province of qualitative data. A second example of qualitative research here indicates how this can be done.

It is over three decades since Willis (1977) published his widely celebrated and yet widely criticized book *Learning to Labour*, a canonical piece of ethnographic research into the operation of resistance theories at work in education. Here is not the place to examine the several criticisms that it has attracted (e.g. for being over-selective in its focus and sampling; for neglecting alternative perspectives; for misrepresenting the working class; for choosing extreme cases; for understating feminism and the actions of significant other females; for understating issues of race; for its determinism). Rather it is held up as an outstanding example of qualitative research that identifies causation through the combining of action narratives with structural (working-class), cultural and sub-cultural factors.

Willis was concerned to investigate 'how working-class kids get working class jobs and how others let them', and, to undertake this, he conducted ethnographic research using participant observation with a gang of white, working-class males in their final time at a secondary school in the middle of England and thence into their early experiences of work. This gang he termed the 'lads', indicating their group solidarity in resisting the authority of the school and their enjoyment of social life both inside and outside school. Through being with them in many contexts and situations in and out of school, he was able to report several characteristics of their sub-cultural lifestyle, for example:

- opposition to, and subversion of, authority, and rejection of conformity: clothing; smoking and telling lies; drinking;
- resistance to the dominant ideology that emanates from the school;
- celebration of the informal group, in contrast to the formal arrangements of school;
- rejection of the conformist students in the schools (termed the 'ear'oles', as they both had the ear of the teachers and listened to the teachers);
- rejection of formality – deciding which lessons to attend; creating their own schedules; and coming to school in order to 'have a laugh', disrupt the teachers, meet their friends, and to regard school as a setting for their social lives rather than their academic development;
- regarding excitement as that which took place largely out of school (except for baiting the teachers and having fun with their friends at school), and for which they needed ready money;
- rejection of the literary tradition and qualifications;
- celebration of manual, anti-intellectual activities;
- living for the present, with no deferred gratification;
- rejection of the coercion which underlines the teaching paradigm;
- sexism and male chauvinism, calling girlfriends 'the missis';
- racism.

When he followed the 'lads' into their first employment willis found several 'elective affinities' and key points of resonance between the culture that they had created at the school and the culture into which they moved in employment, for example:

- manual, often factory-based, waged labour that put immediate cash into their pockets;
- male chauvinism and sexism in the workplace (not least with the pin-up nude female pictures on the factory walls);
- resistance to the dominant ideology that emanated from the bosses;
- attempts to gain informal control of the work process by subverting managerial attempts to control the workplace;
- rejection of coercion in the workplace;
- shirking work/absenteeism/taking time off;
- rejection of the conformists in the factory;
- rejection of 'theory' and certification;
- no break on the taboo of informing on your friends (those in the same situation as yourself);
- speaking up for yourself;
- being oriented to the present;
- rejection of mental labour and celebration of manual labour.

Willis's conclusions and answers to his research question are clear: working-class kids get working-class jobs because that is what they choose and what they are influenced to choose by the values that they hold. His 'lads' see through the social construction of what is deemed valuable by schools and powerful sectors of society and the scorn of working classes (his discussion of 'penetrations'). The 'lads' seek to have immediate gratification, to live for the present, to have money, excitement, sex and power, and to reject theory, authority, conformity and academic qualifications. In valuing these matters and rejecting other values, they deliberately, intentionally, agentically choose to go into the kinds of work that will enable them to perpetuate those values, i.e. working-class, waged, manual, factory work, but nevertheless which will keep them at the bottom of the heap in society (his discussion of 'limitations'). These values, coupled with the specific kinds of work into which the same values lead them, guarantee that they will end up as working-class, largely disempowered adults, i.e. the cycle of working-class membership is reproduced.

Despite the criticisms, Willis's research is a fascinating account of causation at work in qualitative research. He succeeds in 'getting inside the heads' of the actors in the situation (the 'lads'), in understanding and presenting their perspectives on the world – their 'definitions of the situation' – and in establishing the causes of their behaviour at school, their post-school options and the lifestyles that they adopt. He identifies the *driving* causes (the sufficient causes) in their individual and collective psyches and how these influence their lifestyles at school and beyond. Here is a piece of research that impressively combines micro- and macro-accounts of group and sub-cultural behaviour.

Further, Willis's work integrates action, agentic narratives with structural accounts. By blending the participants' own definitions of the situation with the researcher's definition of the situation, the reader is provided with an account that both theorizes the causative processes at work and identifies the sufficient conditions for the causation to operate. His work is an example of overdetermination at work in causation and of understanding causal processes at work.

Further examples of qualitative causal data are given in Chapters 5 and 6.

Using tracers in qualitative research

Hage and Meeker (1988: 195) suggest that, in order to understand causation and causal processes at work in qualitative or ethnographic research, it is possible to use 'tracers'. A tracer is a specific focus of observation 'that allows one to follow more easily the causal processes which connect various state variables' (ibid.: 195–6), e.g. to see what happens with it and in relation to it in specific settings and over time.[6] They give examples of tracers, such as (a) money (e.g. its supply, passage, exchange); (b) decisions (e.g. who, how, relations to power and organizational centralization); (c) an idea (e.g. its flow, distribution, uptake, impact, relatedness to innovation); and (d) meanings (e.g. people's definitions of the situation, symbols, status). In educational research tracers might include conformity, freedom, autonomy, staff–student relationships, resources, planning, assessment, teaching strategies, resistance, and so on.

It is possible to see who uses a tracer or comes into contact with it, how it is used and interpreted, what effects it has on those who come into contact with it, similarities and differences in interpretation and the effects of such similarities and differences, and what additional features it illuminates and brings into focus (just as a tracer is designed to assist the aiming of a bullet).

Implications for researchers:

- Qualitative research can combine participants' own definitions of the situation and causation with those of the researcher's providing overall accounts of causation.
- Qualitative research can combine action narratives with structural accounts in explaining causation.
- Qualitative research can use 'tracers' to identify causal processes.

Taking stock

What we see, then, in the analysis of probabilistic causation in this large chapter is that it entails consideration of a very wide range of matters.

- A must be logically independent of B to permit causation to be established.
- The term 'cause' is an umbrella term for many causes.
- The term 'effect' is an umbrella term for many effects.
- Reasons, intentions, volitions and motives may or may not be the same as causes.
- A catalyst may be the same as a cause.
- The description of a cause is not necessarily the same as the cause itself.
- Causation is learned by the experience, custom and habit of constant conjunction rather than logical connection.
- Causation is inductive, not deductive.
- There are many variants of cause and effect:

  - A causes B;
  - A may cause B and C (one cause, many effects);
  - A causes B and C, but B does not cause C;

- C may be caused by A and B (one effect, many causes);
- A causes B, which causes C, which causes D (a causal chain);
- A causes B but not C or D, as C or D are caused by other causes.

- There are many variants in the temporality of cause and effect:

  - A causes B, and A precedes B in time;
  - A causes B, but A may continue after B has started, an effect may commence before the cause has stopped;
  - A may cause B, but they may be simultaneous, i.e. A may not precede B in time;
  - A may cause B, acting backwards in time (although this is questionable).

- The timing of the effects of a cause may be unclear, delayed, instantaneous, immediate, cumulative, decayed and long-term.
- The full effects of a cause may not be revealed in a single instance, as an effect may be a covering term for many effects.
- Temporality and causation are intimately connected but separate; one can have causation without a temporal dimension.
- A may determine or entail B, and B may depend on A, without there being causation between A and B (the supervenience issue).
- Causation is more fittingly regarded as a process rather than a single event.
- In a causal chain a cause (A) can cause effect (B) which, in turn, can become a cause (e.g. of C).
- An effect may be caused by one or more causal lines.
- Causal lines, strictly speaking, are separate but, empirically, they may interact with each other.
- Causation may be shown in a single instance rather than repeated instances.
- The trigger of a cause is not the sole cause, but only the last cause in a causal chain.
- Causes take place in the context of specific circumstances.
- Causes have direction (from causes to effects), though sometimes it may be unclear what the direction of causation might be.
- Causation may be asymmetric (A causes B but B does not cause A).
- There may be an infinite number of causes and effects, depending on how far back one wishes to go in time and how wide one wishes to go in terms of contexts.
- Reducing the number of component causes can be addressed by identifying necessary and sufficient conditions.
- Necessary and sufficient conditions vary from context to context.
- Determining necessary and sufficient conditions in the human sciences may be difficult.
- Even though there may be regularities of cause and effect from context to context, there are also differences.
- Association – correlation – does not establish causation.
- Covariance is not the same as causation.
- Causation may be direct and indirect.
- The strength of causes may lie in their relation to each other in an individual instance or in relation to their incidence in the wider population.
- The presence of causes affects their relative strengths in a specific context, and the absence of some of these causes in the same context may raise the relative strengths of others.

- The relationship between cause and effect may be linear, non-linear, curvilinear and indeterminate (e.g. chaotic).
- Causes cannot be taken in isolation; they may need to be taken together (compound causes – i.e. they only exert causative force when acting in concert).
- Causes cannot be taken in isolation; there may be interaction effects between them.
- In many cases, probabilistic causation may be a more fitting view of causation than deterministic or regularistic causation.
- Causation requires rival hypotheses and explanations to be tested.
- The effects of some causes may be offset, e.g. reduced, overridden by other causes present.
- The effects of some causes may be masked by the presence of others, but nonetheless causation may be occurring.
- Induction periods and latent periods are part of a causal sequence.
- An effect is not the same as a change; it can be a non-change.
- Effects can be overdetermined (i.e. any of several causes present may bring about the effect).
- Quasi-causation embraces the absence of events, which may bring about effects.
- To discover the effects of direct and indirect causes requires holding causes fixed (controlling for variables) and screening off causes from each other.
- Whilst probability often concerns identifying likelihood, the strongest probability is not always the same as the strongest causation.
- It is important to control for the effects of variables, i.e. to hold them constant (matched) so that fair attribution of causality and the weight of causal variables can be assessed.
- Screening out involves controlling variables.
- Causal forks – conjunctive (open and closed), interactionist and perfect – indicate different kinds of causal relation.
- Statistical tools such as crosstabulations, correlation and partial correlation, regression and multiple regression, and path analysis can be used to assist in the analysis of causation.
- Direct, indirect, antecedent, intervening and combined influences of variables on outcomes can be calculated using statistical tools.
- Controlling for variables can occur in both quantitative and qualitative research.
- It is important to avoid the ecological fallacy in interpreting data.
- Action narratives complement generalized variables in accounting for causes and effects.
- Qualitative research can provide in-depth accounts of causal processes.
- Qualitative data can be ordered and organized to suggest causation.
- Qualitative research can provide action narratives and multiple definitions of the situation and the causation of effects, through participants' and researchers' eyes.
- Tracers can be used to assist the identification of causation and causal processes.
- Causation lies in the assumptions behind models rather than in the statistical tests of those models.

Given this complexity, it would be invidious to suppose that a particular intervention will necessarily bring about the intended affect. Any cause or intervention is embedded in a web of other causes, contexts, conditions, circumstances and effects, and these can exert a mediating and altering influence between the cause and its effect.

Chapter 4

Approaching cause and effect

Introduction

Social science and educational research often asks 'why?'. Causation, explanation, reasons and purposes all feature here. Detecting causation or its corollary – prediction – is the jewel in the crown of social science research (Glymour 1997: 224). Measures of association, however strong, do not establish causation. Indeed prediction (future orientation) may not be possible even if causation (explanation of past and present events) is successful, not least as the conditions and contexts change, e.g. societal, economic, educational. Survey research, however monumental the sample sizes might be, may not help in establishing causation. Statistical processes may not necessarily help either; for example, structural equation modelling, however attractive, is not fulfilling its early promise of establishing causation (Goldthorpe 2007a: 121). Indeed the benefits of high-level statistical analysis such as multi-level modelling are suggested to be 'dubious' (Gorard 2007). As Rudduck (1981: 49) remarked several years ago, statistical methodology often combines 'great refinement of process with crudity of concept'. Statistical methods, argues Goldthorpe (2007a: 17), cannot simply 'crank out' causal explanations of phenomena from numbers, however regular they may appear in combination or correlation. Regularity is not causation.

That said, Ayres (2008) demonstrates the power of prediction, probabilities and regularities yielded by data sets from extremely large samples and sub-samples, particularly when the analysis takes account of regression techniques and standard deviations (two standard deviations accounting for 95 per cent of the population). These are important in evidence-based education and may be more reliable than human intuition (e.g. ibid.: chap. 7), though Ayres underlines the importance of humans in the process of initial hypothesis generation (ibid.: 124). Similarly, Hage and Meeker (1988: 21), countering the criticisms of statistical processes, indicate that path analysis and structural equation modelling may offer useful analyses of causal paths, though they are clear that these may have problems (e.g. stepwise regression techniques may lead researchers to ignore some underlying causal processes (ibid.: 104)).

However, numerical analysis is not alone in falling short of establishing causation. We should not be seduced into thinking that qualitative ethnographic research is an automatic panacea. Indeed many case studies and ethnographies, or pieces of qualitative research, are sometimes little more than inconclusive, quiet self indulgences of their authors' egos – stories masquerading as research. Their contribution to establishing any useful causation (or even to approaching being remotely interesting) is sometimes impossible to discern, and how they further social science, educational research and theory generation and testing is sometimes opaque.

We should not be surprised that the search for causation is elusive. People have different motives, and, further, dynamical systems theory and its sometime derivatives in chaos theory and complexity theory remind us that we live in an emergent, non-linear, multivalent, orthogonal, multivariate, multiply causal, subjunctive, multiply causally directional, and endlessly changing world. Searching for simple causation is erroneous. Statistical processes, of whatever architectonic splendour, baroque sophistication and rococo elaboration, may offer only limited help.

Is the search for causation passé – yesterday's modernistic agenda for today's putative post-positivist, postmodern world? Surely not. Indeed Goldthorpe (2007a), with robust evidence, argues for a careful, rational, cumulative view of knowledge and a renewed search for a sophisticated understanding of causation. In this, his advocacy of the need to test rival theories (ibid.: 120) is powerful, and parts of this chapter are indebted to his work.

Seeking and testing causal theories is fundamental to much educational research. We can ask, for example, whether the increasing association between education and occupational status is a result of

1   meritocracy and the move away from ascription and towards achievement;
2   increased credentialism (qualifications becoming the first filter in job appointments);
3   lean-and-mean employment practices (reduced numbers of workers in a business/institution/company/organization combined with greater demand on those who are employed);
4   increased skill level requirements;
5   increased competition for jobs;
6   limited employment and career prospects (the supply side);
7   increasing demands (the demand side); or
8   a range of diverse individual motives that are not caught in simple, generalized independent variables.

Theories must be put to the test of rigorous evidence.

Behind variables and their patterning are individual motives, intentionality, choices and agency, however constrained. As Marx so tellingly observed, we create our own history, but not in circumstances of our own choosing. An unassailable causal theory – and theory generation and testing is surely the goal of much research – is the consequence of scrupulous data analysis, data interrogation, data evaluation, and theory testing. It should also ensure that: (a) the right questions are being asked in the first place (the research design and operationalization); (b) individual and collective motives, purposes, reasons and personally indicated causes are factored into research; and (c) theory is being used to interrogate the world. Consciously or not, we use causal theory and theories to investigate the world and act in it; as Lewin (1951: 169) remarked: 'there is nothing so practical as a good theory'. The concern here is not only to identify 'what constitutes evidence', but 'evidence of what', and to ensure that appropriate questions and evidence are embraced in research design that can establish causation. This argues for mixed methodologies and for ensuring that individual motives are included as essential ingredients in the research.

This echoes the advocacy of combining different ways of investigating causation (Maxwell 2004; Eisenhart 2005: 245): both of *what* affects what (e.g. experimental approaches) and of *how* A affects B (e.g. ethnographic, narrative and qualitative approaches).

Goldthorpe argues cogently that researchers should continue to concern themselves with the discovery and testing of causation rather than abandoning the enterprise. In this same enterprise, individuals matter – their motives and agency – and it is essential to understand how these become part of laws and patterns of behaviour.

Implications for researchers:

- Data on their own, be they numerical or non-numerical, are insufficient for establishing causality.
- Causation requires a causal theory.
- Causal theories are probably not simplistic.
- Causation remains relevant in a complex world.
- Theories should contribute to the cumulative development of knowledge.
- There are many possible causal theories to explain one effect.
- Rival theories need to be generated and tested.
- Theory generation and testing require evidence.
- Care must be taken to ensure that evidence is evidence of the theory being tested.
- Causal theories must include reference to individuals and to their agency, motives and action narratives.

How, then, can the researcher establish causation? There are three questions that might usefully be pursued here:

1   How can we establish the likelihood of a cause?
2   How can we determine the effect of a cause?
3   How can we determine the cause from an effect?

This probabilistic type of causation takes various forms. For example, likelihood

(a) may involve consideration of the case of B, given A, in contrast to B, given not-A (the counterfactual argument);
(b) may involve statistical analysis (inferences from observed regularities);
(c) involves consideration of the balance of probabilities given the conditions and relative strengths of the causes (both positive forces – promoting the effect – and negative forces – inhibiting the effect);
(d) derives from theoretical analysis, previous research and modelling.

These are potentially complicated matters, and the search for cause and effect, as suggested in the preceding chapters, is tricky. Item (a) focuses on observed regularities and the inferences that can be made from these, though inferences may not demonstrate strict causation. It is also contingent on the answers to items (b) and (c). Item (b) concerns the careful control and manipulation of variables, e.g. in an experimental approach, action research, or an interventionist approach, and seeing the effects of these (discussed in Chapter 5). Item (c) is much more open than item (b) in its implications for research, and concerns the setting up of putative causal mechanisms and processes and subjecting these to rigorous testing and to the testing of rival explanations (discussed in Chapter 6). Item (c) is akin to the forensic investigation of causes by careful detection and reconstruction of events. Item (d) indicates that construct validity of theories should build on previous research and studies.

Implications for researchers:

- Decide whether the intention is to look for the likelihood of an effect from a cause and/or the likelihood of a cause from an effect.
- Decide whether the focus of the research is on the effect of one or more causes or the cause(s) of an effect.
- Causation research is strongly theory-based.

Stages in identifying causation

One can set out a set of simple stages in investigating causation.

Stage 1: Establish what has to be explained.
Stage 2: Construct a theoretical explanation of the causation.
Stage 3: Test the causal theory.
Stage 4: Draw conclusions.

Hage and Meeker (1988: 43) argue that 'a test of a causal theory requires the three parts of general law(s), initial conditions, and (derived from them) statements of observable regularities.' Whilst this may be somewhat positivistic, it nevertheless signals that theory construction is an essential ingredient of establishing causation, and that theories need to be operationalized. How this can be done is addressed in the following pages.

Stage 1: Establish what has to be explained

Before we can consider causation and what is the explanation (the *explanans*) we have to ensure that we know exactly what it is that the causal explanation is seeking to explain, i.e. the *explanandum* (that which has to be explained). This takes us directly back to the first chapter, in which advice was given to ensure that we are really looking at the cause and not its proxy (the description of a cause). We may say that the striking of a match was the cause of a fire, but that is incomplete, as the fire was caused by a multiplicity of factors that are not alluded to in the simple statement of a match being struck.

Goldthorpe (2007a: 8) suggests that theorizing about causation may start from observed regularities in empirical data, for example frequencies of association (Hume's 'constant conjunction', 'contiguity' and 'priority', and Kim's (1993a) examples of entailment, determination and dependence in the supervenience relation). The regularities to be observed may derive from numerical data, measures of association, regression analyses, multivariate analysis, and a plethora of high-level statistical procedures, but, Goldthorpe implies, these may not offer *causal* explanations. They may hint but not prove. Behind the models of structural equation modelling, regression analysis, multivariate analysis and other statistical procedures lie theories of social processes and causal mechanisms; the models are not the theories (cf. Goldthorpe 2007a: 84). Models model and only portray, describe and instantiate theories.

That said, this is not to decry the value of large numbers, of regularities or of statistical techniques. As Goldthorpe remarks (2007a: 19–20), in 'causation as robust dependence' (e.g. finding strong cause-and-effect links) causal explanations are derived from statistical treatment of data, and the larger the data set and the greater the appropriacy of the sampling, the greater is the confidence that can be placed in the results.

Regularities and repeated chains of events may not be the focus of the research. A causal investigation may be much more singular (e.g. a case study or a single focus), for example: 'Why is Sarah having so many problems in her social adjustment in class?', 'Why is this class of students performing so well in science?', 'Why does Stephen cry during mathematics lessons?', 'Why is this new teaching style not improving student motivation?', 'Why is this school principal so unpopular?'.

Implications for researchers:

- Clarify the *explanans* and the *explanandum*.
- Consider investigating the causes and effects of regularities.
- Consider examining the causes and effects of singularities.

It is commonly heard that ethnographic or qualitative data may indicate the explanatory processes that numerical data lack. This may or may not be true. Qualitative data, of various hues (e.g. ethnographic, phenomenological interactionist, interpretive, naturalistic, qualitative observational or interview data), may or may not provide such explanations. They may be no less prone to the limits of induction that plague numerical analysis – observing a putative causal mechanism once does not ensure that it is actually true. Case studies and qualitative data have no privileged status for theory generation in comparison to numerical analysis. They may still only describe (perhaps from a greater number of perspectives – the participants' different perspectives – than is often the case in numerical studies), and the *theory* that derives from them may be no more than a summary of the observations. Ethnographic data, case studies, interactionist accounts, naturalistic and phenomenological studies can give rise to theories and can be the test-bed of theories in the same way as numerical data.

Further, given the plethora of data available in qualitative research, the discussion of the basis for their selection for inclusion or exclusion is significant, or else the reader has no way of knowing how partial, biased, selective and representative (of the case or situation in question) they are, and therefore no way of ascertaining whether the causal mechanisms in question constitute the necessary and sufficient causes and conditions in the situation and whether other causal chains, lines or processes might have greater strength (the balance of probabilities and likelihoods discussed in the previous chapter). Like numerical data, qualitative data should be subject to the canons of probability, careful identification of causation, the strengths of causal probabilities and testing as advocated for numerical data; it is only that the data types differ. Indeed, if one is seeking to establish generalizable laws of causation, then qualitative data may be disadvantaged over large-scale numerical data sets that derive from probability samples.

A narrative or a description is not the same as a theoretical explanation, and, even when it is derived from qualitative data, a theory is no less exempted from testing than are those that derive from numerical data. The test of a theory, as Einstein remarked, should be in circumstances and with data other than those that gave rise to the theory, otherwise there will be circularity: if we use the same data to test as to formulate the theories, then the theories would all be confirmed (cf. Green 2002: 17). Theory *derivation* – e.g. grounded theory – is no substitute for theory testing and validation. Behind individual and qualitative data should stand theory, just as for numerical data.

Returning to the four-stage model outlined above, stage 1 is essentially *descriptive* and *analytical* rather than explanatory, bringing into being those matters that are seeking investigation and explanation. This may be in terms of observed regularities, of a sequence of non-repeated events (a story, narrative, unfolding situation), or simply of an event or process.

Implications for researchers:

- Recognize that neither numerical nor qualitative data may necessarily provide causal explanations.
- Qualitative research has no privileged explanatory potential over numerical research.
- Qualitative data may provide useful accounts of causal processes.
- Numerical and qualitative data may provide the context for testing causal explanations.
- Decide and describe exactly what is the focus, what has to be explained.

Stage 2: Construct a theoretical explanation of the causation

Data, both numerical and qualitative, may be necessary but insufficient for theory. Though having large samples may be more helpful than having small samples in establishing the regularities that the theory may wish to explain, large samples alone may provide little solace. An international newspaper carried an interesting column: a large number of people in Asia believed that a teapot had healing properties (*South China Morning Post* 2008) and they worshipped the teapot; however, does that cause the teapot to have healing properties, and does it mean that the teapot actually has healing properties? Of course not. The number of believers is irrelevant; their views are subjective and perception-based and do not establish causation. Causation, though probabilistic, does not lie in numbers alone. There is a need for a causal mechanism to be explained, and magic, belief or wishes may not feature here.

Implications for researchers:

- Causation is not a function of subjective belief.
- Causation is not a function of sample size.

Large samples may be entirely appropriate or, indeed, inappropriate for the research in question. If the focus is on a specific instance, case, event or chain of events, then a large sample may be misplaced, unfitting and irrelevant. The issue here is of theory construction rather than of sampling. Consider the case of Dibs, in Axline's (1964) touching study of a little boy discovering himself through non-directive play therapy. Here the sample was one (N = 1), and this was entirely appropriate. Indeed Goldthorpe (2007a) discusses the problems of studying globalization where, as the world under study seemingly becomes smaller, N approaches 1.

Following on the heels of the observation, the researcher constructs a possible explanation of what is causing these: the causal mechanisms. In this sense the theory is a *construction* rather than a derivative. Here is a place for quantitative, numerical data, establishing regularities (e.g. through surveys) that may warrant further investigation from the basis of theory. It is not enough, Goldthorpe avers, to establish 'mindless correlations and associations' (2007a: 12); they have little or no explanatory power. Correlations exist, but answering the question '*why*' is a matter of causal theory construction, of conjecture, testing, refutation and demonstration.

Here, is a place for qualitative data that establish narratives and well-explicated and described situations and circumstances. These also stand in need of explanation and a theoretical foundation if causation is to be established. Theory generation or construction may follow from observations (or, indeed, if we accept Popperian analysis, then even our initial observations are theory-driven; as humans we do not have theory-free observation). As Nietzsche (1973) remarked, in *Beyond Good and Evil*: '[t]here is a point in every philosophy at which the "conviction" of the philosopher appears on the scene'. A significant starting point for examining causation is theory. Put simply, we have to ask ourselves what is actually happening in the situation and why. One definition of a theory is that it is a possible causal explanation, to be tested.

Where does a theory come from? How does one begin to establish a theory? Clearly there are many starting points. One may be through observation (e.g. of observed regularities, of an association of events), another through reflection and creativity (e.g. Mitroff 1983). A further starting point may be through asking a 'what if' question (e.g. 'If assessment were to become more authentic, would it increase student motivation?', or 'Does repeating a year at school improve student performance?'), and yet another might be less concerned with regularities but a single instance – 'Why did such-and-such happen?' or 'Why is such-and-such happening?'.

Implications for researchers:

- Theories are constructed to provide causal explanations.
- Narratives, correlations and regularities are neither theories nor evidence of causation.
- Identify the starting point for gathering data to inform theory generation and testing.

Goldthorpe (2007a: 119) contends that quantitative analysis on its own is probably unable to establish causation, and that behind quantitative analysis, indeed logically prior to it, are action narratives. Indeed he argues that it is mistaken to think that it is *variables*, rather than *individuals*, that do the causing or the acting, or to regard individuals as being only the 'locale' for the variables to do their work. *People* and the choices they make create and contribute to the variables, patterned responses and nomothetic observations that numerical analysis and methodologies so prize. Yet, so often in educational research, e.g. surveys and experimental research, the individuals are lost in the aggregates and averages and their motives for answering a questionnaire in a particular way are not explored; the individuals, as Goldthorpe avers, become simply 'the locale for the variables to do their thing' (ibid.).

Let us take as an example the widely documented issue of why teachers leave teaching voluntarily. Many causes are cited, for example: work overload; stress; student indiscipline; low pay; low status; poor career and promotion prospects; government initiatives; school management; poor resources and facilities; difficult parents (e.g. Smithers and Robinson 2001) – i.e. they leave to get away from something rather than being attracted by something else (ibid.: 40). Whilst no one might wish to question this, the main cause is that teachers *decide* that they will leave; they leave because they decide to leave. The personal decision is the cause, though, of course, behind this are several contributing causes and conditions, and the decision is the last stage in the causal chain or causal line, as discussed in Chapter 2 of this book. The point here is that the decision to leave is part of an action narrative rather than being solely a matter of variables.

The desire to identify and manipulate variables may become yet more problematic. Say that one identifies 'sex' as a variable; there may be occasions where it may have causal power, but consider how often it is the case that one's sex actually *causes* a particular outcome. There may be a *relationship* between, say, sex and performance in mathematics, but that is a very different matter from saying that one's sex causes one's performance in mathematics to be whatever it is (cf. Holland 1986: 946). It may be that the female brain and the male brain differ in the ways in which they process information and react to conditions (indeed there is evidence of this, e.g. Gurian and Ballew 2003; Weiman 2004; Sax 2005), just as the ongoing Minnesota studies of monozygotic twins reared apart from each other indicate the power of genetic factors over environmental factors (e.g. Bouchard *et al.* 1990), but this may not mean that sex is a causally relevant factor in mathematics performance. Sex cannot *cause* attainment (cf. Goldthorpe 2007a: 200). Indeed, if sex is taken to be a biological category and gender is taken to be a cultural category, then it may be that one's *gender* may influence one's mathematics performance (e.g. cultural expectations about the performance of girls in mathematics) more than one's *sex* (a biological property). Indeed one may question whether, indeed, sex is actually a variable at all, as it is a nominal category and cannot be manipulated (varied in degree, quantity or level) in the way that a continuous variable, e.g. a level of income or the number of years in schooling, might be manipulated. A variable must be able to vary. Sex may be an attribute rather than a causal variable.

That said, Hage and Meeker (1988: 32) suggest that terms such as 'sex' are, in fact, proxies or shorthand for a range of variables, for example, attitudes, behaviours, opinions, preferences, aspirations, dislikes, social interaction, cultural conditioning, socialization patterns, and so on. They also give the example of 'age' (ibid.: 62). Whilst this is a true variable, being able to vary, it may be used as a shorthand indicator of a range of states, for example, physical strength, qualifications, emotional maturity, seniority, decrepitude, legal status, position in a life cycle, employment prospects, and so on.

> ## Implications for researchers:
> - It is individuals, not variables, which do the acting and the causing.
> - Human agency is a key element in theory generation and testing.

Returning to the issue of individual accounts of causality that lie behind variables, consider, for example, a piece of research that strives to establish the causation between the principal's approachability and the school's quality. Imagine a survey conducted in a large school where a questionnaire item asks 'How approachable is your school principal?'. Let us say that 100 teachers respond 'very approachable', 50 teachers respond 'quite approachable', and 20 respond 'very unapproachable'. The researcher might conclude that the school principal is, overall, approachable. But let us say that, of the 100 teachers who responded 'very approachable', 40 of them had to complete the questionnaire in the presence of their principal, who collected the responses and read them; 20 of them were seeking promotion in the school; 10 of them had their contracts coming up for renewal by their principal; 20 were newly appointed teachers who were still uncertain about their principal; and only 10 genuinely found the principal to be approachable. They all answered 'very approachable' but, for very different reasons, many of them entirely disconnected from approachability. Now let us say that a principal's approachability was hypothesized to be a cause of the high quality of the school and that the approachability of the principal was found to be high in this school; would it be fair to say that, in this case, the cause of the high quality of the school was the principal's approachability? Clearly not. In this case only 10 per cent of responses could be relied upon to be telling the truth. The different individual causative motives leading to the same outcome variable are presented in Figure 4.1.

Or consider a piece of research that strives to address the causation between perceived importance of gaining advanced qualifications and securing employment. Imagine the questionnaire item that asks 'How important is it for you to gain advanced educational qualifications in securing employment?'. Let us say that, of the 100 students who completed this questionnaire item, 65 said 'very important', 15 said 'quite important' and 20 said 'of no importance'. The researcher is surprised at the high number of students registering 'of no importance'. How correct is it to suppose that gaining advanced educational qualifications was not particularly important for students in securing employment? The answer is that we don't know from the data here. We need to know the motives behind the responses given. For example, of the 20 students responding 'of no importance', eight of them might be going into a family business regardless of qualifications; three of them might have connections that would be providing them with work; three of them know that if they said 'very important' then it would place an impossible financial strain on their families, so they preferred to say 'of no importance'; three of them felt that the risks of failing outweighed the possible benefits; and three felt that time spent studying was time away from earning in terms of going immediately into employment without advanced qualifications. The results can be shown diagrammatically, as in Figure 4.2.

Behind the variable 'How important is it for you to gain advanced educational qualifications in securing employment?' lies a range of different causal motives; these are the causes, not the variable itself. We cannot say that 20 per cent of the students saw no important causal relationship between gaining advanced educational qualification and securing employment. They saw the causal relationship but, for various reasons

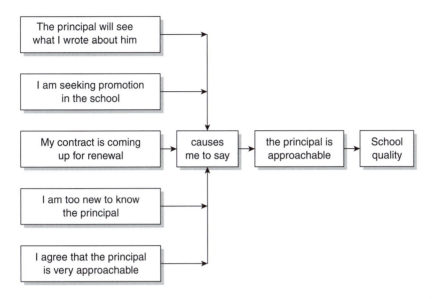

Figure 4.1 Different causal motives behind the same response

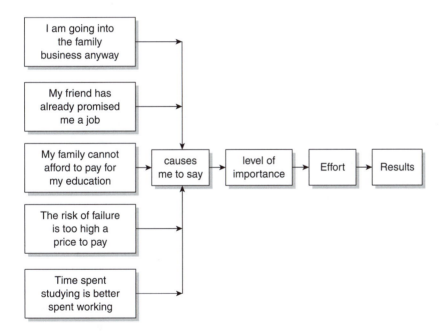

Figure 4.2 Same effect, many causes

(true causes), accorded it little significance. The moral of the story: identify the *real* causes involved in the individuals concerned, and do not be satisfied simply with an aggregate variable that may not demonstrate accurate causation (i.e. the ecological fallacy; see Chapter 3). The variables derive from real causes, the real causes lie in individual motivations and action narratives, and these individual motivations and action narratives reside within the constraints and conditions in which such motivations and action narratives are embedded. The variables are a summary descriptive label that both conceal and embrace a possibly very wide range of causal factors.

Behind the individual causal motives there also lie theoretical causes. For example, one could suggest that individuals weigh up the costs and benefits before deciding on a course of action, i.e. they behave in a way that accords with rational choice theory, maximizing their personal benefits. They have goals and purposes, and take the most suitable steps to realize these in the circumstances and conditions that obtain in any situation.

For example, Tam and Morrison (2005), researching undergraduate employment amongst Chinese university students, found several possible causes of students taking part-time jobs, for example:

- to gain money to pay for education fees;
- to keep debt to as low a level as possible;
- to pay for living expenses;
- to have extra spending money;
- to gain job- and related skills experience;
- to understand the world of work;
- to gain greater confidence for entering the employment market;
- to learn transferable skills (e.g. time management) that improve their studies;
- to improve transferable skills (e.g. interpersonal skills) that suit different kinds of employment;
- to make them attractive in the subsequent employment market;
- to inform their choices on which form of employment to seek;
- to improve their own financial management skills.

On the other hand some students deliberately did not take part-time jobs, fearing that taking one would:

- detract from their study time;
- make them too tired to study properly;
- cause them to miss teaching sessions;
- negatively affect their grades;
- miss deadlines for submission of work;
- lead them to drop out of university;
- bring too great an overload and stress;
- reduce their opportunities for extra-curricular activities;
- expose them to negative behaviour from employers and employees.

One can see that behind the variable and the causal line between (a) 'students' percep-tions of part-time work' and (b) 'taking part-time work' lie many different motives, action narratives, conditions and constraints. Ultimately the decision that students make – whether or not to take up part-time employment – depends on the interplay of conditions, constraints and individual motives, i.e. different action narratives, different purposes, different motives, different reasons, different causes.

Examining a little further the potential power of variables, rather than individuals, to provide causal explanations, consider the independent variables, for example, of income and socio-economic status on educational attainment. How can income or socio-economic status cause educational attainment? These may be necessary but not sufficient conditions in which actual causal processes are embedded. Behind these variables lie human actions, as well as individual and social *processes*, *decisions* and *interactions*, and action narratives are required to explain the causation. Variables on their own, and their relationships (e.g. independent to dependent), do not necessarily establish causation, as causation concerns the action of the humans that lie behind, or are influenced by, such variables. Variables may not establish the true *processes* of causation (cf. Goldthorpe 2007a: 84), even if they are process variables.

Let us return to the opening example of this chapter – the increasing relationship between education and occupations; the opening discussion indicated seven possible system-level causal explanations:

1   increased meritocracy;
2   increased credentialism;
3   lean-and-mean employment practices;
4   increased skill level requirements;
5   increased competition for jobs;
6   increasingly limited employment and career prospects;
7   increasing employment demands.

However, behind each of these possible system-level causal explanations lie different action narratives that may explain why an individual does or number of individuals do what they do in respect of securing the increasingly strong link between education and occupation. The task of research is to understand the action narratives behind the variables and possible explanations. Behind the link between the variables 'education' and 'occupation' lie different 'story lines', different theories, different 'action narratives' (cf. Goldthorpe 2007a: 121). Which apply, and how strongly, is/are subject to empirical test. Without the identification of different story lines, theories and action narratives, causal inference is impossible. Even if one were to place numbers on each of the possible explanations, these, on their own, do not constitute the theories, only data to be interrogated by theory. As Goldthorpe remarks (ibid.: 122), theory precedes the data, rather than proceeding from them. The structure of the most elegant and convoluted structural equation modelling and path analysis is derived from prior theory and prior causal modelling.

Implications for researchers:

- One variable may be the consequence of a range of individual contributing causes and motives.
- Behind variables are humans, and it is they who act causally.
- Behind individual causes lie theories.
- Variables may not be true causes.
- Working with variables alone may overlook causal processes and necessary action narratives.
- Research has to evaluate the relative strengths of rival causal explanations.

The story of the relationship between education and employment is complicated by a whole range of process variables, for example: the kinds of qualifications that the applicant has and how he or she obtained them; the proceedings in the job interview; the process of application; the filtering of the applicants; the behaviour of the job interviewer and the interviewee; the match between the applicant's preference and what is on offer; the sex, age and ethnicity of the applicant and the interviewer; the personalities of the applicant and the interviewer; how the applicant presents himself/herself at interview; the organization's ethos and values; whether the applicant is offered a job; and so on. There is a myriad of factors about which the blunt independent variable of 'education' and the dependent variable of 'occupation' are simply silent. Goldthorpe (2007a: 194–5) argues cogently that it is misconceived to suppose that education *causes* occupation or income in any simple way. Education is the context, the locale, the condition in which employment prospects are embedded. One might change educational practices, but these might make little or no difference to employment opportunities and practices, as the major causes of the latter might lie in arenas other than education. One could reduce educational inequality without disturbing occupational or income inequality (cf. ibid.: 195–6).

Let us consider an example of 'variable' research that, whilst offering some useful causal explanation, understates the importance of action narratives.

A worked example of cause and effect: low attainment and future life chances

In 2008 Howieson and Iannelli published a report entitled '*The effects of low attainment on young people's outcomes at age 22–3 in Scotland*'. As its title suggests, the research is concerned with identifying cause and effect – in this case the putative cause of low attainment at the end of compulsory schooling and its effects on what happens as a result for the former students when they are 22–3 years old. It is an interesting example of an attempt to link micro- and macro-level analysis, society-level factors, school-level factors and employment factors. From the article a causal sequence can be modelled, and this is presented in Figure 4.3.

Figure 4.3 and the research report itself present a depressing picture of the effects of low attainment. Low attainment, it is stated, particularly compared to high attainment, leads to long-term negative labour market consequences, traps young people in a 'precarious and disadvantaged status', reduces their chances of gaining further education, and reproduces cycles of disadvantage, social exclusion and socio-economic position. It is a key predictor of early leaving, low earnings, poor and unstable employment and marginalization in society. The negative situation reported is shown to be more severe for females than it is for males. The research uses sophisticated statistical analysis to inform its conclusions. Indeed it indicates several causal antecedents of the low attainment, albeit in very general and summary terms (e.g. emotional, social, parental factors). So far, so good.

However, whilst lines of causation can be drawn from the research, there is a fundamental question that is not answered: 'Why is what is happening actually happening?' There is a putative causal link between low attainment (B) and a range of outcomes (C); however, between the two there is a myriad of other causal factors that are operating, for example the range of psychological states, personal choices and personal decisions that the young people are making, about which the research is silent.

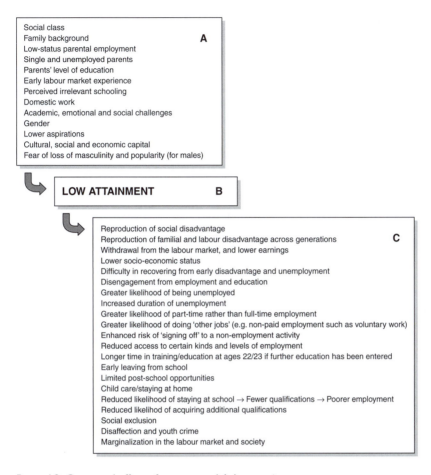

Figure 4.3 Cause and effect of young people's low attainment

One can ask why is it that the young people are low attainers in the first place; box (A) in Figure 4.3 suggests some possible factors, but these do not tell us the psychological states of the young people, their decisions, motivations, constraints, wishes and choices. Similarly, once they have reached the situation of low attainment, we are told nothing about the psychological states of the young people, their decisions, motivations, preferences, expectations, beliefs, constraints and wishes, and the choices they make that lead to the outcomes reported in (C) (cf. Woodward 1997: 302–3). For example, whilst their low attainment, poor employment and poor life chances may be due to their being trapped in cycles of disadvantage, it may be that these same factors are caused by a range of other factors:

- their sheer laziness, with indolence operating at all stages, whilst their successful counterparts are willing to make more effort;
- their low staying power;
- their poor commitment;

- their low aspirations and defeatist attitude;
- their low ability;
- their fear of failure and risk aversion, such that they do not put themselves in a position of having to take difficult examinations;
- their inability to cope with stress;
- their perceptions of the low importance of qualifications;
- their sense of despair, a sense of hopelessness, maybe brought about by poverty;
- their rejection of everything that school stands for, for example authority, academic learning, obedience to certain rules, and so on;
- their lack of motivation as they see that, regardless of their level of education, there are very limited employment prospects where they live.

These are personal matters that mediate the macro-level analysis provided, and it might be that the analysis in the research is a disguised exoneration of the young people's unwillingness to take personal responsibility. In other parts of the world young people would seize the opportunity to study whilst those reported on here are simply indolent and complacent. I am not suggesting that this is the case, but the research is silent on these matters, and so one has to take it into consideration. It may be that the psychological states of the young people in question lead to their poor employment through low attainment or through other channels, i.e. it is less the low attainment than the *experience* of low attainment or the experience of a range of personal factors that leads to low attainment and to poor employment and the negative cycles of social and economic reproduction reported in the paper. It may be that behind low attainment is a factor driving both the latter and subsequent poor employment and life experiences (Reichenbach's 'interactive fork'), and low attainment is a correlate, not a cause, of poor employment and life experiences. How do we know that the outcomes reported are due to low attainment and not to a host of other factors (particularly as the study mentions that other students in the same socio-economic position were successful in gaining more qualifications)? (That said, Howieson and Iannelli relate levels of attainment (low, medium and high) to different employment prospects and levels of income at ages 22–3.) Perhaps the factors reported are only the circumstances, the conditions, the context in which the real causal factors are located, rather than being the causes themselves.

Put simply, there is a range of additional factors that may be operating, both on the low attainment (B) and on the outcomes (C). This renders the model useful but incomplete. There is a range of personal and psychological variables that are not mentioned before (A), between (A) and (B) and between (B) and (C). The process – the causal chain – is incomplete here. Further, one could argue that (A) indicates predictors – proxies – rather than causes and, indeed, that (B) is a predictor – a proxy for a whole range of personal and psychological factors – rather than a complete cause. If we really wish to know why low attainment is caused, and why, in turn, low attainment causes the outcomes with which it is associated in the research, then we have to get inside the heads, the hearts, the personalities, the choices, motivations, expectations, wishes, decisions, constraints, that reside within the individuals concerned. We have to combine macro- and micro-factors in attributing causation of the low attainment, and we have to move from micro- to macro-factors in attributing causation between the low attainment and the outcomes found.

Rather than the persona-free, decision-free, choice-free, motivation-free, personality-free, expectation-free, wish-free, constraint-free input–output model adopted in the research, one can model a whole range of examples of other causal pathways, and these are presented in Figure 4.4. One can see that the directions of causation are various, and that known and unknown additional factors (e.g. personal factors and decisions) could be exerting significant causal power on the causes and outcomes observed. There is an action narrative, a set of personal and agentic matters, to be included in the causation that are currently absent from the analysis, and it is these that might require the attention of policy makers in addition to the focus largely or solely on raising the attainment levels of the young people in question.

Hence, what we have here is a putative set of causes, a set of associations rather than causal links and causal chains. Running through the whole analysis are people, yet their sentient, rational, motivational, decision-making selves are missing from the analysis. This is an example of Goldthorpe's (2007a: 119) 'variable sociology', in which, he suggests, it is mistaken to believe that it is the variables rather than the individuals who are doing the acting or causing, or that the individuals are only part of the *context* in which the variables do their work. Clearly the research abides by Mellor's (1995) principle that causation must raise the chances of an effect without guaranteeing it. However, the research, though important, given that its title draws attention to 'the effects of low attainment on young people's outcomes', is incomplete in its account of causation.

Figure 4.4 indicates just a few of the multiple lines of causation that might be acting instead of, or as well as, the lines of causation suggested by Howieson's and Iannelli's research. The use of boxes containing question marks hints that there may be a host of other factors that are operating in the situation that the research does not address. Put simply, once one takes into account the need for action narratives and personal motives, the situation of causation suddenly explodes into an almost infinite number of causes and their influence on the effects indicated in the research. If one wishes to recommend interventions to improve the situation of the young people in question, then this is to question the simplistic decisions that are frequently made by policy makers.

Implications for researchers:

- Consider the variety of possible lines of causation between variables.
- Consider action narratives and individuals in accounting for causation and its effects.

To consider independent variables such as income or socio-economic level as causes is to rehearse the 'black box' notion of causation: we know the input and we know the outcome, but the causal processes between the two – the genuine causation – are unexplained or unaddressed here. We have to scratch below the surface to look in context at human intentionality and individual behaviour, and these may not be regular, consistent, uniform or repeatable, but, rather, may depend on the circumstances at a particular time, with a particular person or groups of people in a particular context and operating in particular conditions. Humans have values, beliefs, intentions, motives, opinions, attitudes, desires, expectations, wishes, constraints, purposes and objectives that may vary markedly from person to person, and which are not caught in the simplistic sets of independent variables that often constitute a causal model. Models may be silent on these. It is perhaps

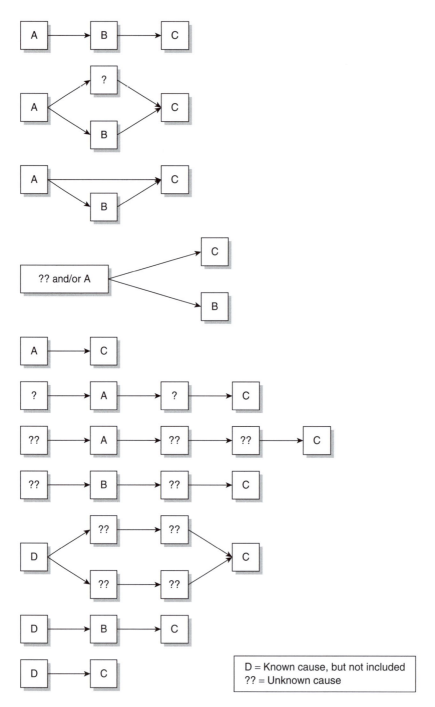

Figure 4.4 Modelling causes and effects of low attainment in young people

overstating the causal situation to believe that a simple intervention – a cause – could bring about a particular or desired effect in such mutable and unrepeatable circumstances. Yet, unfortunately, it is this same approach that fuels much policy decision making and replaces careful, qualified and tentative suggestions with blunt assertions of the value and causation of such-and-such an intervention. If only it were that simple!

Implications for researchers:

- Ensure that causal processes complement input–output models of causation.
- Recognize the significance of intentionality, agency, values and beliefs in causal behaviour and in investigating it.

The discovery of individual action narratives exacts its price. As can be seen from the examples above, the more one investigates the causal processes and action narratives that lie behind the aggregate – general – variables and their interrelationships, the more one becomes immersed in increasingly complicated interactions and complexity. How can any patterns and regularities emerge from such a complicated array of individual actions, let alone be researched? How helpful is it to consider actions and causal action narratives at the level of individuals when the intention may be to understand regularities? Of course, the first does not preclude the second; it is possible to identify emergent patterns and regularities from individual behaviours, but the price is high, for example, requiring the detailed 'constant comparison' of grounded theory – i.e. ensuring that all the data are accounted for and that all the data fit the theory without exception. It is possible, for instance, to show that education has an effect on a person's employment, regardless of the many variables embedded within education and employment and the causal processes that link the two.

One the one hand there has to be a trade-off between manageability, fairness to the phenomena – the *explananda* – the theory that is being tested and the participants in the research. This reality advocates caution in claims made for the research. It may not 'prove' such-and-such; it counsels against overstating conclusions about causation, understating the boundaries, limits and applicability of the research.

On the other hand one may be able to derive and observe sufficient regularities, despite differences, to make useful generalizations. There may be sufficient conditions and action narratives in common to render generalization of cause and effect possible. This is common practice in drug therapy research, where not only are the major benefits identified, but so are their side effects. A single intervention in poor countries, for example, the abolition of school fees, may have a dramatic effect on gender equality, e.g. the enrolment of girls in school may rise.

The issue at stake here is that, even though there may exist countless different action narratives, this does not preclude major causes from being identified and the consequent interventions from being initiated.

So here we have a tension that researchers will need to address for themselves: how to embrace the necessary level of detailed, perhaps individualistic, causal mechanisms and processes at one end of the continuum, and how to identify regularities, general causal mechanisms and processes at the other end of the continuum.

Implications for researchers:

- There is a tension between a level of necessary causal detail and manageability in the research.
- Having copious detailed causes does not preclude the generation of general theories of causation, indeed it may support them.
- Some causes may override other local, more specific causes.

In saying that behind variables lie humans, a strong claim is being made for micro- to macro-accounts of causal events to be provided, rather than macro- to micro-accounts. Individual behaviour is rarely entirely determined – functionally or structurally – by external systems and structures; rather it is informed by them but also structures them. Human agency operates within structural constraints or conditions, or, to use the terminology from Bourdieu, humans agentically produce 'structuring structures' that in turn become firm 'structured structures' and are influenced by such 'structured structures'. This rehearses the agency/structure debate in sociology (e.g. Giddens 1984; Layder 1994) and this is discussed in the next chapter.

The issue becomes one of connecting individual actions (psychological matters) to social actions (sociological matters). Educational research draws on both; in this sense it is cross-disciplinary in a way that psychology and sociology on their own are often not. This is arguing for the need to identify how individual behaviours and actions emerge from, and also give rise to, social structures. How do social structures enter what Bourdieu (1977) terms the 'habitus' of actors (their subjective dispositions, values, opinions, beliefs, attitudes and principles that are formed out of objective socialization and everyday experiences of the external world)? In turn, how do the actors' own subjective dispositions, actions, behaviours, values, opinions and principles form the objective social world? Is it that the micro causes the macro? Is it that the macro causes the micro? Is it that they cause each other? Is it that it is not causality at work but simply supervenience, the macros supervening on the micro, or the micro supervening on the macro, i.e. that changes in individuals correspond to, or vary with, changes in society and vice versa, without any causal connection or relation being involved?

How do external structures 'get inside the heads' of individuals and affect their behaviour? For all that Marxian analysis so far has failed in its prediction of the overthrow of capitalism by communism, and that this revolution would occur amongst the working classes in industrial centres and cities, at least Marx did what many theorists have failed to do: connect the macro with the micro and offer an explanation of how the external world and its structures entered the consciousness and agency of actors. His theory of false consciousness, whilst risking casting individuals in the role of 'ideological dopes of stunning mediocrity' (Giddens 1979: 52) and understating their awareness of their own condition (Eagleton 1991), nevertheless succeeds in linking micro and macro where many attempts have either failed or not even been tried.

In trying to explain how individual actions account for social formation, Sawyer (2005: 43) cites Hayek's view that 'social phenomena must be explained in terms of individuals', and that social formations, groups and phenomena emerge from, even though they may not be reduced to, individual actions. This smacks of the famous line attributed to the former UK prime minister Margaret Thatcher, that 'there is no such thing as society', revealing her affiliation with Hayekian economic theory. Hayek's (1942: 288) example is of how tracks 'in a wild, broken country' may not be set up expressly and deliberately but simply grow from – be caused by – the actions of hundreds of people who are seeking the best way across the country and who, by happenstance, tread the same routes. Harford (2008: 138) indicates how individual stones rolling down a hill constitute a landslide; the individual stones affect each other. Individual actions combine to make social structures (Coleman 1990: 19). As Sawyer (2005: 89) remarks, institutions are no more than complex networks of interacting individuals, and these interactions and practices make up the institution, no more and no less. The task of the researcher is to examine how these regularities – e.g. the tracks across the 'wild, broken country' – came into being, i.e. discovering the causal processes that led to their existence. The tracks become the *explananda*: those things that need to be explained.

The argument here is that it is individuals who bring about regularities and structures, so any causal account has to delve into individual causal processes. As Goldthorpe (2007a: 87) suggests, if individual processes are at work, generating regularities, then we should not only discover what these processes are but also identify any other processes that may be at work that are contributing to, or bringing about, an effect – i.e. identify causal lines and causal chains.

However, a problem arises in individualistic accounts, in that they may not engage *social* causation. As Durkheim (1982) remarks, there are 'social facts' that are both external to individuals and have causative power over them. There exist social rather than individual causes of behaviour, and 'methodological individualism' risks overlooking these. Sociological accounts of causation are not the same as psychological accounts, and educational research needs to embrace both.

The issue becomes one of accounting for the *separate* power of social facts to influence individual behaviour. Social groups and societies and their behaviour are not simply aggregates of individual behaviour writ large (cf. Sawyer 2005: 142); they have a separate ontological status and existence. Just as the combination of hydrogen and oxygen makes water, so water has its own emergent existence that is not reducible to hydrogen and oxygen; the whole is greater than the sum of its parts. As Comte remarked, we can no more decompose society into individuals than we can decompose a line into specific points (ibid.: 38). There is a powerful argument against reductionism of macro-features to micro-elements. In educational research terms, this argues for the need for researchers not only to examine the causal effect of macro- on micro-determinants, and vice versa, but to link the two in providing the *explanans* of the *explanandum*.

Sawyer makes a powerful case for researchers to provide understandings and explanations of the *processes* – the mechanisms – by which social phenomena emerge from individual action and by which individual action emerges from, is caused by, social phenomena and structures. For Sawyer, the interactional paradigm is incomplete because it finds uncomfortable the idea that emergent social phenomena might be irreducible to individual behaviours (2005: 201), and, indeed, it fails to indicate the mechanisms by which social structures affect individual interaction (ibid.: 205), just as the structure paradigm is incomplete because it does not theorize the processes of social emergence, i.e. it does not provide a causal explanation of the role of interaction in determining social structures (ibid.: 206). For Sawyer, an account of behaviour has to incorporate both.

The interaction paradigm has to provide a causal account of social emergence, and the structure paradigm has to provide a causal account of individual behaviour; the causal processes and mechanisms of the one on the other need to be established, not least in respect of accounting for ephemeral and stable structures and emergent and stable individual behaviour (Sawyer 2005: 210). In this enterprise, Sawyer avers, it is not sufficient to provide an account of processes of emergence; it is necessary to ensure that the account is causal. Echoing the work of Bourdieu and Giddens three decades earlier, he restates that a central problem in sociology is to indicate how the purposive and intentional actions of individuals combine and cause system-level behaviour, and how those purposive and intentional actions in turn are affected and formed by the constraints and influences from the system (ibid.: 216). Agency affects structure, just as structure affects agency; micro affects macro, just as macro, affects micro.

Taken together, the comments heretofore reaffirm the age-old case for setting aside shibboleths of macro- and micro-analysis and for combining these in providing causal accounts of *explananda*.

Agency and intentionality must feature in accounts of causation (Eisenhart 2005: 256), and these often give supremacy to qualitative approaches (e.g. Maxwell 2004). Theory development – stage 2 in the identifying causation – has to integrate micro and macro.

Implications for researchers:

- Some theory generation may proceed from the micro to the macro in identifying individual action narratives that contribute to more general causal theories.
- Some theory generation may proceed from the macro to the micro in identifying individual action narratives.
- Supervenience is not the same as causal dependence.
- Some theories may not be reducible to individual accounts 'writ large'.
- Behind action narratives lie causal theories.
- Causal connections must be made between individual and social behaviours and actions, and vice versa.
- Explanatory accounts of phenomena should include both macro- and micro-elements, and the connections between them.

Stage 3: Test the causal theory

Testing the causal theory is a process that comprises three elements:

(a) evaluating how effectively the causal theory explains, and is consistent with, all of the data (the 'theoretical saturation' of grounded theory (Glaser and Strauss 1967)), such that any further data can be accommodated within the existing theory rather than changing it;
(b) constructing and evaluating rival causal theories or explanations, and identifying whether they provide a better, more complete causal explanation of the data, preferably in respect of different data (i.e. whether they fit the data better than the initial theory);
(c) identifying how the causal theory might be falsified, and testing that falsification.

The possible charge that this is positivist and scientistic, advocating the 'scientific method', can be resisted. The 'scientific method' may itself be scientistic, and there may be other ways of proceeding in science, and, indeed, the methods indicated here are the ways in which humans learn, not only the ways in which humans learn scientifically. Further, the generation and construction of theory is a highly creative act, perhaps serendipitous and inspirational (Mitroff 1983). 'Testing' too often has become a term of abuse, like positivism, and perhaps it triggers the stock criticism of being positivistic, smacking of control mentalities, using reductionist – atomistic – procedures and paradigms, isolating and manipulating variables in a highly instrumentalist, anti-human and non-realistic way, reducing behaviour to independent and dependent variables and a blind belief in the power of numbers. This may be correct, but that is not to eclipse its potential value, and it is also not the whole story; indeed, cause-and-effect and causal chains may be premised on independent and dependent variables, and this is a strength. But such a view of testing may also be mistaken: there are countless non-positivistic tests – indeed, trial and error is a powerful way of learning. So let us put prejudice on one side and continue to use the term, though widely rather than narrowly.

Testing the theory applies to both quantitative and qualitative research. Qualitative research is not somehow exempted from testing. Similarly, reliability and validity, though perhaps their canons of operation may be different for quantitative and qualitative data, are requisites for the tenability of a theory. Whilst, for quantitative data, reliability may concern stability, replicability and consistency (Cohen *et al.* 2007: chap. 6), whereas in qualitative data it may concern authenticity, honesty, depth of response, candour and honesty, this not only underlines the importance of reliability for both data types, it also raises the question of why the canons of reliability for quantitative data may not apply to qualitative data, and vice versa.

Just as reliability applies to all different data types, so does validity, of whatever hue: construct, content, concurrent, ecological, criterion, consequential, cultural and so on (see Cohen *et al.* 2007: chap. 6). No data types or methodologies for research and for testing theory are exempt.

Testing a causal theory involves not only seeing if that causal theory holds true, but seeing the conditions in which it may or may not hold true, how to falsify it, how to test for and evaluate rival causal explanations, what the results of the falsification of the proposed causal theory and the testing of rival causal theories show, and how robust the causal theory is in the face of a Popperian 'severe test'.

Implications for researchers:

- Qualitative data are not exempted from the requirement of testing to establish the status of the causal explanation.
- Causal theories must accommodate, embrace and fit all the data without exception.
- Causal theories must be subject to empirical test.
- There are several kinds of empirical test.
- Rival causal explanations must be considered and ruled out, perhaps through testing.
- A causal theory must indicate how it can be falsified.
- A causal theory cannot be tested with the same data that gave rise to the theory.
- Causal explanations must demonstrate reliability and validity.
- It may be appropriate to use canons of reliability and validity from quantitative data for qualitative data, and vice versa.

A worked example of considering rival causal theories: the case of the Chinese learner

The following section provides an extended worked example that indicates the importance of providing rival causal explanations of an observed effect. Let us consider an example of a widely observed phenomenon: why it is that East Asian students seem to outperform their Western counterparts in international tests of educational achievement, particularly when the teaching and learning styles that are employed seem to be of questionable quality (the paradox of the Chinese learner, discussed below).[1] In this worked example many references are provided; these are included to indicate that causal explanations can draw on other data and research – cumulatively – to provide empirical support for, and testing of, causal theories.

The paradox of the Chinese learner is intriguing for Westerners and Chinese alike. In a nutshell, it questions why, despite using rote learning, memorization, repetition, constant testing, large classes, competitive motivation, examination orientation, authoritarian and didactic teaching and learning methods, passivity and compliance – in short, despite the presence of putative negative features of teaching and learning, together with a supposed absence of many positive features – Chinese students consistently achieve more highly than their Western counterparts, are highly adaptive, prefer high-level, meaning-based learning strategies, and engage in deep learning. Several studies[2] reinforce this East Asian phenomenon, as do the results of the Programme for International Students Assessment (PISA) studies of educational performance (OECD 2004, 2007).

The first stage of investigating causation is to establish that the putative phenomenon actually exists. Here the evidence of achievement is clear: Stevenson *et al.* (1990) report superior achievement by Chinese students in comparison with American students. Stigler and Perry (1990) indicate that, in a test of mathematics, the highest-scoring American students outperformed only one of the 20 classes in Taipei from the first grade upwards, and this applied to all branches of mathematical reasoning. Stevenson *et al.* (1990) state that Chinese students obtained significantly higher scores in mathematics and reading than did their American counterparts. Cai (1995) found that Chinese students scored considerably higher than US students in computation and simple problem solving in mathematics. Lau (1996), Bond (1996) and Wong and Wong (2002) summarize much research to indicate the outstanding performance of Asian students, particularly in mathematics, in comparison with students from other nations and cultures. Lee (1998: 48–9) reports that students in Taipei, Sendai and Beijing significantly outperformed Chicago students in mathematics at grades 1 and 5, a difference of over 30 per cent at grade 1 and 45 per cent at grade 5, and that Beijing students scored highest compared with students in Taipei, Sendai and Minneapolis in arithmetic and algebra at grade 4.

The International Association for the Evaluation of Educational Achievement in 1980 found that, for mathematics, the performance of the top 5 per cent of American students matched that of the top 50 per cent of Japanese students (Stevenson and Stigler 1992: 31). Hong Kong twelfth-grade students in 1987 had mean algebra scores of nearly 80 points, whilst for American students it was 40 points; for elementary functions/calculus the Hong Kong students scored 60 points, compared with the 30 points scored by their American counterparts. Students in Taipei consistently outperformed students in Minneapolis and Chicago at first-grade and fifth-grade levels for mathematics in 1980 and 1987 (ibid.: 35). Hong Kong students gained the highest scores in the second International Study of

Educational Achievement in Mathematics (Robitaille and Garden 1989). China topped the list for the 1992 International Assessment of Education Progress (Lapointe *et al*. 1992).

The Trends in International Mathematics and Science Study (TIMMS) (1999) places Singapore, Korea, Taiwan, Hong Kong and Japan above the United States in mathematics and science (Gonzales *et al*. 2000). The 2003 TIMMS study, too, presents a very clear picture of the regularity with which East Asian student outperform their Western counterparts (Mullis *et al*. 2003: 16–17).

The Programme for International Student Assessment (PISA) study (OECD 2004) reports that, for 2003, in mathematics, students from Korea, Japan, Hong Kong and Macao overall were in the top six of the 40 countries taking part, with Hong Kong first, far ahead of the United States. The Programme for International Student Assessment (PISA) 2006, involving 57 states/countries/territories, also provides evidence of the regularity with which East Asian students outperform their Western counterparts.

The phenomenon is regular across time and across country/territory. Though here is not the place to discuss the strengths and weaknesses of such studies, nevertheless they indicate neatly high levels of this kind of achievement by East Asian students. However, there are some difficulties in providing explanations in such studies of Chinese learners and their achievements; indeed, the supposed paradox may not be as paradoxical as it appears (see also Dahlin and Watkins 2000: 67),[3] and attempts to unravel it to date can be characterized by a neglect of consideration of a range of possible explanations.

There are several possible causal explanations for these findings (why East Asian students do well in international tests of achievement despite questionable pedagogical practices), and these lie in the terms of social, cultural, pedagogical, curricular and economic factors. There is a need for researchers to seek robustness by examining all possible explanations of this phenomenon and, thereby, to operate Popper's principle of falsifiability as the touchstone of rigorous science in the field. The *explanandum* is the phenomenon recounted above. What is the possible *explanans*? What might be the causal explanations for the paradox outlined above? The discussion below provides ten possible causal explanations of the observed regular phenomenon here, the *explanandum*.

Explanation 1: The premises of the paradox are incorrect

This view argues that rote, repetition and memorization do not preclude, indeed they can lead to, understanding, deep rather than superficial learning, high-level cognitive strategies and the creation of a 'deep impression' of material on the Chinese learner's mind (Dahlin and Watkins 2000). Rote learning and memorization, several authors argue (e.g. Stevenson and Lee 1996: 134; Gu 2001: chap. 13; Lee 2005; Salili *et al*. 2001: 223–5), are not mindless recitation and stuffing the head with little-understood matters, but are part of the process of creating a bright and clear understanding of something – seeing through it (Au and Entwistle 1999). Indeed it may be a Western misperception to regard such pedagogies negatively, as the *order* of learning differs between East Asian and Western cultures. Gardner (1989, cited in Biggs 1996a: 55) suggests that, in Chinese education, learning the skill precedes creating the new work, rather than vice versa (as in some Western cultures), and Cai (1995) indicates that Chinese and US syllabuses differ in the timing of the introduction of different mathematical concepts and processes. Studies suggest that the premises of the paradox may be misconceived (e.g. Biggs 1996a; Dahlin and Watkins 2000: 67).

Explanation 2: Putatively discredited practices actually work

A second explanation is that the methods of teaching and learning, so swiftly maligned in the paradox, actually work. They produce the results. Though the teaching and learning practices may smack of a discredited behaviourism, nevertheless they seem to be producing high levels of achievement on international tests, i.e. it may be an empirical truth even if it is unpalatable to certain educationists.

Explanation 3: East Asian students are brighter than others

A third possible explanation is that Chinese and East Asian students perform better in the international tests of educational achievement because they are brighter – more intelligent or more capable – than others (see Lynn 1988; Chan 1996: 104–7; Stevenson and Lee 1996: 129–31). In this explanation, the tests have done their job well and display effective item discriminability, showing which students in which countries are more able than others. Though this may be absurd or unpalatable to some, smacking of eugenics or the genetic fallacy, nevertheless, in the world of *possible* explanations, it is a possible explanation.

Explanation 4: East Asian students and teachers work hard to ensure that the methods produce positive results

Stevenson and Stigler (1992: 54) suggest that school is far more central to the lives of most East Asian students than of American students. Stigler and Perry (1990: 335) report that students in Taiwan spent significantly more time in school than American children (a third more school days) and, on average, 1.5 times more hours each week on studying. For mathematics and language, fifth-grade students in Taiwan spent 11.2 hours and 11.4 hours each week respectively, whilst their American counterparts spent 8.2 and 3.4 hours each week respectively. Time-on-task was higher for Chinese students (90 per cent compared with 83 per cent for Americans), as was time with the teacher (91 per cent compared with between 87 and 49 per cent for Americans). Stevenson and Stigler (1992: 53) record that, whilst American students spend half the days each year in school, for Chinese students it was two-thirds. Stevenson et al. (1990: 96) found that the Chinese mathematics curriculum was not only more advanced than its American counterpart, but that children in Taipei spent more than three times the amount of time each week on mathematics than did their American counterparts.

The commitment by East Asian teachers and students to the teaching and learning methods employed extends beyond school hours to homework (Stigler and Perry 1990: 346), private tutorial centres (e.g. Stevenson and Stigler 1992) and extra-curricular classes (a huge industry in East Asian cultures (Bray 1999, 2006)), to buttress up this approach, i.e. to make sure that it works in bringing about high levels of achievement. Brand (1987) reports that Asian American students spend, on average, 11 hours each week on homework, compared with seven hours each week by other students. Stevenson et al. (1990: 43) state that students in Taiwan spent, on average, four times longer each day on homework than their American counterparts. Whilst first graders in Minneapolis spent an average of three minutes on homework each day, for Taipei students it was 40 minutes; whilst fifth graders in Minneapolis spent an average of 20 minutes on homework each day, for Taipei students it was 78 minutes. Stevenson and Stigler (1992: 61) report that students in Taipei spent, on average, 1.9 hours each day on homework and .6 hours each day on play, compared with .8 hours and 2.4 hours respectively by students in Minneapolis. Cai (1995: 26) mentions that 72 per cent of students from China spent two hours or more on mathematics homework, in comparison with only 37 per cent of US students.

This hard work is reinforced by the pressure cooker system of high competition, significant amounts of testing (Morrison and Tang (2002) report students taking up to two tests each school day) and an emphasis on achievement through effort and application rather than ability (Lee 1996). Hard work, as Lee remarks, is part of the Confucian Heritage Culture (CHC) feature of 'perfectibility through effort'; there are no ceilings on achievements other than those determined by effort, or its lack. Stevenson and Stigler (1992: 106) state that American students gave up faster than Chinese students when faced with a difficult problem, and that, for fifth-grade mathematics students in Taipei, 77 per cent solved the problems that they attempted whilst for American students it was only 51 per cent. Hong (2001: 112) found that low-ability Hong Kong students often worked harder than high achievers.

Given this deep-seated cultural resonance between the virtues of hard work, achievement motivation and the school experience of drill, rote, memorization and repetition, effort and application, it is hardly surprising that Chinese students perform well.

Explanation 5: Students perform well despite poor teaching and learning strategies

Taking the CHC further, it could be that the teaching and learning methods cited are, in fact, highly inefficient, but that students' sheer hard work overcomes the problems with them and that this compensates for the poor teaching and learning experienced. Witness the hours and hours of homework that East Asian students undertake from kindergarten upwards (Stevenson *et al.* 1990; Stevenson and Stigler 1992); one would be seriously alarmed if these hours of work did *not* produce results. Salili *et al.* (2001: 230–2) report that Hong Kong students continue to spend more time on studying than Canadian students, even though their teachers marked their performance much more harshly than did the Canadian teachers.

Conversely, several studies (e.g. Stevenson *et al.* 1990; Stevenson and Stigler 1992; Hatano and Inagaki 1998: 82; Lee 1998) suggest that pedagogical strategies for mathematics in Chinese and Japanese schools, far from being poor, are focused, engaging, interactive, problem-oriented, explanatory, thought-provoking, concept-based, procedural, response-oriented, and designed to ensure understanding much more than in American schools. If this is so then part of the paradox evaporates.

Explanation 6: The value of schooling and education

Lee (1996), Gow *et al.* (1996) and Pratt *et al.* (1998, 1999) note the CHC's affirmation of the value of, and respect for, education. Stevenson *et al.* (1990: 6) indicate that academic achievement is accorded a more central place in Taiwan than in America, and Stevenson and Stigler (1992) and Gow *et al.* (1996) reassert the Asian emphasis on scholastic achievement. Hatano and Inagaki (1998: 96) suggest that Asian culture accords great significance to mathematics learning. This is further supported by theories of human capital in which, as Woodhall (1997: 220) reports, investment in human capital through education brings greater returns to individuals in developing rather than developed countries such as those of Europe and the West. One can still educate oneself out of poverty in East Asian countries (e.g. Stevenson and Lee 1996), a feature which is less clear-cut in those developed nations of the West in which chance plays a significant role (see Jencks 1972; Halsey *et al*. 1980; Woodhall 1997). East Asian students may still look to education as a passport out of poverty and towards improvements in life chances.

This is compounded in East Asian societies, in which there is restricted access to higher education and in which competitive entry is strong for secondary education (Stevenson's and Lee's (1996: 129) comments on mainland China) and scarce university places (Gow *et al*. 1996: 115–16; Stevenson and Lee 1996: 134). Little wonder it is, therefore, that students strive to perform highly. In situations of limited university places, the zero-sum model still operates: my gain is your loss, and students, keenly aware of this, must beat the others in order to succeed. And they succeed by outperforming their rivals in tests and examinations. In schools too, teachers, students and parents use marks as measures of people; one has to strive be top of the class.

Explanation 7: The contents of the tests are suited to the contents of Chinese students' learning and curricula

The reason why Chinese learners do so well may be because the items that appear in the tests conform to the contents of Chinese students' curricula (e.g. Cai 1995; Wong 2000). This rehearses the familiar issue that whether students do well or badly in tests depends on the similarity between the syllabi/curricula followed and the test contents. Put simply, Chinese students may do well in international tests of performance because the latter measure those items at which they excel and which they have studied. They are like school. Indeed Stigler and Perry (1990: 341) comment that Chinese teachers emphasize fast and accurate performance and getting the right answer, with 17 per cent of mathematics time spent on mental calculation, a phenomenon not found at all in American classrooms. The argument here is that it is precisely because of the teaching, learning and curricula to which Chinese learners have been exposed that they do well. There is no paradox at all, as they all complement each other very comfortably.

Explanation 8: Chinese students are good test takers

In this explanation Chinese students may be schooled into the culture of tests and may become excellent test takers even though the results may have few and limited spillover effects in real life. Stigler and Perry (1990: 342) indicate that 7 per cent of all segments of mathematics lessons in Chicago were devoted to evaluation, but the figure was 18 per cent for students in Taipei. Chinese students, tested *ad nauseam* (Lewin and Lu 1990; Morrison and Tang 2002) may be excellent test takers in competitive, examination-oriented education systems (e.g. Gow *et al*. 1996). It is hardly surprising that they do well in international tests; they have been groomed for them on a daily basis in a marks and test-oriented culture.

Students, and their parents and teachers, are caught up in the regimen of marks and competition, in which (perhaps caricaturing the situation for conceptual clarity) either one is top, or nearly top, or one is a failure, with the concomitant shame brought to family and school. As Lee (1996) remarks, in Chinese culture, not doing well is not only a personal matter; it is also letting down the family and one's teacher in a society in which such relationships are highly significant and sensitive.

Explanation 9: The Hawthorne effect

Students across the world rise to the occasion of an examination. Chinese students may be no different from others in this respect; indeed, given the emphasis on competition, frequent examinations and high-stakes testing in East Asian contexts, it would be surprising if the Hawthorne effect (e.g. reactivity) were not considerable here, perhaps even stronger than in other parts of the world. With so much hanging on 'performance' (not least for university entrance) (and Salili (1996) and Shi *et al.* (2001) suggest that 'performance' and 'achievement orientation', rather than, for example, task goals, are powerful features of Chinese learners), it would be remarkable if Chinese students were *not* to take examinations very seriously.

Explanation 10: The results are signifiers of Chinese culture

There are several features of the Confucian Heritage Culture (CHC) and its educational manifestations, including, *inter alia*:[4]

- modesty, conformism, docility, obedience to authority, unquestioning 'filial piety' (regardless of actual teacher behaviour), loyalty, respect for elders;
- concern for 'face' and relationships, and motivation through the avoidance of a 'sense of shame' and the gaining, giving and saving of 'face';
- respect for education and academic excellence;
- imitation (mimesis) as a requirement for learning and development;
- the malleability of human behaviour;
- 'perfectibility through effort': there are no ceilings on performance, and success is possible if enough effort is exerted, rather than because of innate ability;
- increased effort pays dividends in performance;
- persistence and perseverance: the need continually to strive, never give up and never be satisfied with present performance, even when it is already of high quality;
- the value of hard work for the application of ability;
- an acquisitive and accumulative view of knowledge: a banking conception;
- hierarchical student–teacher relationships, with respect for, and a lack of challenge to, the rank and the teacher/authority/seniority, i.e. the teacher as the authority and decision maker;
- the operation of a control model of teaching and learning;
- tests, grades, competition and cramming;
- four R's: reception, repetition, review, reproduction;
- drill, rote, memorization, recall, repeat;
- four M's: meticulousness, memorization, mental activeness, mastery;
- little tolerance of ambiguity (the search for the single 'right answer', as in a test).

Whilst it is dangerous to provide simplistic lists of characteristics *as if* they were exact and empirically true, nevertheless, for conceptual and heuristic clarity, the conjuncture of the putative CHC and educational practice might ensure that the methods of rote, memorization, drill and repetition work here to effect student achievement. Culture and educational practices are sympathetic to each other and mutually potentiating.

These ten possible explanations suggest that researchers should not foreclose prematurely the investigation into the paradox of the Chinese learner and spectacular performance, and that a rigorous investigation should weigh the evidence, the warrants and the alternative causal explanations of the phenomenon. Which one or ones explain most fully and fittingly the situation found is an empirical question. Simple or single explanations of this multi-layered phenomenon are elusive.

What we have in this worked example is a clear case of causal 'overdetermination', as discussed in Chapter 3. Any one of the ten explanations might constitute a sufficient but unnecessary condition for the outcome, but together or in combination they overdetermine the outcome.

The extended example here points the researcher to the need to identify different rival causal theories, to test them, and to evaluate the outcomes. Maybe only then is one in a position to claim the robustness of the causal explanation adopted.

Implications for researchers:

- Identify possible rival causal explanations.
- Refer these rival theories to the relevant literature and range of evidence.
- Test the theories to see which explain the data most fittingly.
- Seek disconfirming as well as confirming evidence of the causal explanation.

Stage 4: Draw conclusions

Conclusions derive from evidence. One has to be careful to ensure that overgeneralization is avoided, and therefore it is essential to remain within the confines of the parameters of the research. For example, it would be ridiculous to claim a generalizable effect from a limited case study or a non-probability sample. Equally it would be ridiculous to claim a generalizable effect to a whole population if the sample – however large – did not represent that population.

Further, conclusions must stem from an evaluation of rival causal explanations of the *explananda*. After the rival explanations have been given and their status evaluated, what remains of the causal theory – does it remain intact, or does it stand in need of modification, refinement, extension, abandonment, and so on? Which theories are best supported?

Implications for researchers:

- Do not overgeneralize.
- Keep the conclusions within the boundaries of the data, research and evidence.
- Eliminate rival causal explanations.

There are threats to the regularity or probabilistic nature of cause and effect, and account must be taken of these in understanding causation.

Taking stock

This chapter has argued that causal explanation is a fundamental purpose of educational research. Causation lies behind the construction, testing and evaluation of research, and robust research requires the testing not only of the theory in question, but of possible rival theories. The chapter has also argued that 'variable research' offers an incomplete account of causal processes, and that human intentionality, values, attitudes, goals and purposes lie behind variables and are significant contributors to an understanding of the causal processes at work in a situation. This entails moving from micro- to macro-analysis of causation and human behaviour. Further, the chapter has pointed out that manageability – and its corollary: the reduction of necessary detail in establishing causality – sits uncomfortably, but not impossibly, with the need to provide generalizations for educational research into cause and effect. Action narratives are important features of causal theorization, though it is recognized that behind these lie further causal theories. In this context, reference was made to rational choice theory as one explanation of why humans behave as they do in selecting the causal processes that they do (and Chapter 6 returns to this).

The extended example of explanations of the success of East Asian students in international studies of educational achievement, despite discredited pedagogical practices of rote, memorization and drill, was provided as a worked example of the need to consider, test and evaluate rival causal explanations for phenomena. The example provided ten possible interpretations, each of which was seen to provide a possible causal explanation, and it was suggested that interpretations, individually or in combination, can determine and overdetermine the effect – the high performance. The chapter has set out a four-stage process for identifying causation, and has worked through each stage of this model to suggest its practical implications for researchers.

Chapter 5

Determining the effects of causes

Introduction

Since the behaviourism of Skinner, the idea that a given stimulus could produce a predictable response has captivated social scientists. If we can determine the effects of causes then we are in a powerful position to judge 'what works', to make predictions and to exercise some control over events. The idea is clearly of merit. The practice is more complicated. Can we really know the effects of causes? This chapter examines issues involved in trying to understand and explain the extent to which an intervention – a cause – might predict its outcome – an effect. If we could establish a firm nexus between the two then this could be invaluable for educationists. The process is one of informed inference and accepting the 'best yet' suggestion of causation, in the knowledge that it might be superseded or imperfect.

Three major approaches to determining effects from causes are explored in this chapter: action research; a range of experimental approaches; and participant and non-participant observation in qualitative research. Behind these lies what Goldthorpe (2007a: 196) terms 'consequential manipulation' – the ability to determine effects (the dependent variable) by the careful manipulation of causes (the independent variable(s)). Here the approach is decidedly interventionist rather than non-interventionist (though there are exceptions, which will be discussed below): the researcher introduces and maybe manipulates an intervention, perhaps under controlled conditions, and then sees the effects of that intervention.

Manipulating causes

There are several meanings of the term 'manipulation' here, for example:

1 introducing a new variable whilst the other factors continue to be uncontrolled;
2 introducing a new variable whilst other factors are controlled;
3 removing a variable whilst other factors continue to be uncontrolled;
4 removing a variable whilst other factors continue to be controlled;
5 altering the amount of an existing quantity of a factor (e.g. reducing or increasing it);
6 maintaining the amount of an existing quantity of a factor whilst other factors are altered;
7 extending a factor, i.e. adding to it;
8 contracting a factor, i.e. removing some aspects of it;
9 modifying a factor (e.g. changing its nature and quality as well as its quantity);
10 changing a variable in a way that leaves others undisturbed;
11 applying (1) to (10) in respect of more than one variable at a time.

Table 5.1 Resources, student motivation and examination results

Independent variable	Level 1	Level 2	Level 3
Availability of resources	Limited availability (1)	Moderate availability (2)	High availability (3)
Student motivation for the subject studied	Little motivation (4)	Moderate motivation (5)	High motivation (6)

Implications for researchers:

- Consider causal manipulation in determining the effects of causes.
- Causal manipulation has many meanings, and the exact meaning to be used requires clarification.

The intervention may be singular and unvaried (e.g. the introduction of a new method of teaching in a school or class), or varied (different amounts of the new method of teaching). This latter is akin to the medical researcher who examines the effects of different levels of a new drug: a little, a moderate amount, a large amount, and so on, perhaps on continuous, sliding scales of quantities and strengths. A little amount may have no effect, a moderate amount may effect a cure, and a large amount may be lethal! A similar methodology could be used in education, for example if one wished to investigate the effect on performance in an examination of different levels of availability of resources and student motivation in respect of the subject studied. This is shown in Table 5.1.

The research could examine the nine possible combinations of these: 1+4; 1+5; 1+6; 2+4; 2+5; 2+6; 3+4; 3+5; 3+6. (An example that followed the same principle was given in Chapter 3, concerning class size and interactive/non-interactive teaching.) Tables 3.12 and 5.1 deal in absolute values/nominal variables – (a) interactive teaching and non-interactive teaching (Table 3.12), and (b) three levels of each variable (levels 1, 2 and 3 (Table 5.1) – rather than continuous variables (e.g. on a sliding scale rather than in three categorical levels). An example of continuous variables might be to examine the effects of age and motivation on mathematics performance. Here the two independent variables are continuous and their effects vary, for example Figure 5.1. In the example here the difference for motivation in mathematics is not constant between males and females, but varies according to the age of participants, and there is an interaction effect between age and sex.

Implications for researchers:

- Decide whether the causal variables are nominal (fixed) or continuous.
- Decide on the amount of the cause to be manipulated.
- Recognize that the effects of causes may not be linear.

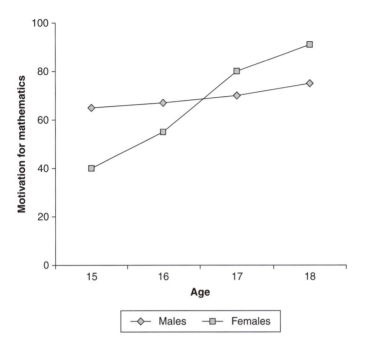

Figure 5.1 Mathematics scores by age and sex

Let us not always assume that the same cause always produces an effect or even a similar effect. Even with Pavlov's dogs in the early days of behaviourist psychology this was not always the case – some of the dogs simply gave up on the experiment and ceased to respond, others became confused and ended up howling, whilst others completed the test satisfactorily. The same intervention may work wonderfully well in one class but may fail disastrously in another: same cause, different effect. Even with the same class, exactly the same cause may produce a different effect: the effect of repeating an activity may be greater boredom, hostility and resentment by students; by contrast, on the second time round it may raise motivation, produce even better results and provide much more in-depth learning than on the first occasion. (This questions the reliability that can be placed in 'repeated measures' experiments (Cohen *et al.* 2007: 281–2). These are designed, quite correctly, to eliminate order effects, but, nevertheless, may suffer from their own problems, with the repeat bringing unreliability rather than reliability into the frame.) The point here is that the cause itself (the intervention) may be necessary but not sufficient to produce the required effect, or it may not produce a similar, repeated effect, and this depends on the surrounding conditions (e.g. the receiving parties in the interventions).

A series of studies on English-language teaching failed to show any changes consequent to an intervention. In one instance the move towards greater collaborative and cooperative work in English lessons made no measured difference to students' scores in English tests (Ao 2006), and in two other instances the move towards a communicative language teaching approach made no appreciable difference to students' performance in English tests (Lai 2004; Ho 2007). In these cases there was an intervention but it made no difference. In the cases of English, though the interventions were made, it was suggested that the participating classes of students were so conditioned by years of the routine practice of traditional, didactic, grammar translation-based teaching that a short-term intervention had no real impact on upsetting years of conditioning. We do not know, however, what the test results would have been without the intervention – they may have been the same, or lower or higher, or variable, depending on the students involved. We return to this point later in the chapter.

Interventions may produce an effect, but it is too small and short-lived to be noticed, or is offset by more powerful factors, or the timing of the post-test is too soon or too late, or that changes are occurring but not in the ways anticipated, and so on. There are many reasons why no differences might be observed, even if they are actually present: researchers may have been looking for a difference in the wrong places or with instruments that may not have found effects that were actually present. The issue concerns:

(a) what the effects would have been without the intervention (they may have been the same, or lower or higher, or variable, or different, depending on the students involved);
(b) the group concerned cannot be both involved and not involved in the experiment.

How can we handle these two matters? A central means of addressing this issue concerns sampling or, being more precise, randomization or matched sampling. The idea is that we have two groups, a control and an experimental group, who are matched in terms of all the relevant factors (e.g. age, ability, sex, socio-economic status). This is usually done by having some form of probability sample (e.g. a random sample or a random stratified sample). We address this further in the discussion of experimental approaches below, but firstly the chapter addresses action research.

Implications for researchers:

- The same cause, with either the same group or a different group, may produce a different effect.
- Effects are not stable functions of causes.
- An effect may be present, but unnoticed.
- Consider how long an effect has to last before it is deemed to be an effect.
- Consider the most suitable timing of the observation/measurement/evaluation of the effect.
- Sampling is a critical factor in determining cause and effect.
- Causal manipulation to determine effects can occur in action research, experimental research (*par excellence*) and participant and non-participant observation.

Action research

One common example of interventionist approaches (manipulating a cause to produce a particular effect) lies in action research. The teacher or group of teachers (a) identify a problem that they are experiencing; (b) consider a range of possible interventions to address the problem; (c) evaluate these on the basis of practicability, preferability, capability to solve the problem, and so on; (d) opt for one of the putative solutions/interventions; (e) put it into practice; and, at a suitable point in time, (f) judge the extent to which the intervention has worked in solving the problem. It all seems very neat and straightforward.

For example, teachers may indicate that they are experiencing difficulties in the students' levels of concentration and motivation in reading. So they undertake an intervention to try to stimulate motivation and concentration in reading. They (1) provide more books; (2) display the books in a more interesting way; (3) talk to the students about their reading habits and preferences and then purchase materials to suit these; (4) provide for longer periods of sustained reading time; (5) use the books as central to significant parts of the school work; (6) take students to the local library on a regular basis. The result is that the students' levels of concentration and motivation rise; the action research has worked.

But has it? The situation may not be such an open-and-shut case. How do we know, for example, that it was the intervention that caused the effect? Maybe it was the weather, or the time of year, or the children's diet (and research from the University of Cambridge has produced startling results concerning the beneficial effects of Omega 3 on children's learning), or the pressure of upcoming examinations, or parental pressure, or increased teacher concern and pressure, or possible incentives (e.g. to be 'top of the class' in reading, with a reward attached), or teachers' changed behaviour, or a hundred other reasons. Maybe the intervention was not the best intervention that could have been introduced (but there is no way of telling, other methods having been ruled out). Maybe the students' mood and attitudes to reading simply changed over time (i.e. they would have changed regardless of the intervention) as they matured. The problem in action research is that, even though there is an intervention and an outcome, the causal relation has not been established, as there are insufficient or insufficiently strict controls, checks and balances in the procedures. It is weak. A possible cause is identified (the intervention), possible causal processes seem to have been followed (the several contents of the intervention (1) to (6)) and there is an outcome. However, it is not causation that has been established, only a set of conditions. It is the optimism of ignorance, hope or putative probability.

Action research can be considered to be a quasi-experimental approach without the rigour of the experimental method, as it often lacks controls (e.g. of the variables involved) and external points of reference; it has some of the characteristics of an experiment but not all the necessary and sufficient conditions for it to be considered a 'true' experiment. Indeed action research may be of a qualitative rather than a quantitative nature.

Action research is not of a singular kind. It is an umbrella term that embraces many approaches. An alternative approach within action research could be more rigorous, for example using a truer experimental method, with control and experimental groups and controls on independent, process and outcome variables. However, given that action research typically involves teachers working in their own domains (e.g. their own classroom, their own school), the risks of contamination can be immense. For example, (a) the control and experimental groups may speak to each other, or interact with each other; (b) in an effort to control the variable of 'the teacher', the same teacher may teach both the control and the experimental group, but her behaviour with, and attitude to, each group may differ; (c) the control group may react badly (negatively) to not experiencing what they see the experimental group experiencing. There are many possible contaminating factors here.

Are there alternatives to action research that might provide a more careful and sustainable account of causation and causal explanation? Fortunately there are, and the chapter turns to these.

> **Implications for researchers:**
>
> - Action research can identify the effects of causes, but it risks lack of rigour and reliability.
> - Action research lacks the external controls that could indicate causation more accurately.
> - Action research can take several forms, one of which is closer to a true experiment.

Experimental methods

Whilst experimental approaches may be powerful, they may be the stuff of the physical rather than of the social sciences, and social science often deals more in non-experimental approaches. That said, experimental approaches, if they can be used, may yield robust results. Determining the causes of effects is often addressed by using experimental methods. In a 'true' experimental method, the procedures are thus.

- Randomly assign subjects to two matched groups – control and experimental (such randomization being a way of allowing for a range of variables).
- Conduct a pre-test to ensure that the control groups and experimental groups are matched (the parity issue) on the variables considered important.
- Identify, isolate and control variables, whilst excluding any other variables.
- Administer the intervention to the experimental group whilst holding every other variable constant for the two groups.
- Manipulate the independent variable as required (e.g. vary its values).
- Ensure that the two groups are entirely separate throughout the experiment (non-contamination).
- Conduct a post-test and compare the results of the control and experimental groups (often in terms of the comparing average results of the groups on the pre-test and the post-test).

The idea here is that, as all the possible variables have been isolated and controlled, any observed effect can only be caused by the intervention. Further, by random allocation of participants to either a control or an experimental group, the problem of controlling the countless variables operating on, and in, participants is overcome. Randomization and random allocation are key features of the 'true' experiment.

Randomization is a key, critical element of the 'true' experiment; random sampling and random allocation to either a control or an experimental group is a central way of allowing for the additional uncontrolled and, hence, unmeasured variables that may be part of the make-up of the groups in question (cf. Slavin 2007). It is an attempt to overcome the confounding effects of exogenous and endogenous variables: the *ceteris paribus* condition (all other things being equal); it assumes that the distribution of these extraneous variables is more or less even and perhaps of little significance. In short it strives to address Holland's (1986) 'fundamental problem of causal inference', which is that a person may not be in both a control group and an experimental group simultaneously. Random stratified sampling allows certain desired controls to be placed on the random

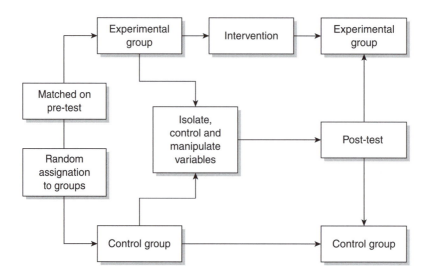

Figure 5.2 The 'true' experiment

sample. As Schneider *et al.* (2007: 16) remark, because random allocation takes into account both observed and unobserved factors, controls on unobserved factors, are thereby unnecessary.

The 'true' experiment can be represented diagrammatically as in Figure 5.2. If students are randomly allocated to control and experimental groups and are equivalent in all respects (by randomization) other than one group being exposed and the other not being exposed to the intervention, then, it is argued, the researcher can attribute any different outcomes between the two groups to the effects of the intervention. Schneider *et al.* (2007: 11) argue that, whilst randomization may indicate the effects of an intervention, and its magnitude, nevertheless it does not indicate either the causal mechanisms and processes at work or the settings.

Let us consider a case of an experimental approach, in which an attempt at causation was made, to see if a particular cause produced a particular effect. In 2004 Schellenberg reported the results of an experiment that was conducted to test the hypothesis that having music lessons enhances IQ (i.e. a 'far transfer' effect). Put simply, does music make one smarter? The research initially identified two possible transfer effects: near transfer (that which occurs between highly similar contexts and domains) and far transfer (that which occurs between domains that have less in common). The research reported previous findings that were consistent with the hypothesis that music lessons promote intellectual development. The research investigated whether this included, for example, other forms of intelligence, such as verbal memory, spatial ability, reading ability, selective attention, and mathematics achievement. The research recognized a possibly confounding effect, such as the fact that other experimental studies had typically compared children taking music lessons with children taking no additional lessons of any kind, so it was unclear whether the observed associations stemmed from musical training or from structured, extra-curricular activities, i.e. the source of the effect was maybe unclear.

To take account of these matters, Schellenberg selected a random sample of six-year-olds in Toronto (N=144), chosen because it was thought that children of that age both

Table 5.2 Two experimental and two control groups

Experimental groups		Control groups	
This group received music lessons of a 'standard keyboard' type	This group received music lessons adopting the Kodály voice method	This group received non-musical artistic activity: drama	This group received no lessons at all

Table 5.3 Experimental results for control and experimental groups

	Experimental groups		Control groups	
	Keyboard	Voice	Drama	No lessons
Full-scale IQ before lessons	102.6	103.8	102.6	99.4
Full-scale IQ after lessons	108.7	111.4	107.7	103.3
Difference	6.1	7.6	5.1	3.9

were sufficiently mature for formal lessons and possessed a 'plasticity' that tended to decline in older children. They were divided into two experimental groups and two control groups, as in Table 5.2. Each child was randomly assigned to one of the four groups, measured before and after the lessons using three tests: (a) an IQ test (the Wechsler Intelligence Scale for Children); (b) a standardized test of educational achievement (the Kaufman Test of Educational Achievement) and (c) a test of social functioning (the Parent Rating Scale of the Behavioral Assessment System for Children). Twelve children (8.3 per cent) dropped out, i.e. the experimental mortality was quite high. In each lesson group (keyboard, voice, drama) two different female professional instructors taught three classes each; each class had six children. The results are presented in Table 5.3.

The calculation of the difference made can be undertaken thus: {post-test for experimental group *minus* pre-test for experimental group} *minus* {post-test for control group *minus* pre-test for control group}. In formula terms this can be written:

Average causal effect $(A) = (E_1-E_2) - (C_1-C_2)$

where:
E_1 = post-test for experimental (treatment) group
E_2 = pre-test for experimental (treatment) group
C_1 = post-test for control group
C_2 = pre-test for control group.

In terms of the numbers, the effect of the cause can be calculated thus:

- between the 'keyboard' experimental group and the 'drama' control group: $6.1-5.1 = 1.0$;
- between the 'keyboard' experimental group and the 'no lesson' control group: $6.1-3.9 = 2.2$;
- between the 'voice' experimental group and the 'drama' control group: $7.6-5.1 = 2.5$;
- between the 'voice' experimental group and the 'no lesson' control group: $7.6-3.9 = 3.7$.

The greatest differences were between the 'voice' experimental group and the 'no lesson' control group, followed by the 'voice' experimental group and the 'drama' control group, then the 'keyboard' experimental group and the 'no lesson' control group, and finally the 'keyboard' experimental group and the 'drama' control group. One could surmise that the most effective intervention was not only the 'voice' method, but with a group that had no drama.

Schellenberg concluded that, compared with children in the control groups, children in the music groups exhibited greater increases in 'full-scale IQ'. The effect was relatively small, but it generalized across the various tests administered. Unexpectedly, children in the drama group exhibited substantial pre- to post-test improvements in adaptive social behaviour that were not evident in the music groups. Schellenberg was careful to bound his study, indicating that it was already well established that simply attending school raises IQ, and that school instruction was particularly effective when classes are small. He concluded that music lessons, taught individually and in small groups, may provide additional boosts in IQ because they are like school and are still enjoyable. The music lesson also involved a range of diverse experiences that could generate improvement in a wide range of abilities. Hence Schellenberg was able to support his hypothesis that some 'far transfer' (to distant domains), as well as near transfer (to similar domains), was caused by music lessons.

At first sight the research appears attractive and robust. One can see that the groups are randomly allocated and matched, that there is an input and an outcome, that average differences are calculated, that variables are isolated and controlled, and that the research conclusions remain within their legitimate boundaries.

However, we do not know about other key factors that might be present but which were not factored into the research, the causal context or conditions. For example, the reader is told nothing about the background musical abilities of the children, their liking for music, the kinds of music that they liked or disliked, their motivations for – and during – their involvement, their attitudes to the interventions, the teacher–child relationships, the interactions that took place between the teacher and each child, their liking for drama, their preferences for extra-curricular activities, their reactions to a battery of three tests, the conditions (e.g. rooms, sound, light, timing, group participation, in which the interventions took place); in short, the reader is not told about a diversity of causal processes and conditions that may have been exerting an influence on the results. They have been neither controlled in nor controlled out. The results are suspect. The research uses only confirming evidence and does not seek, or find, rival, alternative explanations, nor does it seek falsification criteria. It has a hypothesis in mind, it gathers data that support it, and then, lo and behold, the hypothesis is supported. It is a straw man, akin to my supposing that, as in the newspaper example reported in the previous chapter, a teapot has healing powers, so I measure how much faith the worshippers have in its healing powers, I find out the nature, amount and extent of believers and non-believers who have been cured of whatever ailment they say they had and, because the number of believers cured exceeds the number of non-believers cured, I am convinced that the teapot must have healing powers. It is a fiction.

The issue here is that there is a danger that hypothesis testing may be testing the wrong hypothesis. This is important, for it throws into question a fundamental issue in identifying causation. Statistical tests alone, of whatever sophistication, are only as good as the assumptions made behind them, and behind statistical processes lies a model of 'what causes what'. Hence there is a significant risk of circularity in investigating causation: the researcher commences with a model of causation and then tests it, perhaps with high-level statistics, e.g. path modelling, regression analysis, structural equation modelling and suchlike. Indeed the researcher may find regularities, coefficients, effects sizes and signifi-cance levels of monumental power, but these do not prove that the causal model is correct.

Turner (1997) provides a very clear example of this, not in education but in epidemiol-ogy. He showed how two rival theories of the spread of cholera in the nineteenth century (the infection being waterborne and the infection being airborne, depending on the altitude of the streets (the *elevation* law)) could both have been sustained by statistical analysis, as that analysis did not rule out airborne infection, whereas the true cause (the waterborne hypoth-esis) was discoverable by careful analysis of the *mechanisms* of transmission (1997: 40). Statistics might work within a model, but what if the model is incorrect? Real causes might not be the same as statistical variables, and statistics might simply be the new alchemy. Behind causal modelling and statistical manipulation lie theory, assumptions and intuitions which need to demonstrate construct validity. Just because one regression might exist and be more powerful than another does not prove causation; as Clogg and Haritou (1997: 101) remark, social researchers are at risk of deducing from statistics (e.g. regression and path analysis) little more than they have assumed in the first place, i.e. they are tautological and circular, and it should not be a matter of faith that causation is implied by statistics. Faith, they aver (ibid.: 105), is best kept for the Sunday School; social science requires construct validity underpinned by robust theory. Models that predict or fit the data well may have nothing to do with causation or the size of causal effects (ibid.: 110), and statistical assump-tions may have little relationship to causal inferences. Indeed Freedman (1997: 114) com-ments that regression equations have not succeeded in discovering causal relationships.

Turning back to the music example here, the research operates on a simplistic input–output model, with very few causal processes involved, so it is remains dangerous to con-clude that the putative causes actually caused the observed effects. Indeed Hage and Meeker (1988: 55) suggest that the experimental approach may be fundamentally flawed in assuming that a single cause produces an effect. On the one hand the research has the attraction of reporting what is deemed to be a causal result that overrides individuals; however, on the other hand, it has not established causality, only association/correlation, and this is due, in part, to the absence of identification of causal processes. We simply do not have sufficient information to be able to judge causation here. It may be that the set-ting effects are acting causally, rather than the intervention itself, i.e. there is a 'setting effect' (where the results are largely a function of their context) (see Maxwell 2004).

Implications for researchers:

- 'True' experiments are powerful ways of achieving causal manipulation and of determining effects of causes.
- Input–output experimental models provide an incomplete account of causation.
- Process variables and causal mechanisms can be included in an input–output model, and these may influence the analysis of cause and effect.
- It is essential to know the conditions in which an experiment takes place, including the nature of the participants, as these exert an influence on the effects of causes.
- Experimental methods operate on a hypothesis-testing paradigm.
- Behind statistics lie models; behind models lie theories, and it is the theories and models that must demonstrate causation.

The power of the 'setting effect' to exert significant causal determination is revealed in, for example, two classic experiments:

(a) the Milgram (1974) studies of obedience, in which everyday, 'average' humans were led, by the power of the situation and the situational pressure of obedience to the wishes of the researcher and the research situation, to administer supposedly increasingly powerful electric shocks to participants, up to the maximum of 450 volts. Indeed 65 per cent of the participants administered the most powerful shocks, far in excess of the prediction of psychiatrists, who had suggested that around 10 per cent of participants would administer the highest voltage.

(b) Zimbardo's Stanford prison experiment (http://www.prisonexp.org), in which a mock prison was constructed in the basement of the psychology building at Stanford University. The subjects were selected from a pool of 75 respondents to a newspaper advertisement asking for paid volunteers to participate in a psychological study of prison life. On a random basis, half of the subjects were assigned to the role of guard and half to the role of prisoner. Prior to the experiment, subjects were asked to sign a form, agreeing to play either the prisoner or the guard role for a maximum of two weeks. Those assigned to the prisoner role should expect to be under surveillance, to be harassed, but not to be physically abused. In return, subjects would be adequately fed, clothed and housed and would receive $15 per day for the duration of the experiment. The outcome of the study was dramatic. In less than two days after the initiation of the experiment, violence and rebellion broke out. The prisoners ripped off their clothing and their identification numbers and barricaded themselves inside the cells whilst shouting and cursing at the guards. The guards, in turn, began to harass, humiliate and intimidate the prisoners. They used sophisticated psychological techniques to break the solidarity of the inmates and to create a sense of distrust amongst them. In less than 36 hours one of the prisoners showed severe symptoms of emotional disturbance, uncontrollable crying and screaming, and so he was released. On the third day, a rumour developed about a mass escape plot. The guards increased their harassment, intimidation and brutality towards the prisoners. On the fourth day, two prisoners showed symptoms of severe emotional disturbance and were released. On the fifth day, the prisoners showed symptoms of individual and group disintegration. They had become mostly passive and docile, suffering from an acute loss of contact with reality. The guards, on the other hand, had kept up their harassment, some behaving sadistically. Because of the unexpectedly intense reactions generated by the mock prison experience, the experimenters terminated the study at the end of the sixth day; it did not run its full course of time.

In both of these examples, the power of the situation exerted causal force that overrode the natural dispositions and behaviours of the individuals involved. Philip Zimbardo, the leader of the Stanford prison experiment and subsequent expert advisor on the Abu Ghraib prison incidents in Iraq, termed this 'the Lucifer Effect' (Zimbardo 2007), in which everyday humans turn into perpetrators of evil because of the power of the situation. Social pressures determined individual behaviour here, and an input–output model in the experimental method risks overlooking this. As Durkheim (1982) remarked, there are 'social facts'.

> **Implications for researchers:**
>
> - 'Setting effects' and context can exert an enormous influence on an experiment, can mediate causes and effects, and can exert an even stronger causal influence on the effects than the initial cause.
> - Setting effects require attention to detailed causal mechanisms and individual behaviour.

Experimental approaches, when they work properly, are a powerful way of establishing causation in evidence-based education (EBE) (cf. Gorard 2001: 16). For advocates of EBE, the nature of evidence is often of a particular kind only: data are to be derived solely from randomized controlled trials (RCTs) – the controlled experiment with randomization to ensure generalizability (e.g. Boruch 1997; Tymms 1999; Oakley 1998, 2000). Using Campbell and Stanley's (1963) conventions, the highest quality experiment for RCTs is the 'true' experimental design, with pre-test–post-test control and experimental groups and randomized allocation of participants to the groups. Of lesser quality (because of threats to internal and external validity) are the 'one group pre-test–post-test designs (where there is no control group), the *ex post facto* designs (where the direction of causation may not be clear and the lack of controls may compromise reliability (Cohen *et al.* 2007: 268–9)) and the non-equivalent control group design (where there are important differences between control and experimental groups). RCTs, their advocates argue, constitute the 'gold standard of evidence' (Coe *et al.* 2000; Curriculum Evaluation and Management Centre 2000: 1), and the aggregation of small-scale, published and unpublished experiments through meta-analysis (Fitz-Gibbon 1984, 1985, 1996; Cook *et al.*, 1992; Tymms 1999) yields a combined body of evidence whose collective weight is important – despite critics of this approach, who argue that RCTs cannot answer 'all the important questions in educational research' (Eisenhart 2005: 246).

> **Implications for researchers:**
>
> - Randomized controlled trials are a powerful way of establishing causation and its effects.
> - Meta-analysis of randomized controlled trials can combine several studies that may indicate robust causal explanations.

The parallels for evidence-based education through RCTs are:

(a) the Cochrane Collaboration for evidence-based medicine (Sheldon and Chalmers 1994; Maynard and Chalmers 1997), where the systematic review and documentation of well-controlled RCTs contribute to the accumulation of a systematic evidence base. Indeed, the Campbell Collaboration in education is seen as a 'younger sibling' (Coe *et al.* 2000: 2) of the Cochrane Collaboration (see also http://campbellcollboration.org) along with the What Works Clearinghouse in the United States (http://ies.ed.gov/ncee/wwc/).

(b) the moves towards evidence-based policy and practice in health care and social work (cf. Boruch 1997; Davies 1999), which may steer educational research along the lines of the medical model (Dobby 1999; Evans *et al*. 2000: 20).

What we have, then, from the advocates of EBE is a clear argument:

- policy making and practice should be based on 'what works' in education;
- 'what works' in education should be based on the evidence of what works in practice;
- the evidence should be derived from randomized controlled trials (RCTs);
- the weight of evidence from RCTs can be ascertained through meta-analysis.

These are powerful claims, and they need to be defended – and defensible – rather than assumed, as they are not unproblematical. For example, what constitutes 'evidence' is problematical, and certainly may be wider than that derived from RCTs.

Implications for researchers:

- Judging 'what works' is not determined simply by randomized controlled trials, as there are other issues to be addressed, e.g. for whom, under what conditions, and according to what criteria.
- It is important to make clear what constitutes 'evidence' in randomized controlled trials.

Let us examine the case for RCTs a little more, as they exemplify issues in experimental approaches more widely.[1]

Randomized controlled trials in experimental approaches to determine 'what works'

The purposes of RCTs are clear – to establish causation and predictability. Though this is, of course, perfectly honourable, causation, here, is premised on control (Cohen *et al*. 2000: 211) and manipulation. Regardless of the perhaps questionable desirability of predicating human sciences on the scientistic instrumental reason of the natural sciences, with its subject/object split, its notion of value-neutrality, and its procedures for 'doing things to people', there is the *de facto* problem of whether this, in fact, can be done, given the conditionality of social science research discussed in Chapter 3. The impact of complexity theory and chaos theory (Gleick 1987; Waldrop 1992; Lewin 1993; Kauffman 1995) suggests that predictability is a chimera. For example, Tymms (1996: 132–3) suggests that different outcomes might be expected even from the same classes taught by the same teacher in the same classroom with the same curriculum; if something works once there is no guarantee that it will work again. Hence, if utilization is an important focus, then RCTs may have limited utility.

The impact of theories of chaos and complexity here is important, for they argue against the linear, deterministic, patterned, universalizable, stable, atomized, modernistic, objective, mechanist, controlled, closed systems of law-like behaviour which may be operating in the world of medicine and the laboratory but which do not operate in the social world of education. Theories of chaos and complexity contain several features which seriously challenge the value of RCTs in education (e.g. Gleick 1987; Waldrop 1992; Lewin 1993; Morrison 1998, 2008; Cohen *et al.* 2000: 386):

- small-scale changes in initial conditions can produce massive and unpredictable changes in outcome (e.g. the beat of a butterfly's wing in the Caribbean can produce a hurricane in America);
- very similar conditions can produce very dissimilar outcomes;
- regularity and conformity break down into irregularity and diversity;
- effects are not straightforward, continuous functions of causes;
- the universe is largely unpredictable;
- if something works once there is no guarantee that it will work in the same way a second time;
- determinism is replaced by indeterminism; deterministic, linear and stable systems are replaced by 'dynamical', changing, evolving systems and non-linear explanations of phenomena;
- long-term prediction is impossible;
- order is not predetermined and fixed, but emerges unpredictably through self-organization, connectedness and autocatalysis (e.g. Doll 1993);
- social life, education and learning take place through the interactions of participants with their environments (however defined, e.g. interpersonal, social, intrapersonal, physical, material, intellectual, emotional) in ways which cannot be controlled through RCTs;
- local rules and behaviours generate diversity and heterogeneity of practice, undermining generalizability from RCTs about 'what works'.

Complexity theory replaces an emphasis on simple causation with an emphasis on networks, linkages, feedback, impact, relationships and interactivity in context (Cohen and Stewart 1995), emergence, dynamical systems, self-organization and open systems (rather than the closed system of the RCT). Nets and networks replace linear causation (see Figure 2.3). Even if we could conduct an RCT, the applicability of that RCT to ongoing, emerging, interactive, relational, changing, open situations, in practice, may be limited, even though some gross similarities may be computed through meta-analysis. The world of classrooms is not the world of the computed statistic.

Implications for researchers:

- Randomized controlled trials are premised on prediction, control and manipulation; that is their greatest strength and their greatest weakness.
- Causal explanations from randomized controlled trials are no guarantee of their predictive value.
- Randomized controlled trials may misrepresent and underrepresent the significance of the tenets of complexity theory and changing environments.

Further, it is perhaps untenable to hold variables constant in a dynamic, evolving, fluid, idiographic, unique situation (a feature which is recognized in health-care research (Davies 1999: 115)). It is a truism to say that naturalistic settings such as schools and classrooms are not the antiseptic, reductionist, analysed-out or analysable-out world of the laboratory, and that the degree of control required for experimental conditions to be met renders classrooms unnatural settings, yet the implications of this truism are perhaps understated in RCTs. Even if one *wanted* to undertake an RCT, to what extent is it *actually* possible to identify, isolate, control and manipulate the key variables and, thence, to attribute causation?

For example, let us say that an experiment is conducted to increase security and reduce theft in schools through the installation of closed circuit television (CCTV). The effect is a reduction in theft in the experimental school. Exactly what are the causes and the causal processes here? It may be that potential offenders are deterred from theft, or that offenders are caught more frequently, or that the presence of the CCTV renders teachers and students more vigilant – and, indeed, such vigilance might make the teachers and students more security-conscious so that they either do not bring valuables to the school or they store them more securely. The experiment might succeed in reducing theft, but what exactly is happening in the experiment and the school? Are the changes occurring in the teachers, the students, or the thief, or a combination of these?

Of course, advocates of RCTs would respond by saying that the cause is clear – the installation of the CCTV – and that the experiment has generated further hypotheses to be tested experimentally (cf. Coe *et al.* 2000: 4), but this is very far from claiming knowledge of 'what works' or attributing unequivocal causation. Leaving aside the fact that this is not a 'true' experiment, there being no control group, the RCT is still a comparatively opaque 'black box', disabling the identification of detailed causal processes and mechanisms that produce effects (Clarke and Dawson 1999: 52), and it is precisely these detailed processes and mechanisms that we need to know about in order to understand causation.

Proponents of RCTs might wish to argue that, in fact, this does not matter, for the experiment appears to have identified what works (cf. Coe *et al.* 2000: 5) – the CCTV has reduced theft – thereby overriding those other, perhaps less important, variables that might be operating in the situation. However, this is to neglect the central part that *people* play in the experiment – they have perceptions, motivations, attitudes, wishes, responses – and all these have an effect on the experiment. An RCT, as Pawson and Tilley (1993: 8) observe, might be 'splendid epistemology' but it is 'lousy ontology', as programmes are mediated by their participants. People in the programme might choose to make an intervention work or not work, and teachers' and students' motivations in, commitments to, and involvement in an intervention might be the critical factors.

This is a crucial matter, for RCTs require exactly the same intervention or programme within and between the control and experimental groups, i.e. to ensure that the protocols and procedures for the research are observed and are identical. Yet this is impossible. Because sentient people tailor their behaviour to each other, their behaviour will differ, and, therefore, the planned intervention or programme will alter. One question here is the extent to which exactly the same treatments will be occurring in the relevant parts of the RCT or, indeed, in the way in which the intervention or programme was intended.

For example, a teacher may modify, intentionally or unintentionally, a part of a programme or its 'delivery' to suit the students, perhaps because she does not agree with one part of it, or is particularly enthusiastic about another part, or because she is certain that a particular part of the programme, based on her experience of the participants, will not work or will cause other problems in the class. Indeed her classes may be differentially receptive to the intervention, so she adjusts her behaviour. The task for researchers, then, is to retain consistency, yet this could cause the researcher and the practitioner to come into conflict with each other if they give rise to ethical, interpersonal, administrative or management problems on the part of the practitioners. What if the practitioners object to the impersonal 'laboratory conditions' of the research?

The social processes at work in the experiment may be the determining factor, and RCTs may be unable to control for these. This is a well-rehearsed problem in causation – behind or alongside an apparent cause (A causes B) are other causes (e.g. C causes A which causes B, and D causes A and B respectively; see the discussion of causal forks in Chapter 3). The search for simple causation is naïve – indeed it may be the interplay of several causes and conditions that is producing the effects observed (a feature of complexity theory); it is unclear how an RCTs can disentangle this. It is akin to a person taking ten medicines for a stomach pain: he or she takes the medicines and the pain is alleviated, but which medicine(s) was/were effective, or was it the synergy of them all that caused the relief? This may be important if efficiency – value for money – is to be ensured.

That the interaction between the intervention/programme and the setting or the context can exert an effect on the outcome is neither novel nor unnoticed (e.g. Campbell and Stanley 1963). Indeed, during the course of the programme a range of other unanticipated factors might come into play which cannot be 'controlled out' and which might exert a massive influence. Unlike the world of the laboratory, this is the reality of social and human settings, and Slavin (1986) suggests that an RCT undertaken under artificial laboratory conditions might not translate into actual classrooms. It is difficult to see how RCTs handle this issue. This is acknowledged, for example, by Campbell and Stanley (1963), though in the dynamical, non-linear, complex world of classrooms it is impossible to see, let alone measure, how these might be affecting the RCT. The butterfly beating its wings in the Caribbean and causing a hurricane in another part of the world frustrated Lorenz's attempts at long-range prediction of weather patterns (Gleick 1987); so it is in classrooms. Small events cause major upsets and render long-term prediction or generalizability futile. How do we know what the effects of small changes will be on an RCT? We may have knowledge of short-term rather than long-term effects, so the timing of the post-tests is important.

What is being suggested here is the need to identify exactly what is happening in the programme or intervention, i.e. the processes and causal mechanisms taking place. RCTs singularly neglect this; indeed they may be unable to take account of, or are not concerned with, these processes and mechanisms, yet is precisely this sort of evidence that might be important in determining causation.

The importance of context is undeniable, yet where is this taken into account in the RCT? The RCT actively builds outs and excludes key elements of context, as they could 'contaminate' the experiment, yet it could be these very factors that are important and which contribute to overcoming Type I and Type II errors (e.g. finding a spurious difference between control and experimental groups, and failing to find a real difference between control and experimental groups respectively).

Pawson and Tilley (1993) argue that striving to control the influence of extraneous factors by random assignation of participants to control and experimental groups (a procedure advocated by Campbell and Stanley (1963)) is ill-judged, as this prevents researchers from identifying those very conditions that might be contributing to the success or failure of a programme or intervention, i.e. precisely the sort of information that might be useful to policy makers (Clarke and Dawson 1999: 53) (see the discussion of the Schellenberg experiment earlier). As Clarke and Dawson observe (ibid.: 54), it is the people in a programme that cause it to work, not the programme itself. This may be extremely important to policy makers, for it may cause resources and attention to be allocated more efficiently and effectively. For example, if it is the motivation of the participants rather than the actual contents of a programme that are the critical factors in the programme's success, then channelling money, let us say, into material resources rather than into human resources and human resource management (e.g. reducing class sizes or increasing the number of teachers for students with special needs) might be misplaced.

The preceding argument has suggested that simply striving to describe 'what works' neglects the important issues of (i) what works in what conditions; (ii) what are the roles and the behaviours of people and context in contributing to 'what works'; and (iii) why programmes and interventions work or do not work. These are vital factors in establishing causation. These are complemented by the need to clarify: (a) 'what works' for whom; (b) in whose terms 'what works' is being judged; (c) 'against what criteria 'what works' are being judged; and (d) at what cost/benefit 'what works' is being judged.

Implications for researchers:

- The world of the controlled laboratory misrepresents the real world of interacting variables in natural settings.
- Randomized controlled trials may be unacceptably reductionist.
- Randomized controlled trials need to specify the actual causes that are being manipulated and the exact effects that are being determined.
- Randomized controlled trials may indicate what works or does not work, but not why or how.
- There may be many effects in a randomized controlled trial, and it is unfair to be overselective in indicating the effects.
- Some effects in a randomized controlled trial may be undesirable.
- Randomized controlled trials may fail to give an account of the processes and mechanisms at work, and it is these, rather than inputs and outputs, that yield insights into 'what works'.
- In a randomized controlled trial there may be many reasons for, or explanations of, why a cause produces an effect, and account needs to be taken of these.

The perhaps seductive simplicity of the desire to find 'what works' by RCTs disguises a range of complex factors. These are ethical as well as empirical. With regard to ethical questions, one could not say that the end justifies the means, and in practical terms it might be unclear exactly how to judge 'what works' (Levačić and Glatter 2000: 11). I might find, for example, that constant negative harassment of teachers by a school principal might increase the amount of time they spend on lesson preparation, which might (or, indeed, might not) improve lesson quality. However, it might be difficult to defend such behaviour ethically.

Though the intervention in the example here of principal behaviour might be judged a success in the principal's eyes, in the eyes of the staff the intervention is a dismal failure; 'what works' for one party does not work in the eyes of another. This issue characterizes much 'management' literature. Witness the debate about 're-engineering' the company: whilst for managers this makes for a lean, efficient, profitable company it is also a euphemism for massive job losses (Micklethwait and Wooldridge 1997). In Japanese management practices, company bosses see the attractions of the 'virtuous circle' of flexibility, quality and teamwork, whereas the same practices are seen by junior employees as a vicious circle of exploitation, control and surveillance respectively (Wickens 1987; Garrahan and Stewart 1992). It is not that one party is correct and the other incorrect; both parties are correct, but they have different perceptions of the same phenomena. This argues for the need to adopt a multi-perspectival position on observed phenomena. It is difficult to see how RCTs can catch this spread of perceptions in judging 'what works', unless they utilize a range of outcome measures. Increasing homework may be effective according to a school principal, but may demotivate students from lifelong learning – clearly a failure in the eyes of students.

Further, the results might be effective in the short term and in the longer term, but such behaviour might also be counter-productive, as the poor interpersonal relations, the hostile atmosphere, the 'blame culture' and the demotivation of teachers caused by the principal's behaviour might lead to rapid staff turnover and the reduction in teachers' commitment to their work. In the short term, school inspections may improve schools' academic results, but, in the longer term, they can lead to such demoralization of teachers that recruitment and retention rates suffer, which leads to falling academic results. The thirst for improved grades in schools may lead to an initial improvement in performance, but it may also contribute to a testing and cramming culture of nightmare proportions (Noah and Eckstein 1990; Sacks 1999). The timing of the outcome measure, the post-test, is clearly an important factor in determining success here.

This issue of the timing of the post-test rehearses the arguments for identifying curvilinearity in relating factors: in the short term raising stress can improve performance, though in the longer term it is detrimental to health. Drinking coffee can bring temporary stimulation but in the long term can be detrimental. A short, sharp stay in a harsh prison regime might show a brief decline in recidivism, but, in the longer term, it might make no difference to rates of recidivism.

'What works' is a matter of judgement which is based on, or informed by, data from RCTs; the data alone do not speak for themselves. As Gorard (2001: 9) remarks, 'education does not have a single agreed indicator of what works'. Data have to be interpreted, weighed, judged, and considered; 'what works' is a value statement not simply an empirical statement, and to neglect this is to commit a category mistake. Judging 'what works' in causation is as much a statement of value as a statement of empirical outcomes.

There is a problem in RCTs, in that a single intervention does not produce only a single outcome; it produces several. 'What works' is neither absolute nor unambiguous; a treatment for cancer can cure the cancer but it might also bring several side-effects, for example hair loss, amputation, sickness and gross lethargy. The recognition that there are several outcomes of an intervention or programme requires a judgement to be made about the relative importance or priority to be given to each outcome. RCTs neglect this.

The pre-specification of outcomes not only risks missing catching the unintended – and perhaps unmeasurable – effects of a programme, it assumes that outcomes are capable of being operationalized and measured comparatively straightforwardly. Measures may only catch superficiality. An RCT may be entirely rigorous but, maybe as a consequence of meeting the canons of rigour by isolating and controlling important factors out of the experiment, even if causation is shown, it might be in such restricted, local, specific terms as to be non-transferable to other contexts.

Though constructing appropriate measures may simply be a technical matter, this is unlikely to be the sole resolution of the problem, as the judgement of adequate construct and content validity is not decided by measures alone, it is deliberative. RCTs operate only within the sphere of pre-specified goals; in the bigger picture of everyday classrooms what works in an RCT may be incompatible with other factors that are taking place. An intervention programme may raise students' measured achievements in reading but may provoke an intense dislike of books or of reading for pleasure. RCTs are inherently reductionist and atomizing in their focus and methodology; they are incapable of taking in the whole picture (Cohen and Stewart 1995: chap. 6).

The preceding analysis argues for the need to ensure that outcome measures demonstrate validity, that they measure what it is intended they should measure, and that this is interpreted widely and comprehensively. This might be possible in an RCT in the natural sciences that is examining the effects of a particular fertilizer on increased and improved crop yield (Morrison 1993: 44–5) or the action of a particular drug on the human body, but, in interpersonal and personal situations, notions of improvement are ethical and much more wide-ranging. This is not only to suggest that outcome measures should catch actual outcomes, which, of course, they should; it is to recognize that outcome measures will necessarily need to be interpreted comprehensively in social and educational programmes (Rossi and Freeman 1993).

Further, it might be very difficult for the teacher conducting an RCT to avoid the problem of the control groups and experimental groups not coming into contact with each other and, thereby, 'contaminating' the RCT (though this might be ameliorated, for example, by having the control and experimental groups in different schools). The intention may be to operate single blind experiments (where those taking part do not know to which group they belong), double blind experiments (where none of the participants knows to which group they have been assigned or who is receiving the treatment or intervention), or triple blind experiments (where the data are coded in such a way as to prevent those processing the data from knowing to which groups the participants have been assigned). However, one has to ask simply how realistic this is. Nash (1973) shows how quickly, accurately and insightfully students are able to appreciate exactly what is happening in classrooms, and so are teachers. Blind RCTs may be impossible. If this is the case, then reliability and validity might be compromised.

Implications for researchers:

- Judging 'what works' has to address ethical as well as practical issues and contexts respectively.
- The timing of the evaluation/observation/measurement of the effect has to be appropriate.

- Decisions have to be taken on whether effects are short term, long term, sustained, or short-lived.
- Causes and effects may exist in a non-linear relationship.
- Effects may be both negative and positive.
- The same cause may produce many effects.
- Sampling is problematic in randomized controlled trials, there being problems with both large samples and small samples.
- Contamination of the control and experimental groups must be avoided.

With regard to sampling, randomization may not be appropriate in some circumstances. For example, let us imagine a situation where some form of punishment were to be tried in schools for a particular offence. How would one justify not making this a required punishment for all those in the school who committed the particular offence in question? It would offend natural justice (Wilkins 1969; see also Clarke and Dawson 1999: 98) for some offenders to be exempted in the interests of an experiment.

Clarke and Dawson (1999: 130) draw attention to the fact that, in health care, treatments may produce adverse reactions, in which case patients are withdrawn from the experiment. Others might simply leave the experiment. That this contributes to 'experimental mortality' or attrition rates has been long recognized (Campbell and Stanley 1963). Less clear in education, however, is how the problem has been, or might be, addressed (cf. Rossi and Freeman 1993). This might undermine putative parity between the control and experimental groups. As the constitution of the groups changes, however slightly (and chaos theory reminds us that small changes can result in massive effects), so the dynamics of the situation change, and the consistency and comparability of the research protocol, conditions, contexts and contents are undermined. To address this involves identifying not only the exact factors on which assignation of the sample to control and experimental groups will take place, but also a recognition of significant ways in which the two groups differ. The judgement then becomes about the extent to which the dissimilarities between the two groups might outweigh their similarities.

The argument here has suggested that establishing causation and 'what works' begs several serious questions, including:

- defining 'what works';
- whose views to adopt in defining 'what works';
- addressing the complexity and multi-dimensionality of elements in defining 'what works';
- recognizing that 'what works' is a matter of judgement rather than solely of data, and that this judgement is imbued with moral and ethical concerns;
- identifying the kinds of data and methodologies required to understand 'what works';
- addressing the limits and possibilities of RCTs in providing useful evidence of 'what works';
- addressing a range of technical issues concerned with RCTs with regard to sampling, generalizability, reliability and validity.

Indeed, 'what works' may fail to address causation at all; causation is about 'how something works', not only 'what happens'. This is not to argue simplistically against RCTs *per se*; they have their place. Indeed, their ability to address teachers' self-generated problems should not be overlooked (Davies 1999). Randomized controlled trials can provide useful research data on 'what works'. However, establishing causation and 'what works' in an RCT is far from obvious, and, even if it were done, to regard experiments as the sole way of establishing causation 'is absurd' (Eisenhart 2005: 251).

Further issues in experiments

There are several types of experiment and quasi-experiment (see Cohen *et al.* 2007: chaps 6 and 13), including, for example,

- laboratory experiments (controlled, artificial conditions):
    - pre-test–post-test control and experimental group;
    - repeated measures design;
    - factorial design;
    - two control groups and one experimental group pre-test–post-test;
    - post-test control and experimental group;
    - post-test, two experimental groups;
    - pre-test–post-test, two treatment groups;
    - matched pairs;
    - parametric design;
- field experiments (controlled conditions in the 'real world'):
    - one-group pre-test–post-test;
    - non-equivalent control group design;
    - time series;
- natural experiments (no control over real-world conditions).

The preceding discussion has introduced some issues in laboratory-type experiments. In many cases a quasi-experiment, rather than a 'true' experiment, may be more appropriate or, indeed, the only course practicable. A quasi-experiment is where not all the conditions of a 'true' experiment obtain or where random allocation is deemed to be unethical, unfeasible or unwarranted, leading to some comparative studies which attempt to isolate the effects of a particular cause or intervention without using randomization (Schneider *et al.* 2007: 4–5). Cohen *et al.* argue that:

> the field experiment is similar to the laboratory experiment in that variables are isolated, controlled and manipulated, but the setting is the real world rather than the artificially constructed world of the laboratory…. Field experiments have less control over experimental conditions or extraneous variables than a laboratory experiment, and, hence, inferring causality is more contestable, but they have the attraction of taking place in a natural setting. Extraneous variables may include, for example:
> - Participant factors (they may differ on important characteristics between the control and experimental groups);
> - Intervention factors (the intervention may not be exactly the same for all participants, varying, for example, in sequence, duration, degree of intervention and assistance, and other practices and contents);
> - Situational factors (the experimental conditions may differ).

These can lead to experimental error, in which the results may not be due to the independent variables in question.

(Cohen et al. 2007: 274–5)

Further, randomization and matching of control and experimental groups may not be easy in a field experiment. Field experiments may have control over what Campbell and Stanley (1963) refer to as 'the who and to whom of measurement' but lack control over 'the when and to whom of exposure', or the randomization of exposures which is essential if true experimentation is to occur (Cohen et al. 2007: 279). In these circumstances generalization may not be possible. Whilst field experiments have the attraction of being carried out in real situations, these same real situations create their own problems.

With regard to the natural experiment, Cohen et al. argue that 'sometimes it is not possible, desirable or ethical to set up a laboratory or field experiment' (2007: 274). They provide an example of a traffic accident: one cannot stage a traffic accident in the interests of research (though, of course, one can set up a simulation). Goldthorpe (2007a: 212) provides a further example of this, in the case of marital instability and its effects on children, asking whether the children of couples who separate fare better by the break-up or whether they would have fared better if the family had remained together. In this case the effect is the observed behaviour. The difficulty here is that one cannot have the same couple both separating and not separating (Holland's (1986: 947) 'fundamental problem of causal inference'), nor can one break up a family in the interests of the research (i.e. manipulating a causal intervention). However, one can examine children from families who, ceteris paribus, did and did not break up. Children and families who were sufficiently similar on the characteristics deemed to be important could be examined, and then the research could study the effects of separation and non-separation on the children, i.e. careful matching and then studying the two sub-samples to identify the effects.

Holland's (1986, 2004) 'fundamental problem of causal inference' is important. Schneider et al. (2007: 13) suggest that it comes into being once one accepts that a causal effect is the difference between what would have happened to a person in an experiment if he or she had been in the experimental group (receiving the intervention) and if the same person had been in the control group (the counterfactual argument, i.e. if he or she had not been in the experimental group or had not been in the control group). However, this is impossible to test empirically, as the person cannot be in both groups.

Holland (1986: 947) suggests a scientific and a statistical solution to this problem: the scientific solution is to assume invariance or homogeneity (e.g. a block of wood is a block of wood is a block of wood; it can be kept unchanged!); the statistical solution is randomization and the measurement of average effects. Schneider et al. (2007: 13–15) make several suggestions to address Holland's problem.

- Place the person first in the control group and then in the experimental group (which assumes temporal stability (cf. Holland 1986: 948), i.e. the fact that there are two time periods should make no difference to the results, there being a constancy of response regardless of time).
- Assume or demonstrate that the placement of the person in the first group does not affect him or her for long enough to contaminate (affect) his or her response to being in the second group (the causal transience effect) (cf. Holland 1986: 948).

- Assume that all the participants are identical in every respect (which may be possible in the physical sciences but questionably so in the human sciences, even in twin studies: Holland's (1986: 947) *scientific solution*).
- Focus on the *average* results (Holland's (1986: 948) *statistical solution*), for example the *average* scores on the pre-test and post-test, which may be useful unless it masks important differences between sub-sets of the two samples, for example, students with a high IQ and students with a low IQ may perform very differently, but this would be lost in an average, in which case stratification into sub-samples can be adopted. Random allocation to the control and experimental group is one way of addressing this.

In many cases the natural experiment is seeking to establish causes from effects, and we turn to this in the next chapter.

Implications for researchers:

- Laboratory, field and natural experiments are useful, but each has its own variants, strengths and weaknesses.
- Laboratory experiments may be strong on control but weak on the non-laboratory reality.
- Field experiments may be strong on reality but weak on controls.
- Natural experiments are useful where there are ethical or practical problems, and these are often *post hoc*, determining causes from effects.

It is important to raise some concerns about the experimental method *per se*, principally the extent to which it is practicable and desirable in educational research (see also Cohen *et al.* 2007: Chaps 2, 6 and 13). Three main kinds of experiment have been indicated above: laboratory (RCTs), field and natural. Each of these may raise questions of desirability and practicability. The laboratory experiment raises doubts about realism: what happens in the antiseptic, sanitized world of the laboratory may not happen in the outside world of the classroom and school. The field experiment raises doubts about isolation and control of variables, and the natural experiment raises doubts about the accuracy of causal inference, as it is not possible to isolate and control variables.

In terms of *desirability*, one has to question the acceptability of employing a model from the natural sciences (the experimental method is often called the 'agricultural method') in the human sciences, as it smacks of unacceptable control, manipulation and the treatment of participants as instruments and inanimate objects rather than as subjects. Further, if we believe that an intervention may bring benefit to a group, then what right have we to deny it to an experimental group?

In terms of *practicability* there is the issue of how far it is actually possible, even if considered desirable (or not undesirable), to identify, isolate and control all the myriad variables/conditions involved in human behaviour. The examples earlier, of interventions that may or may not produce an effect, depending on the participants and not on the intervention, serve to point out the difficulties faced here. As was mentioned then, the same intervention may produce huge effects, no effects, minimal effects, or diverse effects with different groups at the same time or with the same group at different times.

How do we know whether we have included, excluded, isolated and controlled all the relevant factors? How do we know that the two groups, even if randomly allocated, are matched in terms of all the relevant factors (the only way we have of ensuring an absolute match is to have the same group being both the experimental and the control group, but this is impossible). As was mentioned in Chapter 3, causation concerns probabilities rather than exactitude.

Also in terms of practicability, there are several threats to the internal and external validity and reliability of the experimental method (Campbell and Stanley 1963; Cook and Campbell 1979; Cohen *et al.* 2007: Chap. 13; Schneider *et al.* 2007: 20–6). In terms of internal validity these include history, maturation, statistical regression, testing, instrumentation, selection, sampling, experimental mortality, instrument reactivity, the selection–maturation interaction, motivation and interest in the task, and the conditions of the experiment (see Campbell and Stanley (1963) and Cohen *et al.* (2007: chap. 13) for further explanations here).

Threats to *external* validity are likely to limit the degree to which generalizations can be made from the particular experimental conditions to other populations or settings: failure to describe independent variables explicitly, lack of representativeness of available and target populations, the Hawthorne effect, inadequate operationalizing of dependent variables, sensitization/reactivity to experimental conditions, interaction effects of extraneous factors and experimental treatments, invalidity or unreliability of instruments, ecological invalidity, and inappropriate time scale and timing of the intervention and the post-test (too short an intervention and the results may not show themselves, even though there may be some difference; too soon or too late a post-test and the results may not have shown themselves or have faded away respectively).

External validity also concerns *Type I* and *Type II errors*: a Type I error is committed where the researcher rejects the null hypothesis when it is in fact true (akin to convicting an innocent person); this can be addressed by setting a more rigorous level of significance (e.g. $\rho < .01$ rather than $\rho < .05$). A Type II error is committed where the null hypothesis is accepted when it is in fact not true (akin to finding a guilty person innocent). A Type II error may occur if (a) the measurement of a response to the intervention is insufficiently valid; (b) the measurement of the intervention is insufficiently relevant; (c) the statistical power of the experiment is too low; (d) the wrong population was selected for the intervention. This can be addressed by reducing the level of significance (e.g. $\rho < .20$ or $\rho < .30$ rather than $\rho < .05$). Of course, the more one reduces the chance of a Type I error the more chance there is of committing a Type II error, and vice versa. In qualitative data, a Type I error occurs when a statement is believed when it is, in fact, untrue, and a Type II error occurs when a statement is rejected when it is in fact true (Cohen *et al.* 2007: 145).

Schneider *et al.* (2007: 20–6) also discuss important issues in threats to randomization of allocation, accounting for atypical responses, how to handle different forms of non-compliance (e.g. partial or total participation or non-participation), attrition and reluctance of institutions to participate (addressed, for example by having two or more experiments running simultaneously in two or more schools, with each school participating in more than just one experiment, being a control group in one experiment and an experimental group in the other experiment). They also indicate that the statistical power of the experiment (i.e. its ability to detect a true effect of the intervention) may be increased by having large samples.

Implications for researchers:

- Issues of ethics, desirability and practicability can be paramount in the planning and conduct of experiments.
- There are many threats to the reliability and validity of experiments, and researchers need to address these in the stages of planning, implementation, analysis and drawing conclusions.
- Threats to the reliability and validity of experiments are both internal and external. These may reduce the power of establishing the effects of causes in experiments.

So far, this chapter has considered the determination of effects from causes in terms of the introduction and manipulation of factors in action research and experiments. The story does not remain there, for in everyday life we do not necessarily operate in these somewhat contrived circumstances, but nevertheless causal manipulation is present where researchers are seeking to produce and understand effects. This may take the form of deliberate intervention or everyday causal sequencing. In the qualitative domain this can be evidenced in ethnographic studies in which participant observation takes place. Such an approach – the 'observer as participant' – is more interventionist than that of the 'participant as observer' or the 'non-participant observer', in that the researcher (the outsider) intrudes into the everyday world of the participants, whereas in the latter it is the everyday participants (the insiders) themselves who go about their business and who determine what they will do, largely or completely undisturbed by the presence – or intervention – of the researcher.

Let us take the two cases separately: (a) causation and observation by the natural, internal participants themselves (i.e. excluding the external researcher) and (b) participant observation by the external researcher. Both of these take place in their natural settings, and neither of them involves the level of control and manipulation evidenced in experimental methods.

Implications for researchers:

- Participant and non-participant observation in ethnographic methodologies can yield causal explanations of *explananda*.
- Understanding causation in qualitative research embraces human intentionality and agency.
- Causal explanations of effects in natural settings can be powerful in understanding causal processes.

An example of causation and observation by the natural, internal participants: the participant as observer

In the case of the participant as observer, let us consider the example of the secondary-school principal who, believing that there is inertia in terms of school development that is due, in part, to the staff having too comfortable and consensual a life, deliberately causes disequilibrium amongst the staff by saying that the children's performance in science is not as good as their performance in mathematics, based on test results, that this is unacceptable and that teachers have to shoulder the responsibility for this. Underpinning this action appears to be the belief (the theory?) that disequilibrium in the staff causes school development effects. The staff meeting takes place at which the principal makes his or her announcement about the difference in the mathematics and science scores, the unacceptability of that difference, the apportioning of blame to the teachers, and the need for the situation to change. The staff sit in silence throughout. The principal leaves the meeting. Subsequently he or she watches what happens over time as a result.

Let us return to the staff meeting after the principal has left. Firstly there is mutual support by the staff for each other, united in their rejection of the principal's view that somehow the teachers are to blame for the students' differential performance in science and mathematics. Then an aspiring junior member of staff suggests that there may be some truth in the principal's view, and that it should be considered seriously rather than just being rejected out of hand. At first this causes antagonism from the remainder of the staff, as it is regarded as 'breaking ranks' and that, on these kinds of occasion, staff should close ranks rather than expose themselves to the risk of being divided and, thereby, ruled. But the teacher persists, and the meeting moves towards a decision that possible reasons for the differences will be explored and that a subsequent staff meeting will pool ideas on this and how to address it. The meeting disbands.

The next day there starts a whispering campaign by some staff against the individual teacher who spoke out; this festers and spreads into micro-political antagonisms between the mathematics and science teachers, each blaming the others for what has happened. The mathematics teachers blame the science teachers for causing the ire of the principal and for not doing their job properly. The science teachers blame the mathematics teachers for not standing up to the principal and for not showing solidarity with the science teachers' views that students found science less interesting, less relevant and more difficult, and that there were insufficient science resources or teachers in the school compared with the mathematics department.

Then teachers from other departments become involved, saying that there are major differences between the departments: the mathematics department has more teachers and these teachers are more experienced, they have smaller classes, more teaching periods and more support from parents, and, actually, given the advantages, the students should have done even better than they did in terms of test performance. Other teachers take the opposing view, saying that the science department plans and works together much more collegially and democratically than the mathematics department, that the young science teachers are more enthusiastic than the mathematics teachers, that their teaching strategies are much more active and engaging than the dry, dull, routine, traditional didacticism of the mathematics teachers, and that this is not reflected in naïve tests of performance. The two camps separate into those who value traditionalism and content over those who value experiential learning and process approaches to knowledge.

Other teachers remain silent, apathetic and uninvolved – they want an easy life and do not wish to become embroiled in in-fighting that they see is irrelevant to their own situation; such apathy angers other teachers and positive relationships wither even further.

Time marches on; teachers stop communicating with each other, the two departments become Balkanized, and conflicts and silence between individual teachers, together with cliques, increase. The science teachers feel resentful, and some leave at the end of the year. The mathematics teachers, crowing at their success, do nothing. The principal, observing what is happening, creates a new curriculum development team and promotes some staff to develop the mathematics and science curriculum in tandem. Two years later the results of the student science and mathematics test performance match each other more closely, and are high.

What has happened here? A cause – the creation of disequilibrium – eventually has brought about an effect: school development that leads to the rise in the science scores and the parity between the students' test scores in mathematics and science. It is a more natural rather than a more contrived occurrence/intervention in the way that an experiment is a contrived occurrence or intervention. But the causal chain is much more complex than a simple or single cause leading to a single effect. Put diagrammatically, it appears as in Figure 5.3. What we have here is intentionality at work, agency and reaction. It is obvious, too, that there is no singular or simple nexus between original cause and effect; a causal line or causal process is at work here; between the initial cause and the final effect comes a sequence of contiguous, mediating events that subsequently lead to the effect.

But wait: at exactly what point is the disequilibrium occurring and at exactly what point is the school development occurring? There are neither single nor discrete causes and effects, and this rehearses the point made in Chapter 2, that causes and events may overlap. It becomes clear that manipulating a cause may bring about an effect, but not directly and, indeed, not always as anticipated.

Implications for researchers:

- Between a manipulated cause and an observed effect there are many contiguous causal processes that need to be addressed.
- Causal lines and causal chains can be established in understanding causal mechanisms in qualitative research.
- The relationship between causes and effects can be direct, indirect, mediated and non-straightforward in qualitative research.

An example of participant observation of cause and effect by the external researcher: the observer as participant

In the case of the observer as participant, let us take the example of the researcher who is studying the effects of gender on educational choice amongst working-class girls. Let us imagine that the researcher studies a group of working-class, teenage girls who are considering educational choices and future aspirations (cf. Sharpe 1976, 1994). The researcher goes into a school and takes on a role as a leader of a small, marginal extra-curricular activity, for example an art class. During this activity she holds informal conversations with the girls and discovers, early on, that their aspirations are very limited and traditionally stereotyped: they largely seek low-level service occupations requiring

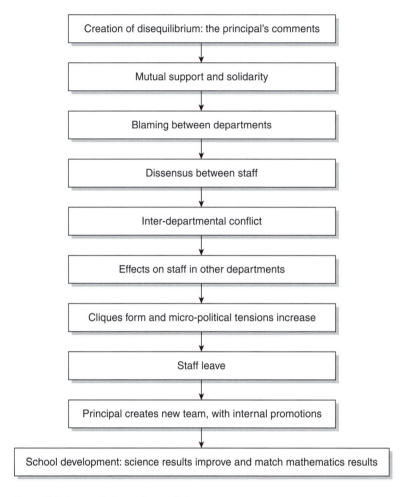

Figure 5.3 A causal chain of many links

minimal educational qualifications or specific short-term training; a steady relationship with a partner or marriage; having children; having fun; and traditional gender-stereotyped occupations, e.g. office work, teaching, nursing, working with children, or hairdressing. The girls say that they are not capable of doing more than this, and that they should only be concerned with 'girls' work'. The researcher raises the question of whether they are content with this prospective situation.

During the course of the time that she spends with the girls, the researcher discusses a range of other possible educational and career options, challenging what she regards as their gender stereotypes and low aspirations. Towards the end of her time in the school she returns to the questions about their educational and occupational choice. This time the same girls indicate that they are considering banking and financial services, professional occupations (e.g. lawyer, doctor, airline pilot), photography, graphic design, journalism, psychiatry, environmental protection work, pharmacy, car mechanics and engineering, fire-fighting, theatre and music. The range of occupations is much wider, the level of demand is higher (requiring extended and high-level education), and the more traditional post-school options are relegated to a much lower position. The intervention – the discussions with the girls – has had an effect: the significant expansion of career options and educational choices.

The cause (the discussions) may bring about the effect directly, indirectly, in a delayed sequence or immediately. Let us say that different events occur in the lives of some of the girls during the initial and the final discussions with the researcher. For example, one girl might discuss the matter with her parents; another might go home and search the internet for possible careers and how to pursue them; another may argue with her parents, who want her to marry and have children; the girls may meet up socially outside school and discuss the matter; another girl may think no more about it; another girl may challenge the researcher and say that it is none of her business.

Further, after the initial discussions, the researcher may realize that, if she were simply to report the girl's low aspirations, conditioning and horizons, then she may be doing little to advance the cause of women in the workplace and in careers, i.e. reporting the situation as it is might be counter-productive to the empowerment and emancipation of working-class girls, may reflect their false consciousness and, in fact, may have the girls presenting themselves in a poor light that may not do justice to their own best interests. So she decides to pursue the issues in subsequent discussions. Whether or not that is a legitimate role of a researcher – a deliberate interventionist strategy, justified on the ethical grounds of 'beneficence' (bringing benefit to the participants) – is outside the present discussion; the point is that she did.

So, between the initial cause and the final effect is a chain of factors, which can be represented diagrammatically as in Figure 5.4. As with the previous example, there is no singular or simple direct nexus between cause and effect; a causal chain/line or process is at work here; between the initial cause and the final effect come a sequence of contiguous, mediating events that subsequently lead to the effect. Similarly, one can observe that the sub-effects contained within the overall area 'effect' commence before all the sub-causes contained within the label 'cause' have been completed. As with the previous example, there are neither single nor discrete causes and effects, again rehearsing Chapter 2's comment that causes and effects may overlap. It becomes clear that manipulating a cause may bring about an effect, but not directly, and maybe not always as anticipated.

Implications for researchers:

- Between a manipulated cause and an observed effect there are many contiguous and simultaneous causal processes that need to be addressed, as they influence the outcomes, the effects.
- Causal lines, causal chains and the interactions of events have to be established in understanding causal mechanisms in qualitative research.
- The relationship between causes and effects can be direct, indirect, mediated and non-straightforward in qualitative research.
- The term 'cause' is an umbrella term for several sub-causes.
- Causes are not necessarily discrete.
- Effects are not necessarily discrete.

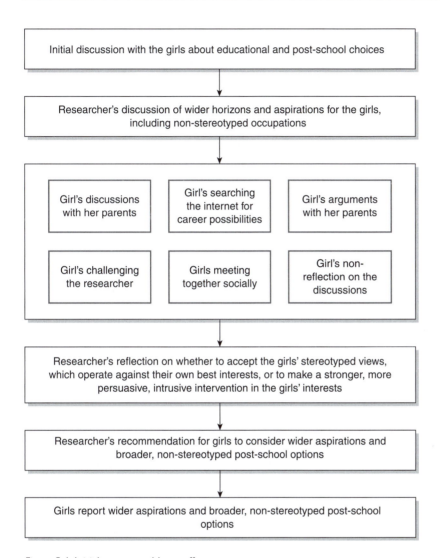

Figure 5.4 Initial causes and later effects

- The term 'effect' is an umbrella term for several sub-effects.
- Causes and effects may overlap in time.
- Researchers must consider the acceptability of a non-neutral researcher, i.e. a researcher who has a substantive agenda or interests (e.g. political, social, ethnic, class, gender, egalitarian) that he or she is intending to pursue through his or her research, i.e. the research is not 'disinterested'.

The timing of data collection points

On several occasions this chapter has alluded to the dangers of poor timing of the measurement or ascertaining of effects: the data collection points. Experimental procedures are prone to problems of timing – too soon and the effect may not be noticed; too late and the effect might have gone or have been submerged by other matters. Experiments typically suffer from the problem of having only two time points for measurement: the pre-test and the post-test, and this leads researchers to focus on 'state variables' rather than causal chains and networks (Hage and Meeker 1988: 171). As indicated in the earlier part of this chapter, these offer little opportunity for identifying causal processes and mechanisms at work. The choice of timing of measurements or data collection for establishing causation is crucial and varies with the purposes of the research. The frequency of the data collection varies with the phenomenon under investigation, the scope of the phenomenon, the overall time scale of the phenomenon, the speed at which the dependent variable is likely to change, and the level of detailed causal explanation required.

Sometimes micro-time is important (e.g. the intervals of just a few seconds, as in the data collection for the ORACLE studies in the 1980s (Galton and Simon 1980)). In other research a longer time frame is more suitable. For example, if one wishes to conduct a panel study (interviewing the same people at different points in their lives, maybe to ask them retrospective questions) then a long time period between data collection points may be acceptable, e.g. three, four or five years. This enables changes in participants' life conditions to have taken place and for these changes to have had effects on their lives, whereas, for example, if the data collection period had been a matter of only a few weeks then no such changes might have been observable. Rather than fixing a specific time, it may be the events themselves that dictate the moment of the data collection, so that, for example, changes are reported when they occur.

The rule of thumb here is that, the more accurately we wish to know the causal sequences, the more frequently and closer together must be the data collection points. As the number of time points for data collection increases, so does the likelihood of making correct causal inferences and establishing correct causal processes, chains, lines and networks. The second rule of thumb is that, the more complex is the phenomenon under investigation, i.e. the more possible causal lines and chains there are in a network of causation, the more time points for data collection might be necessary in order to understand the causation at work. Hage and Meeker (1988: 177) comment that most causal processes are either not observable or not easily observable, i.e. inference overrules description. The shorter and more frequent are the time intervals and times of data collection respectively, the more the causal inferences become a matter of fact rather than of faith.

If we wish to understand causation at work then rich data are necessary. Hence, concomitant with the first two rules of thumb comes the third rule of thumb: the more we wish to understand causation and causal processes, then the more it is that qualitative data may be useful, as they often have much greater explanatory potential than numerical data. Qualitative data can be ongoing and in-depth, and they can indicate causation at work, action narratives and agency within broader conditions and constraints. Consider clinical case studies of individuals, with probing, in-depth interviews, which may have masses of rich qualitative, observational, interview and field note data that, thereby, enable researchers to understand the processes and mechanisms of causation at work in terms of agency and structure (external factors). Participant observation, rather than being an epiphenomenon in the battery of data collection methods, becomes important in understanding causation at work. This is potentiated when used in combination with other qualitative methods (e.g. Hage and Meeker 1988: 179), not least because observation on its own does not establish causation, as much causation is unobservable.

Ethnography may have the edge over experimentation in understanding causation in the real world of education rather than in the laboratory. Indeed representative sampling may not provide any more understanding of causation than a non-representative sample, as – at the risk of tautology – causation is about causes and effects and not about numbers or kinds of people. Further, understanding the mind of one highly disturbed student in detail may yield more about causal processes in deviance than any amount of randomized controlled trials or hundreds of quick-fire answers given to low-level interview questions. The case for qualitative data in the understanding of causation and causal processes is powerful. At the start of this book it was suggested that, as causal mechanisms are not usually observable, the discovery of causes, causal processes and mechanisms is difficult and tentative; in this enterprise qualitative data may even become pre-eminent.

Hage and Meeker (1988: 173), further, argue that, generally speaking, longitudinal data may be more useful than cross-sectional studies in understanding causation and causal processes, not least because causation has a significant temporal dimension. They also consider that quasi-experiments may have the upper hand over true experiments in establishing causation as they can involve multiple time points (ibid.: 172). Similarly, they suggest that that prediction studies may also be useful tools in establishing causation (ibid.: 174), both if the predictions come true and if they do not, and providing that careful planning of the putative outcome of the prediction is undertaken. Indeed they suggest that combining prediction studies with action research presents a formidable means of identifying causation (ibid.) (though they overlook the dangers of the self-fulfilling prophecy here). So the fourth rule of thumb here is that, the more the researcher wishes to understand causal processes, the more methods in combination are useful, each with their own time frames and timing of data collection, i.e. triangulation of time, methodologies, researchers and instruments, even if the price of this is data overload.

Implications for researchers:

- The more accurately we wish to know the causal sequences, the more data collection points are required and the more frequently and closer together these must be.
- As the number of time points for data collection increases, so does the likelihood of making correct causal inferences and establishing correct causal processes, chains, lines and networks.
- The more complex is the phenomenon under investigation, the more time points for data collection might be necessary in order to understand causation.
- The more we wish to understand causation, the more that qualitative data may be useful.
- Participant observation holds a high position in providing data for explanation of causation.
- Prediction studies and quasi-experimental approaches may be useful for gaining understanding of causation, but prediction is not the same as causation.
- The more the researcher wishes to understand causal processes, the more methods in combination are useful, each with their own time frames and timing of data collection.

The problem of personal perception:
the base rate fallacy

It has been argued that causal explanations of the effects of causes have to take account of human agency, intentionality and perceptions. A difficulty arises here, in that humans may not perceive the situation accurately. As Thomas (1928) famously remarked: 'if men [*sic*] define their situations as real then they are real in their consequences'. If I think that there is a mouse under the table then I will act as though there is a mouse under the table, whether there is or not. The problem may be that, in fact, there is no mouse, and my perception is wrong. I may misjudge the situation. As has been seen throughout this book, context and conditions play a large causal role in determining effects. An important message is that humans influence causes; their perceptions of causes, behaviours, events and possible effects exert a causal influence.

People may misperceive and misjudge a situation. A notable example of this is 'the base rate fallacy'. Novemsky and Kronzon (1999) report Kahneman's and Tversky's (1973) example of this in operation. In the example a description is provided of Jack, a 45-year-old man who is married with four children, and who is generally conservative, careful, and ambitious. Jack shows no interest in political and social issues, indeed he spends most of his free time on hobbies such as home carpentry, sailing, and mathematical puzzles (Kahneman and Tversky 1973: 241). In a piece of research, one group of participants was told that this description had been randomly drawn from a pool of descriptions that consisted of 70 engineers and 30 lawyers, whilst another group of participants was told that 'the pool consisted of 70 engineers and 70 lawyers' (Novemsky and Kronzon 1999: 55). The two groups in the research were asked to assess the probability of Jack being an engineer. The results were startling, even counter-intuitive: regardless of the two different pieces of information given about the different make-up of the pool of descriptions, the participants in both groups indicated that there was a 90 per cent probability that Jack was an engineer – they ignored the actual evidence provided and acted on their personal views.

Another example from Tversky and Kahneman (1980: 62) concerns a witness giving evidence in court:

- a taxi-cab was involved in a night-time hit-and-run accident;
- there are two taxi-cab companies in the city: the Green and the Blue;
- 85% of the taxi-cabs belong to the Green company;
- 15% of the taxi-cabs belong to the Blue company.

The witness said that it was the Blue taxi-cab that was involved, and the court tested the witness's ability to identify taxi-cabs under given conditions of visibility. The witness was given a sample of taxi-cabs to identify, half of which were from the Green company and half of which were from the Blue company. The witness identified the taxi-cabs correctly in 80 per cent of the cases and incorrectly in 20 per cent of the cases. The question is raised of the probability that the cab involved in the hit-and-run accident was from the Blue company rather than the Green company (quoted in Harnad 2006: 1).

The exact probability is calculated thus:

$$P(H\backslash D) = \frac{P(D\backslash H)P(H)}{P(D\backslash H)P(H) + P(D\backslash H^1)P(H^1)} = \frac{P(D \mid H)P(H)}{P(D \mid H)P(H) + P(D/H)}$$

$$= \frac{0.80 \times 0.15}{(0.80 \times 0.15) + (0.20 \times 0.85)} = 0.414$$

where:

$P(H\backslash D)$ = the probability that the cab involved in the accident was Blue rather than Green);

$P(D|H)$ = the probability of D, given H;

D = datum: there was no accident; and

H = hypothesis to evaluate: it was a blue cab.

You don't need to understand the mathematics in order to appreciate the point! Most people, it is reported, would say that the probability was about 80 per cent, whereas, in fact, the probability is around 41 per cent (41.4 per cent). They ignore the prior probability $P(H)$, i.e. they ignore some of the details and act on their own judgement rather than on the evidence of the population (Harnad 1996: 1). Koehler (1996: 3–4) argues that people tend to ignore base-rate data and tend to ground base their judgments solely or largely on the similarity between their own personality and the situation (e.g. counter-transference), overlooking the real situation and the real numbers. The point here is that humans may respond to information selectively, and this extends to considerations of causation and effect: humans change causes and effects, based on a range of factors, including their perceptions and understandings. As Morrison (1998: 15) wrote: 'change changes people and people change change', and much of causation is about change.

Implications for researchers:

- Participants and researchers do not always make accurate judgments of situations on the evidence placed before them. Human judgement influences the effects of causes and the interpretation of effects.
- Human behaviour, attitudes, perceptions, values, beliefs, actions and interactions affect relationships between causes and effects, modifying, reducing, increasing and changing both the causes and the effects.

So, can we derive or determine effects from causes? Clearly we can, but only under certain conditions. These include that the lines of genuine causation, the necessary and sufficient conditions and the causal chains or causal lines are established, that causal processes and mechanisms (rather than simply input and output variables) and human agency are included, that alternative explanations for the effects are weighed and eliminated from or included in the discussion as appropriate, that reliability, validity and appropriate sampling have been achieved, that causal manipulation is recognized as not operating like an input–output 'black-box', that causes have several sub-components that need to be addressed, and that antecedents, just as effects, have several sub-components and antecedents that need to be addressed. Causal manipulation to produce a desired effect can operate in action research, experimental research and qualitative research of various hues, both with non-participant and with participant observation.

Taking stock

This chapter has indicated that determining the effects of causes can lend itself to an interventionist strategy in educational research, installing an intervention either to test out a causal influence or a causal model, or because it is already known that it may exert a causal influence on effects, i.e. manipulating variables in order to produce effects. Manipulation takes many forms, and these were indicated at the start of the chapter. The chapter has taken three kinds intervention and examined their nature and potential contribution to determining the effects of causes:

- action research, which has problems of rigour when no external checks and controls are employed such that the attribution of causation may be misplaced;
- a range of experimental approaches, which assume, perhaps either incorrectly or unacceptably, that variables and people can be isolated, controlled and manipulated; and
- participant and non-participant observation in qualitative research.

In addressing these approaches, however, it was indicated that serious attention had to be paid to a range of factors:

- the context of the intervention, as the 'power of the situation' could affect the outcomes and behaviours of participants;
- the same causes do not always produce the same effects;
- inappropriate timing of the post-test measurements of effects could undermine the reliability of the statement of the effects of the cause;
- there is a problem of accuracy, as groups and individuals cannot be in both a group that is and a group that is not receiving an intervention;
- process variables and factors, and not only input variables, feature in understanding causation;
- the characteristics, personae and specific individual features of participants, and their agency, influence interventions and their effects;
- problems of internal and external reliability and validity have to be addressed.

Randomized controlled trials (RCTs) were taken as an example of strongly interventionist approaches, and these, too, were shown to be problematic in determining the effects of causes, for three reasons:

- judging 'what works' on the basis of their findings could be misleading, not least because of the impact of theories of chaos and complexity;
- judging 'what works' is an incomplete analysis of the situation under investigation, and a more fitting question should be 'What works for whom, under what conditions, according to what criteria, and with what consequences for participants?';
- judging 'what works' is a matter of values and not only of performance.

Whilst RCTs can provide data to inform decisions about 'what works', they can indicate unequivocally 'what works'. And although RCTs are one kind of experimental approach, the chapter also indicated several other kinds, for example, laboratory experiments, field experiments and natural experiments. These, too, are prone to problems of reliability and validity.

As an alternative to experimental approaches in determining the effects of causes, the chapter also indicated the possibilities for participant and non-participant observation. Examples were given that indicated the potential for establishing causal chains and causal lines in qualitative educational research.

It was argued that interventionist approaches, and the determination of the effects of causes, risk mixing perception with fact, and the example of the base rate fallacy was provided to indicated how, regardless of evidence, human inclinations may be to judge data and situations on the basis of one's own perceptions and opinions that, indeed, may fly in the face of evidence. Clearly this is only one source of unreliability, and the chapter argued for careful consideration of what actually are the effects of causes, rather then rushings to statements of premature connections.

Chapter 6

Determining causes from effects

Introduction

We observe an event and then we seek to explain its cause. This is commonplace. A person contracts lung cancer; what caused it? There was a traffic accident; what caused it? A school's public examination results are outstandingly high; why? The staff turnover in a school suddenly escalates; why? The researcher is looking for the causes of effects. The determination of causes from effects is rather like forensic investigations in police detection. Detectives work forensically and meticulously, looking for motives, the chain of events, the details of the events, working on clues and hypotheses; so it is with piecing together causes from an examination of the effects. It is provisional, probabilistic, uncertain, and requires scrupulous attention to detail: high 'granularity'.

Unlike the previous chapter, which concerned the determination of effects from causes, i.e. working with causes that one can observe and manipulate, this chapter enters the much more inferential, tentative, hypothetical work of backtracking from effects to possible causes. As Scheines (1997: 189) remarks, we cannot manipulate an effect and hope or expect to change its causes; cause and effect are asymmetrical. Much social science does not have the luxury of being able to conduct a true experiment, and the researcher has to work with non-experimental data (McKim 1997: 11), e.g. surveys, time-series measurements, cross-sectional observations, panel or longitudinal data (Clogg and Haritou 1997: 83) and qualitative studies. As in criminal cases, in working from effect to cause the researcher has to establish 'beyond reasonable doubt' what is being inferred, and similarly, as in legal cases, the 'burden of proof' is on the researcher to establish the cause.

Working backwards from effects to establishing their causes is difficult. As Chomsky's (1959) withering critique of Skinner's behaviourism argued, we simply cannot infer causes from effects, a stimulus from a response. Indeed the successionist conceptualization of causality (Harré 1972), wherein researchers make inferences about causality on the basis of observation, has limitations in really understanding *how* an intervention or set of actions actually work in practice, and yet it is precisely this *explanatory* understanding that is required. The task of identifying causes from effects is not straightforward. Consider the case study that follows.

A case study: Catherine's chemistry

In this fictitious example, Catherine is a Form 5 teenager studying chemistry. At the start of the school year she was keen to learn about chemistry and to understand the subject. She would come to the lessons enthusiastic and motivated; her mother worked in the pathology laboratory of a local hospital, and Catherine's interest was encouraged by her family. At the beginning of the year the chemistry lessons were interesting for the students: the teacher devised work that she knew would engage them, preparing experiments with chemical reactions, and examining the properties of chemicals and their applications in everyday life. After practical work the students would study various formulae and write up the experiments, learning how to operate as 'real scientists' in laboratories.

Catherine enjoyed the work and gained a good understanding of key concepts in chemistry; she willingly followed up the school sessions with homework, which was stimulating, as it built on, applied and extended the school experiences. Chemistry became her favourite subject, and she said that she wanted to become a chemist when she left school, working in the petrochemical industry.

The teacher prepared imaginative and varied teaching and some interesting homework. She discussed with the students how they liked to learn, she listened carefully to what they had to say, and she acted on this. The teacher liked the students and clearly enjoyed the teaching. Catherine's rate of learning of new knowledge was rapid, and her motivation was high. Though there were only three chemistry lessons each week, Catherine would look forward to them and would spend some of her time investigating the topics on her own, reading avidly and searching for materials connected with the chemistry work at school.

The teacher was highly successful and, indeed, six months into the school year she was promoted to another school to become head of the science department. Catherine's new teacher was young, with a degree in chemistry. This was her first job. To be supportive towards the new teacher the school provided close details of the syllabus, together with useful textbooks, details of practical work to do, assessment arrangements, and copies of supporting materials, e.g. worksheets and charts, ideas for teaching chemistry concepts, and computer programs to support teaching and learning.

Shortly after the arrival of the new teacher Catherine's interest in chemistry started to wane. At first her parents thought it was just a reaction to the change of teacher, and that Catherine was mature enough to be able to handle this, given a little time. However, Catherine's marks for, and interest in, chemistry dropped steadily. She complained that all they ever did in chemistry in school was to look at chemical formulae, learn facts from the textbook, and copy notes from the whiteboard. Catherine told her mother that her teacher complained a lot about the class, about how lazy they were and how, because there were only three lessons a week, the students would have to work faster and harder. She said that the teacher had told them that, because they could not be bothered to learn the materials from the book and the whiteboard, she would have to test them more frequently. The effect of this was that Catherine stopped her own private work on chemistry at home and, instead, concentrated on the tests. However, her marks continued to fall.

Catherine's mother asked her what was the matter, and Catherine just started to cry and didn't say anything. So her mother contacted the school and asked to see the chemistry teacher. Catherine's mother met the teacher, who simply told the mother that she should be much firmer with Catherine and force her to study harder because she was poor. Her mother pointed out that Catherine had enjoyed chemistry with the previous teacher, and that she had been very keen on the subject. The teacher simply shrugged this off, saying that at this stage of the year Catherine had to grow up and face the fact that there was some difficult chemistry to be learned, that there was no short cut to this, and it would mean that Catherine would have to study the books and notes much more carefully and learn them. Further, the teacher said that she was shocked at how little Catherine's class of students knew about chemistry, and that it was very important for Catherine to complete the set work or else she would not be able to complete the Form 5 syllabus.

Catherine's mother asked why the teacher had stopped doing practical work with the students, to which the reply came that there was no time for this, and that it was a luxury for which they had insufficient time because they were behind with the syllabus and the students had not learned enough. The mother asked the teacher why she thought Catherine's interest had diminished, and pointed out the change in Catherine's attitude, indeed that she no longer took any active interest in the subject on her own, and that she was bored with learning so many facts, and could not see the point of this. Her teacher simply said that she was not responsible for the students' attitudes, that the students had to 'get their own heads straight' about learning, and that there were things in life which had to be done, whether we like it or not, and that this was an important lesson for Catherine to learn.

The teacher said that she was doing all she could to help the students, telling them exactly what to learn, when to learn, how to learn, and what would be tested, so much that the students almost didn't have to think for themselves. The mother, she said, should be grateful to her for this, not seeking to defend her daughter's poor attitude and results.

Catherine's mother said that she had noticed that the quality of Catherine's work in chemistry had become poor, and that the level of demand seemed to have dropped over time – that her teacher seemed to be accepting poor results. Her teacher said that this was exactly the problem that she – the teacher – was facing, as the students could not be bothered to apply themselves now that the work was becoming more demanding, and that, if she had not lowered her demand, then all of the class would fail. They were not at school simply for fun, and they were not a good class of students. Further, the teacher reprimanded Catherine's mother for even trying to defend Catherine: could she not see, she asked the mother, that Catherine was manipulating her and that the problem lay with Catherine herself?

Catherine's mother told her daughter what had happened. Catherine promised to try harder and to do what the teacher required. Her test scores went up, and she passed. The students' results at the end of the school year were solid, though not excellent; the principal congratulated the teacher. Catherine never followed up her chemistry either in the remainder of her time at school or afterwards.

What are causes of Catherine's decisions never to return to chemistry? Are they, for example:

1   the move away from practical work;
2   the loss of enjoyment of chemistry lessons;
3   unstimulating lessons;
4   arid teaching and learning;
5   overreliance on the textbook;
6   adolescent volatility;
7   Catherine's immaturity;

8   the change of teacher;
9   Catherine's finding something more interesting to do;
10 the decline in Catherine's marks;
11 the reaction of the teacher to the poor standard of chemistry in the class;
12 the reaction of the teacher to the students' lack of application in chemistry;
13 the increase in rote learning;
14 the increase in learning of facts at the expense practical investigation;
15 Catherine's diminishing interest in, and motivation for, chemistry;
16 the increase in tests in chemistry;
17 the new teacher's inexperience;
18 the decrease in the time that Catherine spent at home on chemistry;
19 unrealistic pressure from the teacher;
20 the teacher's negative opinion of Catherine and the class;
21 the mother's intervention at the school;
22 the teacher's overbearing and uncompromising attitude;
23 the teacher's intemperate and harsh response to the mother;
24 the refusal of the teacher to accept blame for the situation;
25 the lowering of the quality of Catherine's work;
26 the pressure to pass;
27 the timetabling, such that insufficient time was available for chemistry;
28 Catherine's wilful and unreasonable behaviour;
29 the fact that Catherine's mother had a profession and there was pressure on Catherine to main the professional class status;
30 the combination or cumulative effects of some or all of (1)–(29) or of other causes.

It is possible to generate a list like this of possible causes in just a few minutes. Clearly it is any or all of these, either singly, in combination, or all together, or, indeed, there may be other causes that are not included here. Which are the strong and which are the weak causes? Which seem more plausible than others? Are there further causes behind the presenting causes (the symptoms), for example: (a) the nature of chemistry; (b) peer group behaviour; (c) theories of motivation, including problems of motivation in teenagers; (d) theories of pedagogy, including traditional teaching; (e) theories of inter-personal relationships; (f) theories of social structure and mobility (the pressure to avoid downward social mobility between generations); (g) theories of the optimization of teaching times; (h) theories of adolescent personality development; (i) theories of agency and intentionality; and so on. There is a huge range of possibilities here. (One potential way of discovering which ones are correct/incorrect/strong/weak, etc., or, indeed if there are others, would be simply to talk to Catherine, using the checklist as prompts and probes, and discovering through an in-depth interview what were the main and subsidiary causes of the observed phenomenon; after all, only Catherine her-self might know the real reasons.)

The example raises exactly the problem of determining causes from the effects described. How does one infer or determine causes from effects from amongst a myriad of possible alternatives? This chapter indicates how the researcher can proceed in deter-mining causes from their effects.

Researchers often start with observations and then work backwards to establish the most likely, plausible, and evidence-supported causes. Backtracking is difficult, and this chapter indicates not only why but how to address some of the difficulties. Previous chapters have argued for the need to establish causal chains, causal processes, to link macro- and micro-levels of analysis, to include human agency and intentionality as well as structural, societal factors in understanding causation, to test rival hypotheses and explanations and eliminate the least fitting of these, and to work with the complicated relationships of cause and effect. This becomes yet more challenging when one is faced with the task of reconstructing and testing hypothesized causation that moves from the effect to the cause. However, this is often the most that researchers can do; they are presented with events and then have to account for them with explanations that hold water. It has also been argued that behind explanations, human behaviour, causes and effects lie theories – of human behaviour, of human choices, of human actions – and these must be part of any causal explanation.

Implications for researchers:

- Determining causes from effects is strongly inferential.
- Inferring causes from effects is a highly tentative and piecemeal activity as it requires backtracking from effects to causes and reconstruction of causal processes.
- Inferring causes from effects requires testing of rival causal explanations and their strength/potency/explanatory potential.
- Causes may not be the same as the symptoms of causes.
- There may be a myriad of causes of an effect, acting singly or in combination.

The difficulty in determining causes from effects is that a particular effect may be the consequence of any number of causes. The task of the researcher is to identify which are the most plausible, which fit the data most satisfactorily, which explanations to discard – and why – and which to retain.

Ex post facto experiments to determine causation

One method of ascertaining causes from effects is the quasi-experiment in *ex post facto* research ('from what is done afterwards'), working backwards from effects to possible causes. Since the events have already taken place they cannot be manipulated by the intervention of the researcher, as in the case of determining the effects of causes. They have all already happened, so the researcher has to hypothesize possible causes and then test them against the evidence, for example by holding factors constant and by controlling and matching the samples.

Cohen *et al.* (2007: 267) make a powerful argument for *ex post facto* research.[1] They contend that sometimes it is not possible, desirable or ethical to set up a laboratory or field experiment: 'an investigator cannot cause one group to become failures, delinquent, suicidal, brain-damaged or dropouts'. For example, let us imagine that we wanted to investigate the cause of different levels of trauma effects on people in road traffic accidents. We could not require a participant to run under a bus, or another to stand in the way of a moving lorry, or another to be hit by a motorcycle, and so on. Instead we might examine hospital records to see the trauma effects of victims of bus accidents, lorry accidents and motorcycle accidents, and see which group seem to have sustained the greatest trauma. It may be that it was the lorry accident victims, followed by the motorcycle victims, followed by the bus victims. Now, although it is not possible to say with 100 per cent certainty what caused the trauma, one could make an intelligent guess that those involved in lorry accidents suffer the worst injuries. Here we look at the outcomes and work backwards to examine possible causes. We cannot isolate, control or manipulate variables, but nevertheless we can come to some defensible conclusions about likelihood.

Cohen *et al.* write that:

> *ex post facto* research is a method that can also be used instead of an experiment, to test hypotheses about cause and effect in situations where it is unethical to control or manipulate the dependent variable, e.g. the effects of family violence on students' performance. We could not expose a student to family violence as it would be unethical. However, one could put students into two groups, matched carefully on a range of factors, with one group comprising those who have experienced family violence and the other whose domestic circumstances are more acceptable. If the hypothesized causation is supportable then the researcher should be able to discover a difference in school performance between the two groups when the other variables are matched or held as constant as possible.
>
> (2007: 264)

The key to establishing the causes is the careful identification of those that are possible, testing each against evidence, and then eliminating the ones that do not stand up to the test, ensuring that attention is paid to careful sampling and to controls – holding fixed some variables.

According to Cohen *et al.*,

> one can discern two approaches to *ex post facto* research. In the first approach one commences with subjects who differ on an *independent* variable, for example their years of study in mathematics, and then study how they differ on the dependent variable, e.g. a mathematics test. In a second approach, one can commence with subjects who differ on the *dependent* variable (for example their performance in a mathematics test) and discover how they differ on a range of independent variables, e.g. their years of study, their liking for the subject, the amount of homework they do in mathematics). The *ex post facto* research here seeks to discover the causes of a particular outcome (mathematics test performance) by comparing those students in whom the outcome is high (high marks on the mathematics test) with students whose outcome is low (low marks on the mathematics test), after the independent variable has occurred.
>
> (2007: 265)

Let us take an example of an *ex post facto* piece of research. Let us imagine that a large secondary school has been experiencing high staff turnover, and researchers are asked to investigate the causes of this. It is observed that the turnover had increased dramatically when a new appraisal and performance management system had been introduced. It is also observed that there is a range of years of experience amongst the staff who left: some had been teaching a long time and some only a very short time, so the researchers wonder whether the number of years of teaching experience is a factor. They gather data

Table 6.1 An *ex post facto* experiment

	Staff leaving the school annually	
	Before the new appraisal and performance management system	After the introduction of the new appraisal and performance management system
<5 years of teaching experience	9	21
5–15 years of teaching experience	14	16
16–35 years of teaching experience	15	17
>35 years of teaching experience	13	22
Total	51	81

from across four years – the two years before the introduction of the new system and two years afterwards – and they present the results as in Table 6.1.

The researchers find a statistically significant difference ($p = .019$) between the two sets of scores (before and after the introduction of the new system). However, they also note that these differences are strongest for the very young staff (new to the profession) and those approaching retirement. They conclude that one cause of the increased turnover may be the introduction of the new appraisal system, but that age is also a possible factor. They hypothesize that young and very old members of staff might resent the imposition of the system, the former finding greener pastures elsewhere and the latter taking early retirement. The problem appears to be at its strongest amongst the younger members of staff. However, behind this phenomenon the researchers also raise the matter of a deeper cause – the tolerance of staff to perceived unnecessary managerialism in education; those least able or least constrained (freer) to tolerate this decide to leave, whilst those with more constraints on them (e.g. bringing up a growing family and hence not able to take serious risks with employment) remain and put up with the new system, regardless of their own feelings. Behind the putative causes lie action narratives, though, in the case here, the researchers did not investigate such conditions or circumstances.

Implications for researchers:

- *Ex post facto* methods can be used to infer causation.
- *Ex post facto* methods are useful when causal manipulation is neither possible nor desirable.
- *Ex post facto* research might indicate the nature of deeper causation that needs to be explored.

In a criterion-group (or causal-comparative) approach to an *ex post facto* understanding of causation, the investigator sets out to discover possible causes for a phenomenon being studied by comparing the subjects in which the variable is present with similar subjects in whom it is absent. Let us imagine, for example, that the researcher is seeking to establish the causes of effective teaching, and hypothesizes that one cause is collegial curriculum

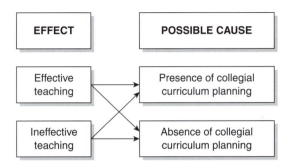

Figure 6.1 Two causes and two effects

planning with other members of the department. The research could be designed as in Figure 6.1. Here there are two criterion groups: (a) the presence of collegial curriculum planning; and (b) the absence of collegial curriculum planning. By examining the difference in effectiveness between those teachers (however one wished to measure 'effective teaching') who did and did not plan their curriculum with colleagues (collegial curriculum planning) one could infer a possible causal difference. But one has to be cautious: at most this is a correlational study, and causation is not the same as correlation. Indeed, as in previous examples in this book, a third cause may be influencing both the effective/ineffective teaching and the presence/absence of collegial curriculum planning, e.g. staff sociability. That said, causal inferences could be made that might warrant further investigation.

In a 'true' experiment, the researcher has manipulative control of the cause and can exercise control by assigning subjects or treatments to groups at random. In the *ex post facto* research situation, this control and manipulation of the independent variable is not possible, and, perhaps more important, neither is randomization. This can compromise the reliability of any causal inference. Further, the researcher cannot know for certain whether, in fact, the causative factor has been included or even identified. Indeed it may be that no single factor is the cause, or a particular outcome may result from different causes on different occasions.

By their very nature, *ex post facto* experiments can provide support for any number of different, perhaps even contradictory, hypotheses; postulating causal hypotheses is dangerous. The investigator begins with certain data and looks for a causal explanation for them; often, however, a number of interpretations may be at hand (see the examples of the Chinese learner and Catherine's chemistry earlier). For example, researchers may find that watching television correlates with low achievement at school. It may be that watching television causes low achievement at school; or, indeed, low achievement at school may cause students to watch more television. Indeed, there may be a third explanation, namely that students who do not do well at school for whatever reason (e.g. ability, motivation) also enjoy watching television; it may be this third variable (the independent variable of ability or motivation) that is causing the other two effects (watching a lot of television or low school achievement) (Cohen *et al.* 2007: 267) (see the discussion of Reichenbach's causal forks in Chapter 3).

Cohen *et al.* (2007: 268–9) also suggest that, even if a relationship has been discovered, there is a problem in deciding which is the cause and which the effect, as there is the possibility of reverse causation. Just because an independent variable precedes a dependent variable in time does not mean that the former causes the latter; this is the *post hoc ergo propter hoc* fallacy (translated as 'after this therefore becomes because of this'). Further, placing subjects into dichotomous groups can be problematic, and, indeed, conclusions may be based on a small sample or a limited number of recurrences. The method may fail to recognize that events have multiple rather than single causes, and it may be impossible to abide by the falsification criterion.

Though the absence of control over the independent variable(s) and the absence of randomization are problematic in *ex post facto* research, some control can be exercised by matching the subjects in the experimental and control groups, though this can also bring problems, as the researcher may not actually know which are the important variables on which the participants should be matched or, indeed, if participants can actually be matched sufficiently.

A further way of introducing control is to try to ensure that the samples are as homogeneous as possible on a particular variable. Cohen *et al.* (2007: 270) suggest that, for example, if intelligence is a relevant extraneous variable then its effects could be controlled by including in the sample only those subjects with a particular intelligence level, i.e. disentangling the independent variable from other variables with which it might be associated, so that any effects found could be associated justifiably with the independent variable of intelligence.

It is important in *ex post facto* research to recognize that there may be several possible, and indeed correct, explanations for the outcomes found in a study. Hence the search for several possible explanations must be conducted, and the explanations tested against the evidence.

Implications for researchers:

- *Ex post facto* methods can be correlational or causal-comparative (criterion grouping).
- *Ex post facto* methods – quasi-experiments – are not as robust as true experiments, as (a) control and manipulation of the independent variables and (b) random sampling may not be possible.
- *Ex post facto* methods are particularly useful if simple connections between cause and effect are implied.
- Correlational research does not necessarily establish causation: covariance may be caused by a third, common, cause.
- Effects may have multiple causes, and this can frustrate the search for simple causation.

Moving away from *ex post facto* research, this chapter provides two worked examples of different ways of determining causes from effects.

Example 1: Class differentials in educational attainment

Goldthorpe (2007b: chaps 2 and 3) provides a very clear example of how to determine causes from effects, and how to test whether the hypothesized causal antecedents and the theories that underpin them provide the most acceptable account of the *explananda*. His work moves beyond the simple elaboration of constructs and concepts (which often masquerade as theory) and identifies and tests causation and causal explanation. His example concerns the 'persistent differentials in educational attainment' despite increased educational expansion, provision and uptake across the class structure (ibid.: 21); it is comprehensive, and is reported in some detail here, as it contains all the ingredients for the educational researcher seeking to establish causation: the causes of the observed phenomena (the effects).

Goldthorpe seeks to provide a causal explanation for his observations, proceeding in several stages:

1   he establishes operationally what it is that he intends to investigate, ensuring that what he intends to examine is actually true: the real case, and not an artificial case;
2   he sets out possible theoretical foundations for his investigation;
3   he examines rival theoretical foundations and, having reviewed each of them, eliminates rival theoretical foundations;
4   he then hypothesizes a causal explanation on the basis of what he takes to be the best theoretical foundation;
5   he sets out the assumptions underlying his causal explanation;
6   he then tests his hypotheses empirically;
7   he draws conclusions based on the test.

Only after that test is he able to provide a causal explanation for his observed effects. In unpacking this further, the example proceeds through the seven stages outlined above.

Implications for researchers:

A seven-stage model for determining causes from effects can be followed:

Stage 1: Establish exactly what has to be explained.
Stage 2: Set out possible theoretical foundations for the investigation.
Stage 3: Examine, evaluate and eliminate rival theoretical foundations, selecting the most fitting.
Stage 4: Hypothesize a causal explanation on the basis of the best theoretical foundation.
Stage 5: Set out the assumptions underlying the causal explanation.
Stage 6: Test the hypotheses empirically.
Stage 7: Draw conclusions based on the test.

Stage 1: Establish what it is that has to be explained

Firstly Goldthorpe observes two regularities (we can term these phenomena 'effects') (2007b: 45).

(a) In all economically advanced societies over the previous 50 years there has been an expansion of education provision and in the numbers of children staying on in full-time education beyond the minimum schooling age (e.g. going into higher education).

(b) At the same time, class differentials in educational attainment have remained stubbornly stable and resistant to change, i.e. though children from all classes have participated in expanded education, class origins and their relationship to the likelihood of children staying on in education or entering higher education has reduced only slightly, if at all, and this applies to most societies.

He includes two more observations (about cross-national variation and gender) (ibid.: 45–6), but this chapter will not focus on these. Goldthorpe, in fact, is establishing social regularities that any causal and theoretical account should seek to explain: the creation, persistence and continued existence of class stratification in modern societies, and the continuing class-relatedness of educational inequality and life chances (ibid.: 24).

Stage 2: Set out possible theoretical foundations for the investigation

Goldthorpe's work is premised on the view that theories are necessary to provide explanatory foundations for how established regularities (in his case, these are social regularities) came to be as they are (2007b: 21). He begins by setting out four different theories to account for social events:

1   Marxist theory, with its emphasis on class struggle caused by the conflict between the owners of the means of production and the social relations of production, and how those contradictions entered the class consciousness of individuals and groups in society and led to the revolutionary overthrow of capitalism (ibid.: 22);
2   the liberal theory of the decline of class consciousness and working-class revolution, to be replaced by social stratification in other forms, increasing social mobility, class decomposition and the reduction of class-based inequality. It seeks to explain how these stem from expanding industrialization and concern for efficiency, increased educational provision, greater equality of opportunity, and the move away from ascription and towards achievement and selection based on a meritocratic form of society (ibid.: 22–3);
3   the cultural theory of class formation and its effects on educational attainment. This derives, in part, from the work of Bourdieu on cultural capital, and, put briefly, argues that schools draw unevenly on the social and cultural resources of members of the society, utilizing particular linguistic structures, regard for education and qualifications, authority patterns, and types of curricula, such that children from higher social locations enter schools already familiar with these social arrangements, so their uptake of the schooling is better than for those for whom schools constitute an alien culture. Equality of opportunity does not guarantee equality of uptake or outcome. Whilst schools formally offer equality of opportunity to all pupils to take up high-status knowledge, there are differential outcomes to this process, dependent on the backgrounds of children (Bourdieu 1976, 1977; Bernstein 1977). Some children will have the background cultural and linguistic capital and 'habitus' – the necessary 'dispositions' and positive attitudes to school, motivations to learning, parental support for education, social advantage, ease in dealing with authority figures, high culture – so that when they meet school knowledge they can engage it comfortably and take advantage of it. For other children school knowledge represents an alien culture and

methodology such that they cannot engage it as easily and hence are disadvantaged. For them the 'hegemonic academic curriculum' (Hargreaves 1989) produces a culture shock. The cultural experiences in the home facilitate children's adjustments to school and academic achievement, thereby transforming cultural resources into cultural capital. Whilst schools formally offer equality of opportunity to all pupils, there are differential outcomes to this process, dependent on the backgrounds of students;

4   rational action theory (also known as rational choice theory). There are several constituent features of rational action theory (for the sake of clarity here this is taken to be synonymous with rational choice theory). These are set out below, and do not derive solely from the work of Goldthorpe, but, for the benefit of readers unfamiliar with the theory, draw on a wider range of literature:[2]

- Human behaviour is instrumental, purposive and consequentialist; humans have goals (not necessarily consciously held) which express their preferences and towards the achievement of which they orient themselves, given all relevant factors that may be out of their control, and anticipating and weighing up the likely consequences of their actions.
- Social phenomena and situations are the consequences of individual decisions and actions.
- Human behaviour seeks to maximize personal benefits (utility) whilst minimizing the costs, calculating and weighing costs and benefits before acting, and then making decisions based on the outcome of such evaluation.
- Human behaviour can be explained and understood in terms of individuals' reasons.
- Primacy is accorded to self-interest.
- Rational people adjust their behaviour to meet the demands and constraints of the present context/society and anticipated/predicted changes in society; they recognize that there is only partial certainty about the anticipated situation.
- Rational people weigh incentives, losses and trade-offs; the best action from a range of alternatives is that which enables the individual to achieve her or his goals with the minimum loss (the profit is the benefit minus the costs incurred).
- Individuals are discrete, purposeful and capable of making choices.
- Humans have sets of preferences or means (utilities) that are hierarchically ordered, i.e. some preferences are stronger than others.
- Human behaviour is decisional; there are decisions and consequences of decisions that are based on information available to the decision maker, who weighs the information, options and potential other players before reaching the decision.
- Rational action provides causal accounts of change and intentional behaviour; individuals change themselves in response to the changes in others.
- When individuals choose which behaviours to perform, they do this on the basis of rational considerations of the 'utility' (the value of the benefit) of a range of behaviours that relate to their hierarchy of preferences, the costs of each alternative (and in terms of foregoing of utilities), and the best way to optimize and maximize utility – which of a set of alternatives is most likely to enable them to achieve their goals.

- People choose what they consider to be the best actions towards the achievement of their goals, in the contexts and according to the constraints that exist and the information that they have and by their most preferred means.
- Social behaviour springs from, and is a composite of, individual choices and behaviours.
- Emergent social phenomena – formations, structures, collective decisions and behaviours – are the outcomes of the rational choices of individuals.
- These emergent social phenomena, springing from individuals' rational behaviour, determine the distribution of resources, opportunities for different behaviours, norms and responsibilities in a situation.
- Rational choice theory is methodologically individualist, i.e. social structures and phenomena are the outcomes of individual behaviours, actions and interactions, though such actions are mindful of social constraints and context.
- Social interaction is a process of social exchange (e.g. of approval, or other kinds of valued behaviours and actions).
- Social systems can be explained in terms of the effects of the system and its properties on actors, the actions of participants in the system, and the combination or interaction of those actions, which lead to systemic behaviour (Coleman 1990: 27).

Here is not the place to consider extended criticisms of rational action/ choice theory.[3] Suffice it to note that:

- rational choice theory contains questionable assumptions (e.g. of the primacy of individual action as the unit of analysis (methodological individualism));
- its definition of rationality is too narrow;
- it does not distinguish clearly enough between individual choices for personal and for social benefits;
- it is unreal in its assumption that people act on the basis of choosing the best options;
- it is too materialist;
- it sits uncomfortably with democracy and social responsibility;
- it does not explain many social phenomena;
- it fails to provide a satisfactory account of rule-following behaviour;
- it is too reductionist, overlooking the complexity of situations;
- its epistemological basis is insufficiently clearly articulated;
- it fails to explain the role and significance of beliefs;
- it is too psychological to stand as a social theory;
- it fails to account for non-instrumental actions and non-consequentialist reasons for behaviour;
- it requires a level of cognitive decision making that many people do not have;
- it offers only *post hoc* accounts rather than predictions;
- it is not falsifiable.

Further,

- not all individual behaviour is individual but is decided in relation to external references;

- not all behaviour is rational (e.g. see the earlier discussion of the base rate fallacy);
- rational choice is often made on the basis of incomplete information, i.e. is not as rational as its proponents would aver;
- there is an overemphasis on preferences and their stability;
- history and power are undertheorized and underestimated;
- rational choice is made on the basis of self-interest and personal profit rather than societal benefit (i.e. social life, the emergence of social groups and institutions, and the causal force of social structures are underemphasized in this theory);
- altruism, cooperation and trust are underemphasized in the theory;
- social phenomena may not be reducible to statements of individual action;
- the marriage of economics, sociology and education in rational choice theory is dubious;
- not all human behaviour is egoistic;
- the importance of irrationality is understated, and irrationality may be an important explanatory factor in some contexts (and context-dependency is an essential ingredient of causation);
- people act without looking to the future;
- decisions made on the basis of rational choice theory overlook questionable assumptions underpinning the theory.

Indeed one can take issue with the view of Homans that 'the secret of society is that it was made by men [*sic*], and there is nothing in society but what men put there', and that social structures are 'simply chains of connected individual actions' that happen to pattern themselves (Homans 1961, quoted in Scott 2000: 9). As was noted earlier, Durkheim's (1982) 'social facts' exist. That said, rational action theory powerfully catches agency as well as structure.

Goldthorpe (2007b) then proceeds to investigate these four theories: Marxist theory, liberal theory, cultural theory and rational action theory.

Stage 3: Examine, evaluate and eliminate rival theoretical foundations

Goldthorpe regards the first two of these theories as essentially spurious in that, in both cases, the *explananda* did not occur. For Marxism, there was no working-class revolution, and, where revolutions did occur, they were neither in the working class nor in the industrial heartlands, i.e. his predictions did not come true. In the face of this Goldthorpe turns to liberal theory, in which it was suggested that there has been a 'withering away' of class (2007b: 23). The liberal theory of society tried to explain this, but, in fact, this too is spurious, as class inequalities continue to demonstrate high levels of stability. Indeed Goldthorpe (ibid.: 24) reports that there is little evidence of greater equality of life chances for individuals from different class backgrounds.

If Marxist and liberal theorists fall at the first fence, then what kind of theory can replace them? Goldthorpe focuses on one area – 'the persistence of class differentials in educational attainment', particularly in the context of increased educational opportunity and its putative weakening influence on class-based determination of life chances – and seeks to explain this from other than Marxist and other than liberal theories (2007b: 25).

Goldthorpe argues that both Marxist and liberal theorists fail in part because they take insufficient account of human agency, action and interaction (2007b: 25) and that humans are far more aware of their situation than false consciousness and ideological delusion would suggest (ibid.: 26) (cf. Eagleton 1991). Hence his self-set task is to explain how the macro-social regularities that he establishes in terms of class and educational attainment are the outcomes of the actions and interactions of individuals. In doing so he is addressing one of the requirements of a theory as suggested above – to incorporate micro- and macro-levels of analysis, human action and structure.

Goldthorpe (2007b: 29–31) then considers another rival causal explanation: Bourdieu's cultural capital thesis (Bourdieu 1976; Bourdieu and Passeron 1977). The cultural capital thesis is not without its criticisms (e.g. Morrison 1995), for example: (a) it operates from a mechanistic, modernistic view of power and domination; (b) it regards human agency as too overdetermined; (c) it is too accepting of domination; (d) it neglects the notions of resistance and contestation; (e) it assumes that the working class is only a pale reflection of the dominant cultural capital; (f) members of the working class have cultural capital also, but it is underrated by dominant social institutions; (g) it assumes that classes are homogeneous; (h) it neglects the mediating effects of gender, ethnicity and class on culture; (i) it overemphasizes the view of educational institutions as sites of *distribution* of cultural capital rather than as sites for knowledge and cultural *production*; and (j) it regards the working class as colluding in their own disadvantage.

Goldthorpe finds cultural theories incomplete in accounting for the continuing disparities in educational attainment over time and as other societal changes have occurred, particularly in the context of educational expansion (2007b: 29–30). He reports evidence to show that children from less advantaged backgrounds have not been excluded from education to the extent suggested by cultural theorists, i.e. education has increased cultural capital, not diminished it.

Hence Marxist theories, liberal theories and cultural capital theories are dispatched in providing a causal account of the effects which Goldthorpe is interested in explaining: the persistence over time of class differentials in educational attainment.

Implications for researchers:

- Ensure that you establish the correct *explanandum*.
- Ensure that the *explanans* – the explanation and its theoretical foundations – demonstrate 'fitness for purpose' by having the potential to include and address all the relevant features of the *explanandum*, e.g. individual action, agency and interaction (micro-features), as well as structure (macro-features).
- Ensure that the theory is comprehensive rather than partial.
- Ensure that agency/intentionality and structure are included in the theory and causal explanation.
- Ensure that micro- and macro-levels of analysis are included in the theory and causal explanation.
- Indicate the main elements and claims of each of the theories under review.
- Test rival theories and eliminate those with the least causal explanatory potential.

Goldthorpe's consideration of rival theories can be represented diagrammatically, as in Figure 6.2. Goldthorpe believes that rational action theory, despite its limitations (and

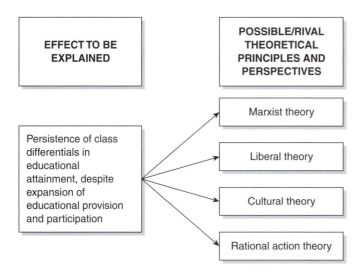

Figure 6.2 Rival theories to explain a phenomenon

he is aware of these), offers the best explanation of the persistence of class differentials in educational attainment, even though there has been increasing educational expansion of provision, participation in education, uptake and overall levels of attainment by class. His analysis is summarized in the account that follows here.

True to rational action theory, Goldthorpe (2007b: 31) places emphasis on aspirations, in particular noting their relative rather then absolute status, that is to say, aspirations are relative to class position, as working-class aspirations may not be the same as those of other classes. Different social classes have different levels and kinds of aspiration, influenced – as rational action theory suggests – by the constraints under which they operate, and the perceived costs and benefits that obtain when making decisions (ibid.: 32). Taking *relative* rather than absolute views of aspiration enables accounts to be given that include the fact of increased provision of, and participation in, education by students from all classes, i.e. class differentials have not widened as education provision and participation have widened.

Goldthorpe (2007b: 32) suggests that the culture theory may account for what Boudon terms 'primary effects', that is, initial levels of achievement and ability in the early stages of schooling. However, he is more concerned with Boudon's 'secondary effects', that is, those effects that come into play when children reach branching points (transition points, e.g. from primary to secondary schooling, from secondary education to university). These have increasingly powerful effects as one progresses through schooling, as they take account of the aspirations and values that children and their parents hold for education, success and life options, i.e. the intentionality and agency of rational action theory, in a way that primary effects do not. Goldthorpe notes that, at each successive 'branching point' (transition point), children from more advantaged backgrounds remain in the educational system and those from less advantaged backgrounds either leave school or choose courses that lead to lower qualifications (hence reducing their opportunities for yet further education).

Aspirations may increase as educational provision and participation expand. Here Goldthorpe (2007b: 33) opines that more ambitious options may be regarded less favourably by those from less advantaged class backgrounds, as they involve: (a) greater risk of failure; (b) greater cost (see also Hanson 2008); and (c) relatively less benefit. In other words, the level of aspiration may vary according to class and the associated levels of assessed cost and risk by members of different classes, and children from less advantaged backgrounds have to be more ambitious than those from more advantaged backgrounds if they are to meet the aspirations and success levels of those from more advantaged backgrounds. Class origins influence risk assessment, cost assessment and benefit assessment – all aspects that are embraced in rational action theory – and these determine the choices made by children and their parents.

> ## Implications for researchers:
>
> - For the theory chosen, set out its key features, derivatives, elements and cognates in respect of the *explananda*.
> - Identify the substantive points that the theory suggests in respect of the *explananda*.

Stage 4: Hypothesize a causal explanation on the basis of the best theoretical foundation

Goldthorpe (2007b: 34) summarizes his theoretical causal explanation of the regular effects that he has observed by arguing that class differentials in educational attainment have persisted because, even though there has been expansion and reform of education, and even though the overall costs and benefits that are associated with having more ambitious options have encouraged their take-up, in practice there has been little concurrent change in the 'relativities between *class-specific* balances': different classes view the costs, risks and benefits differently.

This is his working hypothesis in trying to establish cause from effect.

> ## Implications for researchers:
>
> - Operationalize the theory, suggesting concrete items that can be investigated and tested.
> - Operationalization entails turning general statements into specific, concrete statements that are valid indicators of, or proxies for, the *explananda*.
> - State hypotheses.

Stage 5: Set out the assumptions underlying the causal explanation

How does Goldthorpe test his theory? Initially he draws attention to the ongoing income differentials between classes – indeed, he argues that they have widened (2007b: 35), with manual labourers more prone to unemployment than professional or managerial workers, i.e. the costs of education are still a factor for less advantaged families, particularly at the end of the period of compulsory schooling. At the time when their children come to the end of compulsory schooling, the income of manual workers will already have peaked (e.g.

when they are in their forties), whereas for professional and managerial workers it will still be rising. Costs are more of a problem for manual workers than for professional and managerial workers, i.e. the costs of higher education relative to income, and the consequent effects on family lifestyle if families are having to finance higher education, are much higher for manual workers. This increased proportion of family income to be spent on education for less advantaged families is coupled with the fact that, if children from these families are to succeed, they need even more ambition than their professional and managerial class counterparts, i.e. they are at a potential double disadvantage. Relative advantage and disadvantage are not disturbed, a feature on which liberal theory is silent (ibid.: 36).

At issue here is the point that Goldthorpe makes tellingly, that class position conditions educational decisions made by members of different classes. Different class positions will influence different evaluations of the costs and benefits of education, and these are socially reproductive, i.e. the class position is undisturbed.

Another element of Goldthorpe's argument relates to risk aversion. His view is that a major concern of members of different classes is to minimize their risk of downward class mobility and to maximize their chances for upward class mobility or, at least, maintenance of their existing class location (2007b: 37). This exerts greater pressure on the already advantaged classes (e.g. the salariat) to have their children complete higher education (in order to preserve intergenerational class stability) than it does on the children from less advantaged classes (e.g. the waged). It costs more for the children of the advantaged classes to preserve their class position than it does for children of the less advantaged classes to preserve theirs.

With regard to families in the less advantaged classes, Goldthorpe (2007b: 38) suggests that they regard higher education in a much more guarded light. Not only does it cost less for them to maintain their class position, but it costs relatively more to achieve upward class mobility; their best options might be for vocational education, as it is cheaper and gives a strong guarantee of *not* moving downwards in class situation (e.g. to be unemployed or unskilled). Further, for children in this class, the costs (and likelihood) of failure in higher education could be proportionately greater than those for children from more advantaged families, in terms of:

- the relative costs of the higher education;
- lost earning time;
- lost opportunity to follow a vocational route in which they have greater likelihood of being successful (ibid.) (e.g. if vocational courses are only open to people of a certain age, if financial support would not be forthcoming for 'second time round' applicants, or if applicants were older than a given cut-off age for financial aid);
- loss of social solidarity if a working-class child pursues higher education, the consequences of which may be to remove him or her from his or her class origin and community (ibid.: 38–9).

These factors combine to suggest that children and families from less advantaged backgrounds will require a greater assurance, or expectation, of success in higher education before committing themselves to it than is the case for children and families from more advantaged backgrounds (ibid.: 68).

Goldthorpe is now in a position to set out his causal explanation of the effects (the *explanandum*): the persistence of class differentials in educational attainment despite expansion of educational provision and participation. He summarizes it thus (2007b: 39).

1   Class differentials in the uptake of more ambitious educational options remain because the conditions also remain in which the perceived costs and benefits of these options operate, and these lead to children from less advantaged families generally requiring a greater assurance of success than children from more advantaged families before they (the former) pursue more ambitious educational options.

2   There is a rational explanation for the persistence of these different considerations of ambitious options by class over time, which is rooted in class-based conditions.

The argument is elegant, sophisticated, rooted in theory, explanatory and causal. These are the two main hypotheses that he seeks to test.

Implications for researchers:

- Set out the assumptions on which the causal explanations are based.
- Indicate the directions of causation.
- In the process of identifying causal relations, consider 'reasons for' and 'determined by'.

Stage 6: Test the hypotheses empirically

Goldthorpe then proceeds to test his two hypotheses (2007b: 39–44 and chaps. 3 and 4), adducing evidence about:

- greater working-class sensitivity to the chances of success and failure in comparison to middle class families (p. 40);
- different levels of ambition in working-class and middle-class families (indeed, that the former *over*adapt to their class location (p. 40), being ultra-conservative);
- relative (class-based) risk aversion in decision making, e.g. the risk of failure; the risk of closing options (pp. 55–6);
- the loss of foregone earnings (pp. 53–5);
- the expectations of success and ability (pp. 55–6);
- the evaluation of the potential benefits, value and utility of higher education (pp. 38–9);
- the influences on choices and decision making in different classes (chap. 3);
- the actual choices made by members of different classes;
- the fear of downward social mobility (pp. 53–4);
- the need to preserve, or improve on, intergenerational mobility (pp. 53–4);
- the financial costs (p. 56).

Underpinning his work is the view of rational humans, rational actions and rational choices, outlined earlier, together with a assumption of the existence of a hierarchically ordered class structure (pp. 47–8) and a model of decision making that focuses on decision points (branching points) in an educational career (pp. 48–52). Goldthorpe creates decision trees and then uses these to test his hypotheses. Indeed he recognizes the need to seek to falsify his theory, and he suggests examining 'deviant cases' in this respect (pp. 41–3). That said, he still suggests that more research is needed on the individual action narratives, intentions, actions and interactions at a micro-level that influence decision making in families and children.

> ## Implications for researchers:
>
> - Indicate what needs to be done to test the theory and to falsify it.
> - Identify the kinds of data required for the theory to be tested.
> - Identify the actual data required to test the theory.
> - Identify the test conditions and criteria.
> - Construct the empirical test.
> - Consider the use of primary and secondary data.
> - Consider using existing published evidence as part of the empirical test.
> - Ensure that action narratives and intentionality are included in causal accounts.

Stage 7: Draw conclusions based on the test

Goldthorpe is at pains to evaluate his views (e.g. 2007b: chaps. 3 and 4), citing plentiful evidence from a range of sources to support his conclusions. Indeed he advocates further testing of rival theories, e.g. human capital theory, in order to explain the 'effect' (ibid.: chap. 4). The consolidation of his causal explanation from a range of relevant empirical research and other theoretical models brings very considerable cogency and robustness to his analysis and conclusions.

Goldthorpe finds that class differentials have, indeed, continued to affect the take-up of educational options, and that class differentials in terms of the take-up of more ambitious educational options have been maintained because so too have the conditions in which the perceived costs and benefits of these options lead to children from less advantaged families requiring, on average, a greater assurance of success than their more advantaged counterparts before they decide to pursue such options. There are class differences in terms of relative ambition, risk aversion, perceived costs and benefits, amounts of effort required, assurances of success (and the significance of this), fear of downward social mobility, income, occupational choices, and the need for qualifications. Indeed the decisions that people take are rational (2007b: 39).

Goldthorpe concludes that the results of empirical tests support his explanation of the factors of relative risk aversion and fear of downward social mobility exerting causal power on educational decision making, which, in turn, lead to class differentials in educational attainment being maintained (2007b: 99). He takes care to qualify where his explanation seems to be most fitting, e.g. in its explanation of 'secondary effects' (values, beliefs, constrained choices and rational action within such constraints) (ibid.: 97). Similarly, he identifies areas that require further investigation, e.g. the significant numbers of students from less advantaged backgrounds who are moving into higher education (pp. 95–6) and the need for more information on whether or how far the implied microsocial processes actually are the case (p. 98). He also indicates some possible implications of his views, e.g. the need to combine subjective approaches with the objective 'revealed preferences' approach adopted by economists (pp. 99–100).

Goldthorpe argues that children and their parents rationally pursue their life plans, though these are differentially filtered by class-related constraints and expectations of failure or success in relation to more ambitious educational plans (2007a: 136). He argues that this hypothesis, whilst not being absolutely proven, is better supported than alternative hypotheses (e.g. educational choices being predetermined by culture, class identity and the class structure).

Implications for researchers:

- Identify where the theory has been most and least successful in explaining the *explananda*, i.e. the limits of the explanation.
- Evaluate the theory: how well does it fit and explain all the data (cf. the theoretical saturation' of grounded theory)?
- Identify what needs to be done to provide greater explanation of the *explananda*, and in what areas of the *explananda* this needs to occur.
- Indicate whether the present theory has the potential to explain those parts of the *explananda* that it has not dealt with so far, or whether alternative theories need to be employed.
- Identify where more data are required, and what kind of data they are, in order for the theory to be fully explanatory.
- Consider whether the evidence supports the conclusion about the likelihood of the correctness of the theory and causal explanations, or whether other causal explanations could be equally valid from the data. If so, what are they?
- Have the causal links, causal chains, causal processes and/or causal lines been tracked back effectively and thoroughly in moving from effect back to cause?
- What is the theory behind the cause?

This extended worked example has been selected because it offers a robust, secure account of how to track backwards from an effect to a cause and how to evaluate the likelihood that the putative cause of the effect actually is the cause of that effect. If one were to trace the Goldthorpe model in a diagram, it could appear as in Figure 6.3 (commencing from the top left-hand corner and proceeding clockwise). Goldthorpe meets his own criteria for judging the worth of research: its ability to link with theory and its potential to contribute to the cumulative development of knowledge and the demonstration of explanatory laws. His causal explanation links micro- and macro-explanations, the theoretical basis for which combination he locates in rational action theory. The latter, he avers, both bridges and draws on micro- and macro-accounts, action narratives and structural narratives. It catches intentionality and agency, and indicates how these are influenced by structural features of society (in his case, the class structure).

Implications for researchers:

- Ensure that research and theory are conjoined in the causal explanation.
- Ensure that the causal explanation builds on, and takes further, existing theories and causal explanations, i.e. contributes to the cumulative development of knowledge.

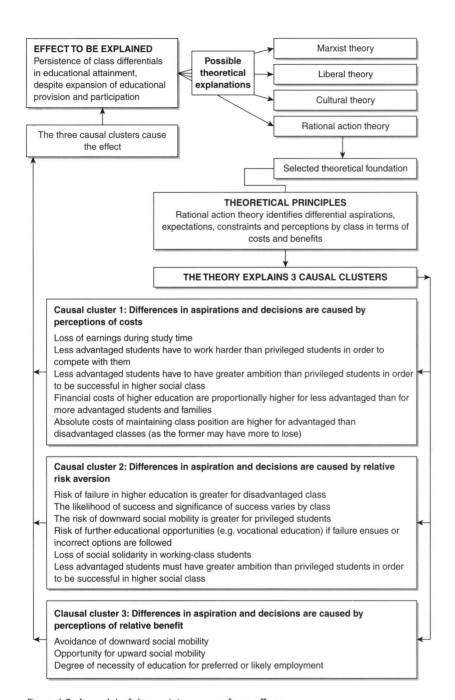

EFFECT TO BE EXPLAINED
Persistence of class differentials in educational attainment, despite expansion of educational provision and participation

Possible theoretical explanations

Marxist theory

Liberal theory

Cultural theory

Rational action theory

The three causal clusters cause the effect

Selected theoretical foundation

THEORETICAL PRINCIPLES
Rational action theory identifies differential aspirations, expectations, constraints and perceptions by class in terms of costs and benefits

THE THEORY EXPLAINS 3 CAUSAL CLUSTERS

Causal cluster 1: Differences in aspirations and decisions are caused by perceptions of costs

Loss of earnings during study time
Less advantaged students have to work harder than privileged students in order to compete with them
Less advantaged students have to have greater ambition than privileged students in order to be successful in higher social class
Financial costs of higher education are proportionally higher for less advantaged than for more advantaged students and families
Absolute costs of maintaining class position are higher for advantaged than disadvantaged classes (as the former may have more to lose)

Causal cluster 2: Differences in aspiration and decisions are caused by relative risk aversion

Risk of failure in higher education is greater for disadvantaged class
The likelihood of success and significance of success varies by class
The risk of downward social mobility is greater for privileged students
Risk of further educational opportunities (e.g. vocational education) if failure ensues or incorrect options are followed
Loss of social solidarity in working-class students
Less advantaged students must have greater ambition than privileged students in order to be successful in higher social class

Clausal cluster 3: Differences in aspiration and decisions are caused by perceptions of relative benefit

Avoidance of downward social mobility
Opportunity for upward social mobility
Degree of necessity of education for preferred or likely employment

Figure 6.3 A model of determining causes from effects

Whilst Goldthorpe's analysis demonstrates the development and testing of a theory in which causes are derived from effects, a second example is presented below that indicates how this may be problematic when causes and effects blur and when effects are overdetermined by causes.

Example 2: When causes become effects and effects become causes: schooling for conformity

This example comes from the author's interpretation of his own observational research in the small Chinese city of Macau. It combines micro- and macro-accounts of an observed phenomenon (conformity in students), indicating how agentic behaviour both conditions and is conditioned by structural forces, and how causes, processes and effects may blur and overlap. It indicates the process of overdetermination at work in producing an effect, in which *conformity* is the cause, medium, outcome and subsequent cause of further conformity in students. Conformity produces the conditions for the reproduction of conformity. It is argued that, in such circumstances, identifying where to break into the cycles of reproduction in establishing causation may be difficult. This rehearses the difficulty of infinite regress in understanding causality (the problem of retreating to the *causae causantes* mentioned in Chapter 2), exacerbated in this instance by the repeated recycling of the same causes and effects. The discussion here also draws attention to some difficulties in the research, and these are included to illustrate problems posed in moving from effect to cause.

The example commences with observed regularities and then offers causal explanations and clarifies the theoretical basis of these (i.e. theories of reproduction). However, in so doing it becomes clear that the distinction between cause and effect gets blurred, as effects change into causes, and, to compound the problem, causes of the same effects, i.e. there is a cycling or circularity of cause and effect at work. A theoretical explanation of these is provided through the twin concepts of 'structuration' from Giddens (1976, 1979, 1984) and 'habitus' from Bourdieu (1976, 1977), and the causal component is seen to be the production and reproduction of conformity in students. The example is qualitative and provides a different perspective from the ways of establishing causation from effects that have been identified in the preceding example. The tone here is deliberately polemical for clarity of the argument.

The example shows that it is possible for cause and effect to be blurred, and determining causes from effects may be highly problematic when effects in turn become causes. In the example of Macau schools, the factor 'student conformity' is both a cause and an effect without its being tautological or circular in argument: conformity brings about the effect of more conformity (Bourdieu's 'structured structure'), and the effect – conformity – conditions the agentic behaviour of teachers and students (Bourdieu's 'structuring structure'), i.e. conformity becomes both the medium for, and outcome of, the reproduction of conformity. The example is of the reproduction of conformity, and that disentangling cause from effect is not always as straightforward as one may wish.

Implications for researchers:

- Include agency and structure in theories and causal explanations.
- Include micro- and macro-analyses in theories and causal explanations.
- Recognize that causes, processes and effects might blur and overlap.

- Recognize that there may be cyclical processes of cause and effect, and that effects in one cycle may become causes of the same effects in a subsequent cycle of events.
- Agentic behaviour and actions are conditioned by, and condition, broader structures in society.
- The same phenomena may be the cause, medium and outcome of events and situations.

The argument here is that Macau's children, from kindergarten onwards, are schooled into conformity. It suggests that this hidden curriculum is difficult to break because it is the consequence of the conjuncture of many powerful forces reproducing the status quo.

Conformity in Macau's schools

If one goes into many Macau classrooms one is struck by several features.

- The physical environment is often sterile and unstimulating; there is a dearth of displays, and what displays exist underrepresent students' work and overrepresent badly drawn, kitsch cartoon characters; the décor is drab.
- The environment is provided *for* the children rather than *by* the children.
- Few areas, if any, of the curriculum are represented in the few classroom displays that exist.
- There are few books or classroom libraries.
- Classrooms are starved of resources or interest, crowded, with children overwhelmingly packed in single or double rows, and working largely alone; where they sit in groups there is little or no group interaction – grouping is a seating arrangement rather than a working arrangement (cf. Galton and Simon 1980).

In many classrooms the curriculum and the work are entirely undifferentiated. The lessons are standardized, driven by standard textbooks, delivered largely through a single mode (the teacher's lecture), reinforced by routine testing (Morrison and Tang 2002), producing standardized, formatted minds (Sacks 1999). All students are required to go through the same material at the same pace in the same way, and classrooms resemble assembly lines or processing factories involved in the mass production of the same standardized goods. Transmission teaching delivers the same uniform product. All the students are expected to reach the same standard (a passing grade), and this is characterized by an overrepresentation of lower order thinking and an underrepresentation of higher order thinking. The teacher tells the students what to think, how to think it, when to think it, and, through testing, how well they have thought. This is control, perhaps done benevolently and caringly, but nevertheless control.

Students and teachers are weighed down by the burden of learning, reciting and repeating facts and information, with huge amounts of marking to be done by the teachers (Morrison and Tang 2002). The knowledge is inert; many children have difficulty in recalling it – they have never used it, and, as brain-based research tells us, one has to 'use it or lose it' (Cilliers 1998: 93).

In terms of pedagogy, there is much didactic, one-way lecturing, with teachers delivering their lecture through a microphone, such that the noise and the teacher's voice are relentless and inescapable. Despite this, students sleep in lessons; they switch off and are switched off learning. The teacher is typically working much harder than the students, and if the students don't pay attention then that is construed as *their* problem, not the teacher's. The lesson is about teaching, not necessarily about learning.

Whole class teaching is accompanied by individual work and very little interaction. Classrooms typically embody differential language rights. Not only does the teacher have more language rights than the students but it is the teacher who decides what these will be, and the teacher monopolizes the talk. As with thinking, the teacher decides who will talk, what they will talk about, when they will talk, and how well they have talked (cf. Edwards 1980). There are very few open-ended questions. Students' learning is passive and responsive, with some 'animating' but little 'authoring' of the curriculum. Students rarely initiate classroom talk; there is little or no choice yet plentiful copying, repetition, drill, exercises and rote learning. When students are asked if they have any questions, there is frequently silence; they have learned to receive without question. This is compounded by a frequently observed phenomenon: the teacher asks a question, there is no response, so the teacher answers his or her own question. There is no need for the students to participate; all they need to do is to sit silently and wait, not disrupt, and everything will be done for them.

In many Macau classrooms one is struck by the amount of choral chanting that takes place, at high volume. Students chant, they shout, with one voice, particularly at kindergarten and primary levels. The quiet hand of conformity is powerfully taught and learned from a very early age. Conformity is 'overdetermined' – rendered inevitable – through the content and structure of lessons.

Many art lessons comprise students copying, or colouring given outlines of drawings; though they may select which colours to use, they have to stay within given lines and boundaries. The agenda for their colouring is pre-set, with no free expression in the *generation* or *creation* of what will be drawn. PE lessons are marked by lines of students performing exercises: an army of trainees. Students have to stay within prescribed boundaries. They are truly being schooled.

Though there is some integrated teaching (e.g. thematic teaching) at the kindergarten stage, from kindergarten onwards students are taught 'lessons'. In many kindergartens and lower primary classes one could as easily be in a secondary classroom, the only difference being in the age of the children; the teaching and learning styles are the same and the organization of the curriculum is largely the same. There is little distinctive pedagogy in each age phase. There are subjects in more than one sense: compartmentalized knowledge and with students subjected to a regimen in whose creation they have no part.

The affective aspects of learning are neglected in many Macau schools: schools are 'serious' places (echoing the Confucian Heritage Culture's emphasis on serious learning (Lee 1996; Hu 2002)), and motivation and enjoyment appear irrelevant: students are there to learn whatever is being addressed by the teachers or the textbook (Morrison and Tang 2002). Students are part of a public performatory culture: teachers are the star performers and have the largest share of each lesson; students are called out to the front of the class – often by a number that has been given to them, rather than by name – to write on the board, or to sing a solo, or to speak, or to recite; the show must go on. Students learn not to challenge the system; they quietly conform to the regime because it is better to keep quiet than to object.

Macau schools do not challenge students (other than to keep quiet), and students do not challenge the system. The system is extensively hegemonic (Gramsci 1971): students and teachers give their more-or-less willing consent to the system (they either overtly support it or do not challenge it), are silenced, and silently conform (Morrison and Tang 2002). Schools are highly hierarchical, closed institutions, with several mechanisms for command, control and surveillance (ibid.), e.g. with CCTV cameras installed. Teachers are on one-year contracts, so they do not risk losing contract renewal by doing anything other than what they are told to do. The hidden curriculum of conformity extends to both teachers and students.

One does not challenge the system, as the benefits of not challenging it outweigh the disadvantages of challenging it. Indeed, one can observe many very young children enjoying the lessons that are teaching them to conform: a society of happy slaves. One of the unspoken features of schooling in Macau is that the students generally have a positive attitude to school and behave well – it would be the envy of many teachers elsewhere to have such learners – and yet these same children are given a diet of dull and unstimulating lessons to be endured in silent boredom. They adhere to a system which represses them. Teachers fail to capitalize on the willingness of their students to learn, but, rather, their tacit compliance and obedience permits poor practice to continue unchallenged.

The 2003 Programme for International Student Achievement (PISA) (OECD 2004: 129) reported that 15-year-olds in Macau scored the lowest of all 40 participating countries in their sense of belonging to school and second highest in their feelings of being 'left out of things'; they felt disconnected from school, an irony in, yet consequence of, a conformist regime. Indeed 39 per cent of Macau's students said 'I feel helpless when doing a mathematics problem', with only 13 countries scoring more highly. Only 57 per cent of Macau's students reported that 'the teacher gives students an opportunity to express opinions' in mathematics, with 28 countries scoring more highly on this issue. Macau's students were fourteenth highest out of the 40 countries in their response to the statement 'I feel helpless when doing a mathematics problem': learned helplessness.

From these observations of regularities in Macau classrooms, a causal account can be teased out through the theoretical lenses of structuration theory and Bourdieu's descriptions of the 'habitus' as applied to classroom life.

Structuration and habitus in Macau schools

Macau's schools provide a clear example of Giddens's structuration theory, informed by Bourdieu's theory of habitus. Conformity is both the medium and the outcome of schooling, reproducing itself in a cycle (Morrison and Tang 2002) through the deliberate but conditioned actions of teachers and students.

Giddens's structuration theory is familiar: in their everyday lives people create and reproduce existing social practices. We exert our own agency and intentionality, creating, producing and reproducing systems through our daily interactions, and, in turn, those systems constrain and influence the ways in which we behave. In our everyday actions we produce and reproduce both constraining and enabling social structures, which are both the medium and the outcome of social production and reproduction (Giddens 1976). Indeed, behaviour is agentic and intentional, and humans construct their social worlds through their actions even though their acts of construction are themselves constrained by the worlds that they have created (Giddens 1981: 54).

For structuration theory, the moment of action can also be the moment of social reproduction as, in our actions, we reproduce the *conditions* of reproduction of the actions (Giddens 1984: 2). Indeed, Layder (1994: 133) writes that humans both 'repeat and reinforce the very conditions that restrict their freedom in the first place'. Through our activities we create and reproduce structural conditions, comprising knowledge, resources, rules, and institutional and societal practices.

For Giddens, routinization and re-creation are powerful forces for reproduction (1984: 2). Though we may act intentionally and deliberately, nevertheless we may end up reproducing the existing social order and social fabric. That said, social structures do not force people to act in particular ways; people are not 'ideological dopes of stunning mediocrity' (Giddens 1979: 52); social structures do not operate independently of the motives and reasons that people have for their behaviour (Giddens 1984: 181). Humans exercise choice and agency.

In Bourdieu's conception, structured structures and structuring structures reside within the *habitus* (1977: 53), defined as systems of enduring *dispositions*. Structured structures, he argues, can generate practices, i.e. they become active as 'structuring structures'. Shilling (2004: 475) cites Bourdieu's remark (1990: 53) that habitus provides individuals with 'predisposed ways of categorizing and relating to familiar and novel situations'.

The habitus is a result of social structures and yet also structures, i.e. changes and influences, behaviour, lifestyles and social systems; it is both a structuring structure and a structured structure (Bourdieu 1986: 170); it both enables creativity and constrains actions and practices, combining action/agency and structure. It is medium and also outcome of social structures and actions, and it dialectically mediates between the objective and subjective aspects of behaviour, structure and agency (Nash 1999: 176; Fuchs 2003).

For Bourdieu, *structured* structures are *ascribed* or given, as in, for example, rules, institutions, roles and behaviours that have a tendency towards self- and system-reproduction, and these are offset by the agency implicit in *structuring* structures, those that are *achieved* or negotiated through the exercise of agency – for example, in roles and practices that disrupt and may eventually replace the structured structures. The interactions surrounding the set of practices are bound by rules; yet, at the same time, such interactions create the rules (structuring structures). As Bourdieu remarks, the habitus is both *opus operatum* (result of practices) and *modus operandi* (mode of practices) (Bourdieu 1977: 18, 72ff.; 1990: 52). Though there is room for action and transformation, nevertheless there is a 'latent determinism' in the concept of habitus (Reay 2004: 432–3; Shilling 2004).

For Bourdieu, the habitus – the store of cultural and subcultural knowledge inside people's heads – conditions their everyday practices and tends to reproduce them (Bourdieu 1977: 3). Such dispositions have to be exercised or they atrophy (Bourdieu 2000: 160), yet keeping them exercised may be socially reproductive (Bourdieu and Passeron 1977). Social structures both constrain and enable the creative dimension of the habitus. For Giddens and Bourdieu alike, structures are both the medium and the outcome of social actions (Fuchs 2003). They constrain practices but are also a result of creative human relationships.

Teachers may be constrained by a system that requires them to behave in certain ways, but they themselves might also set the conditions that constrain them, reproducing cycles of causation. Teachers, not acquiescently but volitionally, exerting their agency, may set up the conditions for the reproduction of the system. The structured structures condition them to behave in particular ways, but teachers may deliberately choose a course of action that guarantees that they will continue to be constrained. The process can be circular, echoing Giddens's view of the routinization of practices, the circularity of agency and structure, and the circularity of causality.

How does this apply to the regularities observed in Macau's schools? How does it help us to understand causation at work here? The structured structures of conformity in the schools – the given practices – themselves are deliberately reproduced in the intentional actions of teachers and students. They become structur*ing* structures in that they are agentically undertaken by the actors, and the structured structures themselves condition the decisions taken by the actors – they are doubly structuring as they also structure the mindset of the actors. The habitus of Macau's teachers and students (as of the parents and school leaders and managers) operates powerfully not only to reproduce the status quo but also to inhibit change; schooling is a conservative force in society (Bourdieu 1976).

The concept of habitus offers an explanation not only for the situation found in Macau but its impermeability to change. Teachers, students, parents and stakeholders have come up through an education system which restricts horizons. They have experienced nothing else but conformity. Little wonder it is that they recycle what they know in this tiny city.   The elements of the habitus in which educational stakeholders operate in Macau combine to render it difficult to change conformity.

Implications for researchers:

- Combine theory with data in providing causal explanations.
- Ensure that the theoretical principles underpinning the causal explanations are fitting, sufficiently comprehensive and powerful.

Clearly in this example the author has his own agenda; the research and the report of the example here are neither neutral nor disinterested. The author has presented a negative reading of the situation and then attributed the observed phenomenon to more or less a single cause (conformity). No rival explanations are presented, and the comments are highly opinionated. The writer has no quarrel with criticisms of this nature; the point of the example lies elsewhere. In this example, conformity is both the cause, medium and effect of the practices in Macau schools. The causal explanation is rooted in theories of reproduction (within the framework of theories of structuration and habitus), and the analysis shows the circular causal effects of conformity – it is the cause, medium and effect of further conformity.

Backtracking from effect to cause may be startling for the researcher, as he or she finds that the cause is also the effect and the medium through which the cause becomes the effect. Cause becomes effect becomes cause becomes effect, and so on. This can be presented diagrammatically as in Figure 6.4. An immediate response to this situation may be that the researcher thinks that he or she has made a mistake and has not found the true cause of the phenomenon observation (student conformity). Whilst this may be true, it may also be that he or she has indeed found the true cause in this non-recursive model, and this cause is part of a cycling of cause and effect at work here, not least through routinization and overdetermination. The researcher seeking the causes of effects may have to face such complications. If, indeed, cyclical processes are at work, as Figure 6.4

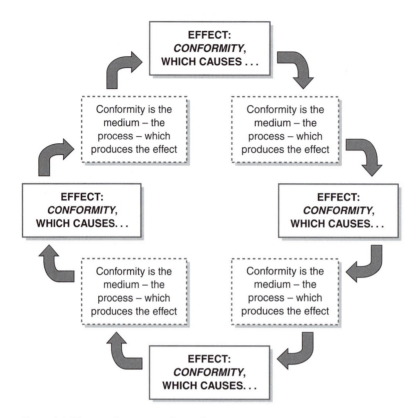

Figure 6.4 The circular nature of causality

suggests, then where does one break into the circle in order to understand causation and to provide a causal explanation? The example here, of causation that recycles and recirculates itself, suggests that it is possible to break in at any point in order to understand causation, since, ultimately, we will arrive back at the starting point, i.e. wherever we start we will eventually discover the circular nature of the causation at work.

The example of schooling for conformity has both strengths and weaknesses. On the one hand it:

(a) draws on theoretical underpinnings for the causal explanation;
(b) combines research with theory;
(c) provides an account of the causal processes and details that give rise to the causal explanation;
(d) infers cause from effect;
(e) combines micro- and macro-accounts and data;
(f) indicates intentionality, agency and structure;
(g) fits the existing data with the explanation.

On the other hand the example contains problems:

(a) it does not fulfil all of the seven stages that were outlined in the earlier part of the chapter, in that it does not review, test or eliminate rival explanations or test the theory and causal explanation with data that did not give rise to the theory in the first place. It addresses stages 1 to 5 of that sequence only;

(b) it risks circularity: the data that give rise to the causal explanation are the same data that are adduced to support the causal explanation; the *explanandum* merges with the *explanans*, and this is illegitimate;

(c) the research is pejorative in that the tone is decidedly negative, putting a gloss on the phenomenon being reported;

(d) the reader is given no insight into the representativeness of the data; there may have been gross selectivity in which data to include and which to exclude, including only those that support the causal hypothesis;

(e) the causal *explanans* may be incorrect in its interpretation of the data. The data may be no more indicators of conformity than they are of class management, or teacher survival in large classes, or simply decent behaviour and tolerance by students, or parental pressure to learn, or of an enabling and caring pedagogy, i.e. the indicators may be proxies for a whole range of causal factors; the values of the researcher may be driving the interpretation rather than the data themselves, and the negative connotation given to conformity is simply the researcher's own construction;

(f) the reader is given no indication of alternative causal explanations or theories, and no new data to test the theories. The question is begged; the causal explanation is begged, pre-empted by the way in which the research is constructed and the data are used.

These are powerful criticisms, and illustrate the difficult, inferential task of establishing causation and then testing to see if the explanation is correct. Considerable reflexivity is required by the researcher in investigating, portraying and interpreting the phenomenon being researched and explained.

Implications for researchers:

- Ensure a theoretical underpinning for the causal explanation.
- Combine theory with research.
- Provide an account of the causal processes and details that give rise to the causal explanation;
- Combine micro- and macro-accounts, intentionality, agency and structure with the data and causal explanation.
- Ensure reflexivity in investigating, portraying and interpreting the phenomenon being researched and explained.

Taking stock

The fundamental problem in determining causes from effects is the uncertainty that surrounds the status of the putative cause; it can only ever be the best to date, and the researcher does not know if it is the best in absolute terms. One effect stems from many causes, and to try to unravel and support hypotheses about these may present Herculean difficulties for the researcher. This chapter has indicated several ways in which causes may be inferred from effects:

- recognizing that a high level of detail may be required in order to establish causation: high granularity;
- identifying causal chains, mechanisms and processes;
- combining micro- and macro-levels of analysis;
- addressing both agency and structure;
- underpinning the data analysis and causal explanation with theory;
- using different kinds of *ex post facto* analysis;
- using correlational and causal-comparative, criterion group analysis;
- ensuring matching of groups in samples;
- ensuring that similar causes apply to both groups;
- adopting a seven-stage process of generating, testing and eliminating hypotheses and rival hypotheses;
- ensuring clarity on the direction of causation;
- using empirical data to test the causal explanation;
- identifying which is cause and which is effect;
- avoiding the problem of overselective data;
- ensuring that the data are fairly representative of the phenomenon under investigation;
- recognizing that cause and effect may be blurred and may overlap;
- accepting that effects may become causes in a cyclical sequence of causation;
- seeking out and recognizing overdetermination at work in causal accounts;
- recognizing the possibility of the reproduction of causality through the recycling of effects and routinization;
- keeping separate the *explanans* from the *explanandum*;
- ensuring that alternative theories and causal explanation are explored and tested;
- drawing conclusions based on the evidence, and the evidence alone.

That the establishing of causes from effects is not only inferential but also complex is evidenced in the final example provided in this chapter, where causes and effects are not only difficult to separate but may recycle themselves in overdetermining a particular effect. If one is examining cycles of reproduction then one is actually examining a snowball effect where in the same causes and effects combine cumulatively to produce a significant phenomenon.

The chapter has argued for the need to review and test rival causal theories and to retain those with the greatest explanatory potential and which fit the evidence most comprehensively and securely. It has also reaffirmed the view that, in order to avoid circularity, testing of rival hypotheses must be done with data that are different from those that gave rise to the hypotheses.

The determination of causes from effects does not have the luxury afforded to causal manipulation in determining effects from causes. Whilst this renders the determination of causes from effects more intractable, nevertheless this is not to say that it cannot be attempted or achieved, only that it is difficult.

Chapter 7

Causation: effective, inconsequential or a lost cause?

Summary of the argument in the book

This book has argued for the importance of determining the effects of causes and the causes of effects. It has indicated ways in which the researcher can proceed in these twin enterprises, but has cautioned that this is not a straightforward enterprise, not least because causation is not often observable. It has argued that deterministic causation may have a place, but that such a place is very small, and that probabilistic causation offers a more fitting characterization of causation in educational research. It has suggested that to infer simple causation is to misread many situations excepting those where massive single causation is clear, and that it is more useful to consider causal processes, causal chains and causal lines, but that these present their own difficulties in establishing causation. Further, it has restated that there is often more than a single cause at work in any effect and that there may be more than one effect from a single cause: an obvious point but one with considerable significance. Causes of effects work in specific circumstances and situations, and account has to be taken of these circumstances and conditions. Understanding of causation may be problematic, as effects may not be direct, linear functions of causes, and because there may be few, many, increasing, reducing, unpredictable, i.e. non-linear effects of causes. Causation was seen to be an inductive and empirical, rather than a logical, matter. The work of Hume and Mill was introduced as an important starting point in understanding causation.

Attention was drawn to the incidence of asymmetry of cause and effect: the cause could produce the effect but not vice versa, though exceptions to this asymmetry were noted. Further, what constitutes a cause and what constitutes an effect were seen to be problematic, and it was suggested that they were better regarded as umbrella terms, under which were sub-causes and sub-effects, causal processes, causal chains and causal lines.

Similarly, a view of causation as implying temporal precedence and succession was suggested, and a brief discussion of simultaneity, entailment and supervenience was provided as evidence of the difficulty with, but need for clarification of, temporal succession (Hume's 'priority'). The relationships, similarities, overlaps and differences between causes, reasons, motives, determination and entailment were also discussed, and the argument was made that, whilst they may all exert causal force in some circumstances, in others they did not. Similarly the confusion had to be eradicated between the actual cause and the description of the cause, the two not being identical. One distinguishing feature of causation was the significance of counterfactuals, i.e. that the absence of X would have led to the absence of Y.

The question was also raised of articulating and operationalizing causes, effects and processes/causal mechanisms, and it was suggested that the terms 'cause' and 'effect' are, in many cases, a shorthand for many sub-causes, sub-processes and sub-effects. Further, it was submitted that causes and effects may only reveal themselves over time. It was argued that causes and effects could be regarded as states and events, but that there was a case for viewing them as ongoing processes, and that, in these circumstances, a cause may overlap temporally with an effect. In this case, it was assested that separating cause from effect might be difficult, even though necessary. Where a cause begins and ends, where an effect begins and ends, when and how causes and effects should be measured, evaluated, ascertained and assessed, were seen to be open questions, requiring educational researchers to clarify and justify their decisions on timings. It was suggested that quantitative data were useful for identifying the 'what' of causation and that qualitative data were useful for identifying the 'how' of causation.

Further, the determination of a cause was seen to be problematic, involving decisions on how far to go back in the temporal causal chain and how wide or narrow to go in the causal space. Problems of causal overload, relevance and manageability were raised in meeting Mill's requirement for all causal antecedents to be included. To address this, the concepts of necessary and sufficient conditions were discussed, and these were placed in the context of separating out triggers (the last cause in a causal chain) from total causation and relevant conditions. Further, it was argued that the pursuit of relevant strengths of a cause was limited to specific contexts and circumstances, that the relative strengths of causes depended on the presence or absence of other causes, and that relative strength might be more usefully determined by examining the presence of the cause in populations rather than in the presence of other causes. The problem was raised of which variables to include, as the exclusion of relevant variables in determining causation was a major difficulty in research. Causes, like effects, might often be better regarded in conjunction with other causes, circumstances and conditions than in isolation. Contextuality – the conditions in which the cause and effect took place – were seen to be a key factor in identifying causation.

It was argued that determining causation through statistical means, though widely used, was highly questionable, as it relied on assumptions that pre-existed the statistics, i.e. that the statistics might only reinforce existing assumptions and models rather than identify causation. Further, it was mooted that linear relationships between cause and effect could take many forms, but that the pursuit of an understanding of linear relations between cause and effect might be misguided, as the effects of causes might be non-linear, and, anyway, that approach tended to deal with singular or a few causes and singular or a few effects, overlooking the interrelatedness and interactions of multiple causes with each other, with multiple effects and indeed with the multiple interactions of multiple effects. Relationships and their analysis may be stochastic, probabilistic and subjunctive rather than linear. Indeed, it was suggested that nets and conditions of causation might be more fitting descriptions of causation than causal lines, chains or ropes.

In establishing causation, the identification of 'causal forks' was seen to be useful, separating covariance and correlation due to a common cause (as in 'conjunctive forks') from the interaction of causes due to the presence of a common cause (an 'interactive fork'), and from the 'perfect fork' (the instance where it is impossible to distinguish between the conjunctive and interactive fork). It was argued that causation is more fittingly described in terms of non-recursive than of recursive models. Further, in attributing genuine causation, the benefits of screening off and controlling for variables (e.g. the presence of a third variable or several variables) were discussed. This was demonstrated with partial correlations and path analysis. The same discussion also indicated some difficulties in this, since identifying which factors to screen off from which implies that it is actually possible to *know* which factors to screen off from which, and, in the case of multiple causality (or in the cases of overdetermination), this may not be possible.

Screening off requires the ability to separate out causes, causal chains and causal lines, and this may be difficult to the point of impossibility. Here it was argued that controlling for the effects of additional variables was advisable if true causation were sought between a putative causal variable and its effect. A range of examples was provided for how to control for the effects of a third variable, and, indeed, for several variables, with both categorical and continuous data. In identifying prior and intervening variables and their influence on the dependent variable, multiple regression analysis and path analysis were introduced, with examples given from Medgraph and AMOS. It was indicated, however, that the strength of these was only as powerful as the causal assumptions which underpinned their modelling.

Caution was advised in order to avoid the ecological fallacy. In arguing for the importance of individual as well as collective, aggregate accounts, it was shown that action narratives and agency were important in accounting for causation and effects, and that 'variable' sociology had limitations if it excluded such action narratives. It was reasoned that, because of a multiplicity of action narratives and individual motivations, there were multiple pathways of causation rather than simple input–output models. In understanding the processes of causation here, the power of qualitative data was noted.

It was argued that causation may be present but unobserved and indeed unobservable, particularly in the presence of stronger causes or impeding factors. Indeed it was suggested that causation could apply in the situation of a non-change just as it applied in a situation of change, that a cause could lower the likelihood of an effect rather than increase it, or even prevent a particular effect.

One way of focusing on a causal explanation was to examine regularities and then to consider rival explanations, rival hypotheses and the theories that underpinned them. The observation of regularities was seen not to be essential to an understanding of causation, and the example of singular case studies was brought forward to exemplify this. The best causal explanation was that which was founded on, and drew from, the most comprehensive theory (e.g. that theory which embraced intentionality, agency and interaction as well as structure, i.e. micro- and macro-factors), that explained all the elements of the phenomenon, that fitted the *explanandum* and data more fully than rival theories, and that was tested in contexts and with data other than those that had given rise to the theory and causal explanation.

A range of statistical treatments was indicated in working with numerical data to understand causation. However, it was shown that statistics alone do not prove causation, and that to believe that they will is to engage in circular thinking. Rather, it is the theoretical underpinnings and assumptions that embody causation, and the role of statistics is to support, challenge, extend and refine these underpinnings and assumptions. Behind the statistics exist theories and models, and it is in the construct validity of these that causation lies. It was the *mechanisms* of causation that should concern researchers rather than solely numbers and statistical explanations.

It was argued that causal explanations that dwelt at the level of aggregate variables were incomplete, as behind them, and feeding into them, lay individuals' motives, values, goals and circumstances, and it was these that could be exerting the causal influence; hence it was suggested that a theory of individual motives might be required in understanding and explaining the causation here. In this respect rational action theory/rational choice theory, though it contained several problems and had received several trenchant criticisms, was considered to provide a useful synthesis of individual agency and the influence of structural features.

Further it was argued that between aggregate independent and dependent variables of cause and effect, respectively, lay a whole range of causal processes, and that these could be influencing the effect and, therefore, had to be taken into account in any causal explanation. The argument was seen to support micro- to macro-analysis and explanation rather than macro- to micro-analysis and explanation. How macro-structural features from society actually entered into individuals' actions and interactions, and how individuals' actions and interactions determined social structures – the causal processes involved – were seen to stand in need of further elucidation, their current status often being seen as the opaque processes in a black-box, input–output model of causation.

Whilst correlation was repeatedly asserted not to be the same as cause, nevertheless it was argued that correlation could assist in suggesting causation. Covariance was also proposed as a possible outcome of a common cause, and the discussion of causal forks was argued to be useful in clarifying this.

The argument was raised for the need to establish the direction of causation, and, concomitantly, it suggested that this may not always be straightforward, as causation can take more than one direction at a time. This justified the use of non-recursive models of causation and of causal nets.

A four-stage model for establishing the effects of causes was introduced, and this drew on the preceding discussion of the need for a theoretical base and careful operationalization, testing and elimination of rival theories and explanations using data other than those that gave rise to the explanation, as well as the drawing and delimiting of conclusions. It was argued that the use of continuous rather than categorical variables might be more effective in establishing the nature and extent of causation.

In examining the effects of causes, three approaches were introduced: action research; experimental methods; and observational research (both participant and non-participant). In these approaches it was argued that causal manipulation through an intervention was possible, but problematic at both definitional and practical levels.

Whilst action research was useful, it was seen to have limitations in the robustness of its methodology and, thereby, the reliability which could be placed in its explanation of causation. There were insufficient checks and balances built into action research for reliability and validity to be assured.

It was argued that experimental techniques, particularly randomized controlled trials, had considerable potency, and that randomization was an important element in determining causation, but that randomized controlled trials were often not possible in education and, indeed, were not immune to criticism. For example, the assumptions on which they were founded were partially suspect, they frequently did not establish the causal processes or causal chains that obtained in the situation, they neglected participants' motives and motivations, and they ignored the context in which the action was located. Indeed it was argued that context could exert a more powerful causal force than the initial causal intervention, and the example of the Lucifer effect was adduced in support of this.

Caution was advocated in supposing that randomized controlled trials, the epitome of causal manipulation in the determination of the effects of causes, would yield sufficient evidence of 'what works', as these, like other approaches, overlooked the significance of context and conditions, of processes, and of human intentionality, motives and agency – in short, of the contiguous causal connections between the intervention and its putative effects. Indeed, it was suggested that even the issue of when and whether an effect was an effect was problematic, and that attention had to be given to effects other than those in which the researcher might initially be interested. 'What works' was seen to be as much a matter of values and judgement as it was of empirical outcomes of causation.

A range of issues in judging the reliability and validity of experimental approaches was also addressed. Amongst these were the acceptability of laboratory experiments that were divorced from the 'real world' of multiple human behaviours and actions. Hence field experiments and natural experiments were introduced as a way of attenuating the difficulties posed by laboratory experiments, though these, too, were seen to create their own problems of reliability and validity.

As an alternative to action research and experimental methods of determining effects from causes, observational approaches were introduced, both participant and non-participant. Whilst it was suggested that these could catch human intentionality and agency more fully than experimental methods, nevertheless they encountered the same difficulty as the preceding approaches, in having to provide accounts of causal processes and causal chains. Further, in addressing intentionality and agency in causal processes and chains, it was also suggested that, whilst perceptions might be correct, they might also be fallacious, partial, incomplete, selective, blind and misinformed. The base rate fallacy was adduced as an example of this. The timing of data collection was seen to be a critical feature in establishing causation, and it was proposed that the greater was the need to establish causal processes, the closer and more frequent should be the data collection points, and that qualitative data could hold pre-eminence over quantitative methods in establishing causation and causal processes. Indeed it was submitted that longitudinal studies might yield accounts of causation that are more robust than cross-sectional studies. In trying to discover causation the use of 'tracers' was also advocated.

It was argued that determining the causes of effects was even more provisional, tentative and inferential than determining the effects of causes, as data were incomplete, and that backtracking along causal chains was difficult. It was possible to generate a huge number of potential causes of observed effects, and the problem was raised of deciding which one(s) was/were correct. Three approaches were set out in tracing causes from effects: (a) variants of *ex post facto* research; (b) a seven-stage sequence of steps to be taken; and (c) identifying the reproductive and recycling nature of cause and effect.

Different forms of *ex post facto* research – quasi-experiments – were introduced, and their strengths and weaknesses considered. Difficulties arose in their sometime inability to control and manipulate independent variables or to establish randomization in the sample, and examples were provided of how to address these problems.

In seeking to identify the causes of effects, emphasis was placed on the need for a theoretical foundation (e.g. rational action theory, Marxist theory, cultural theory, liberal theory, theories of structuration and habitus) to inform causal explanation. It was shown that possible causal explanations should be subject to a Popperian severe test, being evaluated against rival theories and rival explanations, being operationalized in considerable detail (high granularity), and being tested against data that are different from those that gave rise to the causal explanation. Here the work of Goldthorpe (2007b) on social class and educational attainment was held up as an outstanding example. The theory and causal explanation were seen to link micro- and macro-factors, to include agency and intentionality as well as structural constraints, and to contain a level of detail that was sufficiently high in granularity to explain the *explanandum* without concealing or swamping the main points with detail overload, i.e. the researcher was able to distinguish the wood from the trees.

A difficulty for researchers seeking to establish causes from effects was that a cause could also be the medium – the process – and the outcome of a phenomenon, and that effect could, in turn, become a cause of a further cycle of similar phenomena. This was the case in social reproduction and overdetermination, the theoretical foundation for which lay, *inter alia*, in Giddens's structuration theory and Bourdieu's theory of habitus. Where such circular causation exists and how to break into it in order to understand the causal processes at work were important issues for researchers, though it was argued that, eventually, regardless of where one started in a piece of circular causation, the nature of that circularity would be exposed. It was proposed that, even if causation is circular and reproductive, its investigation is still subject to the same criteria as the preceding examples, namely, having a necessary foundation in appropriate theory, operationalization of the theories into causal explanations, testing of the theories with data that differ from those that gave rise to the theory, and testing rival explanations.

In determining causes from effects, attention was also drawn to the inherent danger of overinterpretation of observations, of the projection of the researcher's own views, biases, values on the situation and its interpretation, and of the selective and biased use of data. The call was for as comprehensive a data set as possible, together with reflexivity on the part of the researcher in the investigation, portrayal and interpretation of the phenomenon being researched and explained.

Prospect and challenges

A *leitmotiv* throughout the book is that understanding causation is vital, though it is not straightforward. There are several contemporary matters that might challenge the relevance of understanding and seeking causation in educational and social research. Is there still a role for the investigation and practice of causation in the face of the postmodern society and the emergence of complexity theory?

We live in a postmodern society in advanced capitalism, and this raises the question of how far it challenges conventional understandings of causation (Jameson 1991; Larrain 1994; Layder 1994; O'Neill 1995), since:

- the rate of change is exponential, and the telescoping of time challenges the successionist principle that underpins much of causation. A new event happens before the former event has had the opportunity to become embedded in society, its institutions and players. This suggests that people are thinking less about cause and effect and more about events;

- there is an 'utter forgetfulfulness of the part', 'historical deafness' and the weakening of historicity (Jameson 1991), i.e. people live in, and for, the present and the future rather than seeking background causes. There is a rupture between people's presents and their pasts. Causation does not go away; it is simply forgotten. As Santayana wrote many years ago: 'nothing will have been disproved, but everything will have been abandoned' (1913: 256);
- depthlessness, flatness, visibility, explicitness, clarity and superficiality replace the hermeneutic, the genuine and the deep (Jameson 1991); depth and historical connection are replaced by superficiality and multiple surfaces;
- discontinuity reigns, where society becomes a montage of assorted events rather than causal chains;
- the world of cause and effect is replaced by worlds of discourse, each with their own language games, rules and criteria that are incommensurable with others (Lyotard 1984). No game is privileged, and cause and effect have no privileged status;
- it is impossible, or spurious, to determine regularities and patterns because society and the behaviour of individuals within it are not like that.

If postmodernism poses a threat to the relevance of causation, then this could be seen to be compounded by the emergence of complexity theory and its predecessor in chaos theory. We live on the edge of chaos, and it may no longer be fitting to consider the workings of society, its institutions and the individuals within it in terms of deterministic, mechanistic and linear cause and effect. Najmanovich (2007: 99) indicates that our understanding of society and the behaviours and actions of individuals within it have moved from causation to emergence. In complexity theory, linear causation is replaced by webs and networks of connections, multi-causality, multiple effects and multivalency (see Haggis 2008: 158–60; Olssen 2008: 101). It is no longer appropriate to consider a single cause and a single effect, as causes and effects are plural, multiply connected, with the arrows of causation going in multiple directions, both to and from events; we live in the world of hypertext connection rather than linear connection. The appropriate metaphor is of a web (Capra 1996) rather than a linear chain of causes and effects. We live in a networked rather than a solipsistic society. Reductionism, atomism and essentialism and firm, even absolute, truths are replaced by holism and a causal understanding of the history of systems (Olssen 2008: 101–2).

What if events are not contiguous, but are part of an interconnected but not causally contiguous web? Think of the spider's web. One piece of the web may not touch another piece of the web but nevertheless, in a new twist to transitivity, they are intimately connected. One part of the web does not cause the other part of the web; they are a whole in themselves and the web is a whole in itself and for itself, yet differences in A-properties (the whole web) might also be caused by differences in B-properties (the strands of the web) and vice versa: a re-application of supervenience.

Let us examine our own behaviour. How do we come to be what we are? How do we understand what we are? An event from my very distant past may suddenly resurface today and, non-transitively (or, perhaps more correctly, very weakly transitively, there being so many links, each one subject to many other links and each link being of varying strength and tenacity), may affect my behaviour today. In what sense is it true, or useful, to say that there is a causal connection, that it simply happens that the matter came into my consciousness and that I behaved in the way that I did today? What has happened here is an existential bringing together into a holistic union, a working synthesis, of a range of differentially, loosely, but not necessarily causally connected events that make up my behaviour.

The question that is posed is the extent to which the linear views of causation are upset, challenged or negated by non-linear, web-based complexity. Put simply, how appropriate and fitting is it to work with linear views of causation in a non-linear world? Is linearity a subset of complexity? Does complexity embrace both linearity and non-linearity? Are linear causations and effects a sub-set of complex webs?

Complexity theory does not negate causation; it just renders it more challenging to understand. Complexity theory, rather than abandoning causation, cannot operate without causal connection and explanation, even though emergent self-organized behaviour and phenomena are not predictable. As was mentioned in Chapter 2, predictability and causation are not the same. How, then, can we understand webs of interacting causation?

In this multiply connected world, prediction becomes difficult to the point of impossibility; instability reigns over fixity and certainty. Society and the individuals within it co-evolve (Stewart 2001); they change each other and the emergent new situation is more than the sum of its parts, just as water is more than the blend of hydrogen and oxygen. The closed, mechanistic, linear, deterministic, law-like, clockwork universe of Newton, with straightforward cause and effect, has been replaced by the open, indeterministic, non-linear, relativistic worlds of chaos and complexity (Morrison 2008). Determinism is replaced by autocatalysis that springs from the interaction and ongoing mutual adaptation of the individual and the environment. As Davis and Sumara (2005) indicate, complexity refutes the value of determinism, analytic reduction and the value of the metaphor of the straight line as useful heuristic tools for representing or interpreting phenomena. Linear relations and correlations, linear trajectories and linear narratives make for very poor representations of complex phenomena. The simple regression of one variable or many variables on another may reflect a failure to recognize the multiple, changing, metamorphosing, dynamic society in which we live. Regression is part of yesterday's linear world. Indeed, quantum theory and Heisenberg's uncertainty principle raise major challenges to the domain of 'normal causality' (Salmon 1998: 23), though, as Salmon remarks (ibid.: 24), indeterminism is compatible with causality.

These are commonplace slogans and polemics, but the reality is not as clear as this. Behind the superficial, glitzy, anomic world of the postmodern, and behind the complexity-driven world, lie sentient, agentic and rational individuals, institutions, societies and communities seeking a better life. Postmodernism may be little more than the self-indulgence of the rich (O'Neill 1995). Complexity theory may be wonderful for academics but it does not put food on the table. People still starve and struggle for survival, and causation – be it in forms of positivism or its alternatives – has made, and continues to make, significant contributions to our understanding and quality of life. It is too soon to write its epitaph.

If prediction and causal explanation are not the same, and, indeed, they are not (Clogg and Haritou 1997: 106; Salmon 1998: 5–8), then what is the future of causal explanation? Do current trends in society, do complexity theory and webs of emergent, self-organized, connected networks, signal the demise of cause and effect and its *relevance*? Certainly not; indeed exactly the opposite: they signal the need for an injection of even more thinking about cause and effect. Causation is the antibiotic to kill the excesses of postmodernism. It is required in order to understand the processes of emergence. We have a moral obligation not to abandon causation. Indeed, given its centrality in human learning, we cannot abandon it, even if we wished to; the task is to learn how it works. Complexity and causation are not mutually exclusive; it is just that the relationship between them becomes more difficult to understand. Cilliers (2007: 84) notes that 'we do not have to let go of causality in order to acknowledge complexity'; similarly postmodernism and causation are not mutually exclusive. The postmodern society, institution, community and individual still operate causally; it is just that the conditions and circumstances in which they operate have altered.

The challenge for causation, then, is to reassert itself and to realign itself in contemporary society and decision making. This may require attention to such uncomfortable or unsettling questions as the following.

- Should we focus more on causal processes than on input–output/results models of causation?
- To what extent is it possible to establish causation other than through reduction and recombination of atomistic, individual items and elements?
- How can causation as the understanding of the emergent history of a system, a whole, be investigated?
- How can we investigate multiple and simultaneous causes and their multiple and simultaneous effects in a multiply connected and networked world?
- How can we reconcile causation with unpredictability?
- Does randomness 'trump' causation (Gorard 2001: 21)?
- What use is an understanding of causation if it has little subsequent predictive utility?
- How can we understand causation in holistic webs of connections, i.e. how is it possible to discover or demonstrate causation when looking at events holistically?
- If worlds and networks are to be considered holistically, then what is the appropriate methodology for understanding causation?
- How can we gain further purchase on understanding causation and causal processes in a multi-causal, non-linear world?
- How can causation explain the emergence of new phenomena and higher-order phenomena that arise from the interaction of existing and lower-order phenomena (e.g. within complexity theory) that could not have been predicted from the lower-order phenomena?
- What are the causal processes at work in determining social and macro-structures from the actions and interaction of individuals (the micro-worlds) and, conversely, in determining the actions and interactions of individuals from the structures of society and its institutions (the macro-worlds)? What are their ontologies and epistemologies, and how do we know?
- How can we understand causation (rather than supervenience) when temporality is compacted or when simultaneity obtains?
- How can we attribute causation in a multi-causal and multi-effect world?

- How can we construct models that involve causal, non-causal and random explanations?
- What theoretical foundations can be used to catch agency, intentionality and structure, and their interplay, in understanding causation?

If educational research is to move forward, building on the careful, rational, argued, cumulative development and application of researched and tested theories, and this book has argued that it should, then the understanding and use of causation are here to stay. Causation is fundamental to development. That message needs to ring loud and clear. If you want to know how this comes to be the case, then just ask 'why?'.

Notes

1 The world of cause and effect

1   Hume divides his *Treatise* into different books, each of which has parts; each part has a section, and, within each section, there are paragraphs. Hence the reference here to 1.3.14: 35 indicates Book 1, Part 3, Section 14, paragraph 35. This convention is followed throughout this book.

2 Tools for understanding causation

1   For discussion of space–time causation and branching space–time causation, see Belnap (2002) and Müller (2005).
2   Salmon (1998: 22) and Belnap (2002: 2) replace the word 'necessary' with 'nonredundant'.
3   Belnap (2002: 13) regards the *causae causantes* to be INUS conditions and 'transition events'.
4   For further analysis of whether causes precede events in branching space-times, see Belnap (2002) and Müller (2005).
5   Kim (1993a), Savellos and Yalçin (1995) and McLaughlin (2005) distinguish between weak covariance, strong covariance and global covariance, but this book does not go into the matter here.

3 Probabilistic causation

1   Here is not the place to debate the issue of statistical significance over effect size as it is not germane to the matters in hand, since that debate is more about statistical treatment and analysis than it is about causation; but see Kline (2004) for a full review of the debate and an analysis of different ways of calculating effect size.
2   Lewis's formulation has been criticized (Pinker 2007: 213; Menzies 2008) on the grounds of context-insensitivity (confusing causes, conditions and enablers), 'temporal asymmetry', 'transitivity' (counterfactuals are not transitive), 'pre-emption' conditions (see the example in this chapter of the assassin and the king) and overdetermination (see Chapter 2).
3   This is an example of rational choice theory, discussed in Chapter 6. See also Hechter and Kanazawa (1997).
4   For a critique of Reichenbach, see Salmon (1998: 214–17).
5   As mentioned in Note 1 above, this book will not discuss the debate on, and criticisms of, statistical significance and the value of alternatives such as effect size. However, see Kline (2004) for a full analysis and Cohen *et al*. (2007: 520–5) for an indication of how to calculate effect size.
6   Salmon (1998: 20) sees in tracers an affinity to the 'mark transmission' theory of causality, which, he argues, is a useful tool for understanding causal processes. He also (ibid.: 21) aligns this with Russell's 'at-at' theory of motion and transmission.

4 Approaching cause and effect

1 This examples derives substantially from Morrison (2006).
2 For example: Stigler and Perry (1990); Mayer *et al.* (1991); Stevenson *et al.* (1990); Stevenson and Stigler (1992); Cai (1995); Hatano and Inagaki (1998); Littlewood (1999); Mok *et al.* (2001); Gonzales *et al.* (2004).
3 See: Stevenson *et al.* (1990); Stigler and Perry (1990); Kember and Gow (1991); Stevenson and Stigler (1992); Chan and Watkins (1994); Cai (1995); Gow *et al.* (1996); Biggs (1996a, 1996b, 2001); Marton *et al.* (1996); Au and Entwistle (1999); Pratt *et al.* (1999); Dahlin and Watkins (2000); Biggs and Watkins (2001); and Watkins and Biggs (2001).
4 Ho (1986); Bond (1996); Bond and Hwang (1986); Brand (1987); Stigler and Perry (1990); Stevenson *et al.* (1990); Bond (1991); Stevenson and Stigler (1992); Salili and Hau (1994); Zhang and Carraquillo (1995); Stevenson and Lee (1996); Lee (1996); Lau (1996); Pratt *et al.* (1998, 1999); Wong (1998, 2000, 2004); Littlewood (1999); Gu (2001); Hong (2001), Salili *et al.* (2001); Lau and Roffey (2002); Wong and Wong (2002); Kennedy (2002); Hu (2002) and Lee (2005).

5 Determining the effects of causes

1 The following section uses material from Morrison (2001).

6 Determining causes from effects

1 The following section on *ex post facto* research draws heavily on Cohen *et al.* (2007: chap. 12).
2 For example: Coleman (1990: chap. 1); Turner (1991: 354); Hauptmann (1996); Hechter and Kanazawa (1997); Breen (1999); Scott (2000); Norkus (2000); Green (2002); Boudon (2003); Lovett (2006); Goldthorpe (2007a: 154; 2007b: 141); Jaeger (2007); Harford (2008: 2).
3 For criticisms of rational choice theory, see, for example: Hauptmann (1996); Hechter and Kanazawa (1997); Boudon (1998, 2003); Kiser and Hechter (1998); Somers (1998); Gaertner and Xu (1999); Kara (1999); Zafirovski (1999); Scott (2000); Green (2002); Vanberg (2002); MacDonald (2003); Sawyer (2005); Lovett (2006); Goldthorpe (2007a); Lahno (2007).

References

Ao, I. H. (2006) 'An action research study of English speaking anxiety of Primary Five students in Macao', Unpublished MSc dissertation, Macau Inter-University Institute.

Au, C., and Entwistle, N. (1999) '"Memorisation with understanding" in approaches to studying: cultural variant or response to assessment demands?', Paper presented at the European Association for Research on Learning and Instruction Conference, Gothenburg, August.

Axline, V. M. (1964) *Dibs in Search of Self*, New York: Ballantine Books.

Ayres, I. (2008) *Super Crunchers*, London: John Murray.

Beebee, H. (2004) 'Causing and nothingness', in J. Collins, N. Hall and L. Paul (eds), *Causation and Counterfactuals*, Cambridge, MA: MIT Press, pp. 291–308.

Belnap, N. (2002) 'A theory of causation: causae causantes (originating causes) as inus conditions in branching space-times', Paper presented at the Philosophy of Science Association 18th biennial meeting, Milwaukee; http://philsci-archive.pitt.edu/archive/00000891 (accessed 24 October 2008).

Bennett, J. (1993) 'Event causation: the counterfactual analysis', in E. Sosa and M. Tooley (eds), *Causation*, Oxford: Oxford University Press, pp. 217–34.

Bernstein, B. (1977) *Class, Codes and Control*, Vol. 3, London: Routledge & Kegan Paul.

Berry, W. D. (1984) *Nonrecursive Causal Models*, Beverly Hills, CA: Sage.

Biggs, J. B. (1996a) 'Western misperceptions of the Confucian-heritage learning culture', in D. A. Watkins and J. B. Biggs (eds), *The Chinese Learner: Cultural, Psychological and Contextual Influences*, Hong Kong: Comparative Education Research Centre; Melbourne: Australian Council for Educational Research, pp. 45–67.

Biggs, J. B. (1996b) 'Learning, schooling and socialization: a Chinese solution to a Western problem', in S. Lau (ed.), *Growing Up the Chinese Way: Chinese Child and Adolescent Development*, Hong Kong: Chinese University Press, pp. 147–67.

Biggs, J. B. (2001) 'Teaching across cultures', in F. Salili, C. Y. Chiu and Y. Y. Hong (eds), *Student Motivation: The Culture and Context of Learning*, New York: Kluwer Academic, pp. 293–308.

Biggs, J. B. and Watkins, D. A. (2001) 'Insights into teaching the Chinese learner', in D. A. Watkins and J. B. Biggs (eds), *Teaching the Chinese Learner: Psychological and Pedagogical Perspectives*, Hong Kong: Comparative Education Research Centre; Melbourne: Australian Council for Educational Research, pp. 277–300.

Blalock, H. M. (ed.) (1971) *Causal Models in the Social Sciences*, Chicago: Aldine.

Bond, M. H. (1991) *Beyond the Chinese Face: Insights from Psychology*, Oxford: Oxford University Press.

Bond, M. H. (ed.) (1996) *The Handbook of Chinese Psychology*, Hong Kong: Oxford University Press.

Bond, M. H. and Hwang, K. H. (1986) 'The social psychology of the Chinese People', in M. H. Bond (ed.), *The Psychology of the Chinese People*, Oxford: Oxford University Press, pp. 213–66.

Boruch, R. (1997) *Randomised Experimentation or Planning and Evaluation: A Practical Guide*, London: Sage.

Bouchard, T. J., Jr., Lykken, D. T., McGue, M., Segal, N. L., and Tellegen, A. (1990) 'Sources of human psychological differences: the Minnesota study of twins reared apart', *Science*, 250(6): 223–9.

Boudon, R. (1998) 'Limitations of rational choice theory', *American Journal of Sociology*, 104(3): 817–28.

Boudon, R. (2003) 'Beyond rational choice theory', *Annual Review of Sociology*, 29: 1–21.

Bourdieu, P. (1976) 'The school as a conservative force: scholastic and cultural inequalities', in R. Dale, G. Esland and M. Macdonald (eds), *Schooling and Capitalism*, London: Routledge & Kegan Paul, pp. 110–17.

Bourdieu, P. (1977) *Outline of a Theory of Practice*, Cambridge: Cambridge University Press.

Bourdieu, P. (1986) *Distinction: A Social Critique of the Judgement of Taste*, London: Routledge.

Bourdieu, P. (1990) *The Logic of Practice*, Stanford, CA: Stanford University Press.

Bourdieu, P. (2000) *Pascalian Meditations*, Cambridge: Polity.

Bourdieu, P., and Passeron, J. C. (1977) *Reproduction in Education, Society and Culture*, Beverly Hills, CA: Sage.

Brand, D. (1987) 'The new whiz kids: why Asian Americans are doing so well, and what it costs them', *Time*, 130, 31 August: 42–50.

Bray, M. (1999) *The Shadow Education System: Private Tutoring and its Implications for Planners*, Paris: UNESCO.

Bray, M. (2006) 'Private supplementary tutoring: comparative perspectives on patterns and implications', *Compare*, 36(4): 515–30.

Breen, R. (1999) 'Beliefs, rational choice and Bayesian learning', *Rationality and Society*, 11(4): 463–79.

Cai, J. (1995) *A Cognitive Analysis of U.S. and Chinese Students' Mathematical Performance on Tasks involving Computation, Simple Problem Solving and Complex Problem Solving*, Reston, VA: National Council of Teachers of Mathematics.

Campbell, D. T., and Stanley, J. C. (1963) *Experimental and Quasi-Experimental Designs for Research*, Boston: Houghton Mifflin.

Capra, F. (1996) *The Web of Life*, New York: Anchor Books.

Carrington, L. B., Tymms, P. B., and Merrell, C. (2005) 'Role models, school improvement and the "gender gap" – do men bring out the best in boys and women the best in girls?', Paper presented at the EARLI 2005 conference, University of Nicosia; http://www.cemcentre.org/Documents/CEM/publications/downloads/CEMWeb019%20EARLI%202005%20Role%20Models%20School%20Improvment%20And%20Gender%20Gap.pdf (accessed 2 September 2008).

Chan, G. Y., and Watkins, D. (1994) 'Classroom environment and approaches to learning: an investigation of the actual and preferred perceptions of Hong Kong secondary school students', *Instructional Science*, 22(3): 233–46.

Chan, J. (1996) 'Chinese intelligence', in M. H. Bond (ed.), *The Handbook of Chinese Psychology*, Hong Kong: Oxford University Press, pp. 93–108.

Chomsky, N. (1959 'Review of Skinner's *Verbal Behaviour*', *Language*, 35(1): 26–58.

Cilliers, P. (1998) *Complexity and Postmodernism*, London: Routledge.

Cilliers, P. (2007) 'Why we cannot know complex things completely', in F. Capra, A. Juarrero, P. Sotolongo and J. Van Uden (eds), *Reframing Complexity: Perspectives from the North and South*, Mansfield, MA: ISCE, pp. 81–9.

Clarke, A., and Dawson, R. (1999) *Evaluation Research*, London: Sage.

Clogg, C. C., and Haritou, A. (1997) 'The regression method of causal inference and a dilemma confronting this method', in V. R. McKim and S. P. Turner (eds), *Causality in Crisis? Statistical Methods and the Search for Causal Knowledge in the Social Sciences*, Notre Dame, IN: University of Notre Dame Press, pp. 83–112.

Coe, R., Fitz-Gibbon, C. T., and Tymms, P. (2000) 'Promoting evidence-based education: the role of practitioners', Paper presented at the British Educational Research Association, University of Cardiff, 7–10 September.

Cohen, J., and Stewart, I. (1995) *The Collapse of Chaos*, Harmondsworth: Penguin.

Cohen, L., Manion, L., and Morrison, K. R. B. (2000) *Research Methods in Education*, 5th edn, London: Routledge.

Cohen, L., Manion, L., and Morrison, K. R. B. (2007) *Research Methods in Education*, 6th edn, London: Routledge.

Coleman, J. S. (1990) *Foundations of Social Theory*, Cambridge, MA: Harvard University Press.

Cook, T., and Campbell, D. (1979) *Quasi-Experimentation: Design and Analysis Issues for Field Settings*, Chicago: Rand-McNally.

Cook, T. D., Cooper, H., Cordray, D. S., Hartmann, H., Hedges, L. V., Light, R. J., Louis, T. A., and Mosteller, F. (1992) *Meta-Analysis for Explanation*, New York: Russell Sage Foundation.

Curriculum Evaluation and Management Centre (2000) *A Culture of Evidence*; http://cem.dur.ac.uk/ebeuk/culture.htm (accessed 11 November 2000).

Dahlin, B., and Watkins, D. (2000) 'The role of repetition in the processes of memorising and understanding: a comparison of the views of German and Chinese secondary school students in Hong Kong', *British Journal of Educational Psychology*, 70: 65–84.

Davidson, D. (2001) *Essays on Actions and Events*, Oxford: Oxford University Press.

Davies, H. T. O., Nutley, S. M., and Smith P. C. (eds) (2000) *What Works? Evidence-Based Policy and Practice in Public Services*, Bristol: Policy Press.

Davies, P. (1999) 'What is evidence-based education?', *British Journal of Educational Studies*, 47(2): 108–21.

Davis, B., and Sumara, D. J. (2005) 'Challenging images of knowing: complexity science and educational research', *International Journal of Qualitative Studies in Education*, 18(3): 305–21.

Davis, D. (1995) 'Evidence-based education', *Canadian Association for Medical Education Newsletter*, 7(1): 1–5; http://www.medicine.dal.ca/gorgs/came/clinic.htm (accessed 10 July 2000).

Dobby, J. (1999) 'Issues of quality in research review', Paper presented at the Annual General Meeting of the National Foundation for Educational Research, London: National Foundation for Educational Research.

Doll, W. (1993) *A Post-Modern Perspective on Curriculum*, New York: Teachers College Press.

Dowe, P. (2007) 'Causal processes', in *Stanford Encyclopedia of Philosophy*; http://plato.stanford.edu/entried/causation-process/ (accessed 31 December 2007).

Ducasse, C. J. (1993) 'On the nature and the observability of the causal relation', in E. Sosa and M. Tooley (eds) (1993) *Causation*, Oxford: Oxford University Press, pp. 125–36.

Duncan, O. D. (1969) 'Contingencies in constructing causal models', in F. Borgatta (ed.), *Sociological Methodology 1969*, San Francisco: Jossey-Bass, pp. 74–112.

Durkheim, E. (1982) *The Rules of Sociological Method*, trans. W. D. Halls, New York: Free Press.

Eagleton, T. (1991) *Ideology,* London: Verso.

Edwards, A. D. (1980) 'Patterns of power and authority in classroom talk', in P. Woods (ed.), *Teacher Strategies: Explorations in the Sociology of the School*, London: Croom Helm, pp. 237–53.

Eisenhart, M. (2005) 'Hammers and saws for the improvement of educational research', *Educational Theory*, 55(3): 244–61.

Evans, J., Sharp, C., and Benefield, P. (2000) 'Systematic reviews of educational research: does the medical model fit?', Paper presented at the British Educational Research Association conference, University of Cardiff, 7–10 September.

Fisher, R. (1951) *The Design of Experiments*, Edinburgh: Oliver & Boyd.

Fitz-Gibbon, C. T. (1984) 'Meta-analysis: an explication', *British Educational Research Journal*, 10(2): 135–44.

Fitz-Gibbon, C. T. (1985) 'The implications of meta-analysis for educational research', *British Educational Research Journal*, 11(1): 45–9.

Fitz-Gibbon, C. T. (1996) *Monitoring Education: Indicators, Quality and Effectiveness*, London: Cassell.

Freedman, D. A. (1997) 'From association to causation via regression', in V. R. McKim and S. P. Turner (eds), *Causality in Crisis? Statistical Methods and the Search for Causal Knowledge in the Social Sciences*, Notre Dame, IN: University of Notre Dame Press, pp. 113–61.

Fuchs, C. (2003) 'Structuration theory and self-organization', *Systematic Practice and Action Research*, 16(2): 133–67.

Gaertner, W., and Xu, Y. S. (1999) 'Rationality and external experience', *Rationality and Society*, 11(2): 169–85.

Galton, M., and Simon, B. (1980) *Inside the Primary Classroom*, London: Routledge & Kegan Paul.

Garcia, A. S. (2008) 'Teacher stress in the Macau workplace', Unpublished PhD thesis, Macau Inter-University Institute.

Gardner, H. (1989) *To Open Minds*, New York: Basic Books.

Garrahan, P., and Stewart, P. (1992) *The Nissan Enigma: Flexibility at Work in a Local Economy*, London: Mansell.

Giddens. A. (1976) *New Rules of Sociological Method*, London: Hutchinson.

Giddens, A. (1979) *Central Problems in Social Theory*, London: Macmillan.

Giddens, A. (1981) *A Contemporary Critique of Contemporary Materialism*, Vol. 1: *Power, Property and the State*, Basingstoke: Macmillan.

Giddens, A. (1984) *The Constitution of Society: Outline of the Theory of Structuration*, Cambridge: Polity.

Glaser, B., and Strauss, A. (1967) *The Discovery of Grounded Theory*, Chicago: Aldine.

Gleick, J. (1987) *Chaos*, London: Abacus.

Glymour, C. (1997) 'A review of recent work on the foundations of causal inference', in V. R. McKim and S. P. Turner (eds), *Causality in Crisis? Statistical Methods and the Search for Causal Knowledge in the Social Sciences*, Notre Dame, IN: University of Notre Dame Press, pp. 201–48.

Goldthorpe, J. H. (2007a) *On Sociology*, Vol. 1: *Critique and Program*, 2nd edn, Stanford, CA: Stanford University Press.

Goldthorpe, J. H. (2007b) *On Sociology*, Vol. 2: *Illustration and Retrospect*, 2nd edn, Stanford, CA: Stanford University Press.

Gonzales, P., Calsyn, L., Jocelyn, L., Mak, K., Kastberg, D., Arafeh, S., Williams, T., and Tsen, W. (2000) *Pursuing Excellence: Comparisons of International Eighth-Grade Mathematics and Science Achievement from a U.S. Perspective, 1995 and 1999*, Washington, DC: National Center for Education Statistics.

Gonzales, P., Guzmán, J. C., Partelow, L., Pahlke, E., Jocelyn, L., Kastberg, D., and Williams, T. (2004) *Highlights from the Trends in International Mathematics and Science Study (TIMMS) 2003*, Washington, DC: National Center for Education Statistics.

Gorard, S. (2001) 'A changing climate for educational research? The role of research capability-building', Paper presented at the British Educational Research Association annual conference, University of Leeds, September.

Gorard, S. (2007) 'The dubious benefits of multi-level modelling', *International Journal of Research and Method in Education*, 30(2): 221–36.

Gow, L., Balla, J., Kember, D., and Hau, K. T. (1996) 'The learning approaches of Chinese people: a function of socialization processes and the context of learning?', in M. H. Bond (ed.), *The Handbook of Chinese Psychology*, Hong Kong: Oxford University Press, pp. 109–23.

Gramsci, A. (1971) *Selection from the Prison Notebooks*, ed. and trans. Q. Hoare and G. Smith, New York: International Publishers.

Green, S. L. (2002) 'Rational choice theory: an overview', Paper presented at the Baylor University faculty development seminar on rational choice theory, May; http://business.baylor.edu/steve_green/green1.doc (accessed 19 February 2008).

Gu, M. Y. (2001) *Education in China and Abroad: Perspectives from a Lifetime in Comparative Education*, Hong Kong: Comparative Research Centre, University of Hong Kong.

Gurian, M., and Ballew, A. C. (2003) *The Boys and Girls Learn Differently*, San Francisco: Jossey-Bass, pp. 7–28.

Hage, J., and Meeker, B. F. (1988) *Social Causality*, London: Unwin Hyman.

Haggis, T. (2008) '"Knowledge must be contextual": some possible implications of complexity and dynamic systems theories for educational research', in M. Mason (ed.), *Complexity Theory and the Philosophy of Education*, Chichester: Wiley-Blackwell, pp. 150–68.

Halsey, A. H., Heath, A., and Ridge, J. (1980) *Origins and Destinations: Family, Class and Education in Modern Britain*, Oxford: Clarendon Press.

Hanson, M. N. (2008) 'Rational action theory and educational attainment: changes in the impact of economic resources', *European Sociological Review*, 24(1): 1–17.

Harford. T. (2008) *The Logic of Life*, London: Little, Brown.

Hargreaves, A. (1989) *Curriculum and Assessment Reform*, Milton Keynes: Open University Press.

Harlen, W. (2004a) 'A systematic review of the evidence of reliability and validity of assessment by teachers used for summative purposes', London: University of London Institute of Education EPPI-Centre, Social Science Unit; http://eppi.ioe.ac.uk/cms/LinkClick.aspx?fileticket=oTs5TvawGXw%3d&tabid=116&mid=922&language=en-US (accessed 15 September 2005).

Harlen, W. (2004b) 'A systematic review of the evidence of the impact on students, teachers and the curriculum of the process of using assessment by teachers for summative purposes', London: University of London Institute of Education EPPI-Centre, Social Science Unit; http://eppi.ioe.ac.uk/EPPIWeb/home.aspx?page=/reel/review_groups/assessment/review_four.htm (accessed 15 September 2005).

Harnad, S. (1996) *The Base Rate Fallacy*; http://users/ecs.soton.ac.uk/harnad/Hypermail/Explaining.Mnd 96/0221.html (accessed 2 January 2008).

Harré, R. (1972) *The Philosophies of Science*, Oxford: Oxford University Press.

Hatano, G., and Inagaki, K. (1998) 'Cultural contexts of schooling revisited: a review of *The Learning Gap* from a cultural psychology perspective', in S. G. Paris and H. M. Wellman (eds), *Global Prospects for Education: Development, Culture and Schooling*, Washington, DC: American Psychological Association, pp. 79–104.

Hauptmann, E. (1996) *Putting Choice before Democracy*, New York: State University of New York Press.

Hayek, F. A. V. (1942) 'Scientism and the study of society: part 1', *Economica*, 9(35): 267–91.

Hechter, M., and Kanazawa, S. (1997) 'Sociological rational choice theory', *Annual Review of Sociology*, 23: 191–214.

Hedström, P. (2005) *Dissecting the Social*, Cambridge: Cambridge University Press.

Heise, D. R. (1969) 'Problems in path analysis and causal inference', in F. Borgatta (ed.), *Sociological Methodology 1969*, San Francisco: Jossey-Bass, pp. 38–73.

Hellevik, O. (1988) *Introduction to Causal Analysis*, Oslo: Norwegian University Press.

Hesslow, G. (1976) 'Discussion: two notes on the probabilistic approach to causation', *Philosophy of Science*, 43(2): 290–2.

Hitchcock, C. (2002) 'Probabilistic causation', in *Stanford Encyclopedia of Philosophy*; http://plato.stanford.edu/entried/causation-probabilistic/ (accessed 31 December 2007).

Ho, D. Y. F. (1986) 'Chinese patterns of socialization: a critical review', in M. H. Bond (ed.), *The Psychology of the Chinese People*, Oxford: Oxford University Press, pp.1–37.

Ho, U. M. (2007) 'The effects of CLT on form three students' English learning in a Chinese medium school in Macau', Unpublished MSc dissertation, Macau Inter-University Institute.

Holland, P. W. (1986) 'Statistics and causal inference', *Journal of the American Statistics Association*, 81: 945–70.

Holland, P. W. (2004) 'Evidence for *causal* influence in education research', Paper presented at the annual conference of the American Educational Research Association, San Diego, April.

Homans, G. (1961) *Social Behaviour: Its Elementary Forms*, London: Routledge & Kegan Paul.

Hong, Y. Y. (2001) 'Chinese students' preferences and teachers' inferences of effort and ability', in F. Salili, C. Y. Chiu and Y. Y. Hong (eds), *Student Motivation: The Culture and Context of Learning*, New York: Kluwer Academic, pp. 105–20.

Horwich, P. (1993) 'Lewis's programme', in E. Sosa and M. Tooley (eds), *Causation*, Oxford: Oxford University Press, pp. 208–16.

Howieson, C., and Iannelli, C. (2008) 'The effects of low attainment on young people's outcomes at age 22–23 in Scotland', *British Educational Research Journal*, 34(2): 269–90.

Hu, G. W. (2002) 'Potential cultural resistance to pedagogical imports: the case of communicative language teaching in China', *Language, Culture and Curriculum*, 15(2): 93–105.

Hume, D. (1955) *An Inquiry Concerning Human Understanding*, New York: Liberal Arts Press.

Hume, D. (2000) *A Treatise of Human Nature*, ed. D. F. Norton and M. J. Norton, Oxford: Oxford University Press.

Jaeger, M. M. (2007) 'Economic and social returns to educational choices: extending the utility function', *Rationality and Society*, 19(4): 451–83.

Jameson, F. (1991) *Post-Modernism, or the Cultural Logic of Late Capitalism*, London: Verso.

Jencks, C. (1972) *Inequality: A Reassessment of the Effects of Family and Schooling in America*, New York: Basic Books.

Kahneman, D., and Tversky, A. (1973) 'On the psychology of prediction', *Psychological Review*, 80: 237–51.

Kara, A. (1999) 'A paradox of social rationality: are there contexts where individual irrationality is more conducive than individual rationality to producing rational social preferences?', *Rationality and Society*, 11(2): 187–206.

Kauffman, S. A. (1995) *At Home in the Universe: The Search for the Laws of Self-Organization and Complexity*, Harmondsworth: Penguin.

Kember, D., and Gow, L. (1991) 'A challenge to the anecdotal stereotype of the Asian students', *Studies in Higher Education*, 16(2): 117–28.

Kennedy, P. (2002) 'Learning cultures and learning styles: myth-understandings about adult (Hong Kong) Chinese learners', *International Journal of Lifelong Education*, 21(5): 430–55.

Kim, J. (1993a) *Supervenience and Mind: Selected Philosophical Essays*, Cambridge: Cambridge University Press.

Kim, J. (1993b) 'Causes and events: Mackie on causation', in E. Sosa and M. Tooley (eds), *Causation*, Oxford: Oxford University Press, pp. 60–74.

Kim, J. (1993c) 'Causes and counterfactuals', in E. Sosa and M. Tooley (eds), *Causation*, Oxford: Oxford University Press, pp. 205–7.

Kiser, E., and Hechter, M. (1998) 'The debate on historical sociology: rational choice theory and its critics', *American Journal of Sociology*, 104(3): 785–816.

Kline, R. B. (2004) *Beyond Significance Testing: Reforming Data Analysis Methods in Behavioral Research*, Washington, DC: American Psychological Association.

Koehler, J. J. (1996) 'The base rate fallacy reconsidered: descriptive, normative and methodological challenges', *Behavioral and Brain Sciences*, 19(1): 1–53; http://www.bbsonline.org/Preprints/OldArchive/bbs.koehler.html (accessed 4 April 2005).

Lahno, B. (2007) 'Rational choice and rule-following behavior', *Rationality and Society*, 19(4): 425–50.

Lai, P. C. (2004) 'An analysis of collaborative and cooperative group work for improving students' reading and writing in English and higher order thinking', Unpublished MSc dissertation, Macau Inter-University Institute.

Land, K. C. (1969) 'Principles of path analysis', in F. Borgatta (ed.), *Sociological Methodology 1969*, San Francisco: Jossey-Bass, pp. 3–37.

Lapointe, A. E., Mead, N. A., and Askew, J. M. (eds) (1992) *The International Assessment of Educational Progress Report Number 22-CAEP-01*, Princeton, NJ: Educational Testing Service, Center for the Assessment of Educational Progress.

Larrain, J. (1994) *Ideology and Cultural Identity*, Cambridge: Polity.

Lau, A., and Roffey, B. (2002) 'Management education and development in China: a research note', *Labour and Management in Development Journal*, 2(10): 1–18.

Lau, S. (ed.) (1996) *Growing Up the Chinese Way: Chinese Child and Adolescent Development*, Hong Kong: Chinese University Press.

Layder, D. (1994) *Understanding Social Theory*, London: Sage.

Lee, S. Y. (1998) 'Mathematics learning and teaching in the school context: reflections from cross-cultural comparisons', in S. G. Paris and H. M. Wellman (eds), *Prospects for Education: Development, Culture and Schooling*, Washington, DC: American Psychological Association, pp. 45–77.

Lee, W. O. (1996) 'The cultural context for Chinese learners: conceptions of learning in the Confucian tradition', in D. Watkins and J. B. Biggs (eds), *The Chinese Learner: Cultural, Psychological and Contextual Influences*, Hong Kong: Comparative Education Research Centre; Melbourne: Australian Council for Educational Research, pp. 25–41.

Lee, W. O. (2005) 'Teachers' perceptions of citizenship in China', in W. O. Lee and J. Fouts (eds), *Education for Social Citizenship: Perceptions of Teachers in the USA, Australia, England, Russia and China*, Hong Kong: Hong Kong University Press, pp. 55–92.

Levačić, R., and Glatter, R. (2000) 'Really good ideas: developing evidence-informed policy and practice in educational leadership and management', *Educational Management and Administration*, 29(1): 5–25.

Lewin, K. (1951) *Field Theory in Social Science: Selected Theoretical Papers*, ed. D. Cartwright, New York: Harper & Row.

Lewin, K., and Lu, W. (1990) 'University entrance examinations in China: a quiet revolution', in P. Broadfoot, R. Murphy, R. Torrance and H. Torrance (eds), *Changing Educational Assessment*, London: Routledge, pp. 153–76.

Lewin, R. (1993) *Complexity: Life on the Edge*, London: Phoenix.

Lewis, D. K. (1986) *On the Plurality of Worlds*, Oxford: Blackwell; cited in B. P. McLaughlin, 'Varieties of supervenience', in E. E. Savellos and U. Yalçin (eds), *Supervenience: New Essays*, Cambridge: Cambridge University Press, 1995, pp. 16–59.

Lewis, D. K. (1993) 'Causation', in E. Sosa and M. Tooley (eds), *Causation*, Oxford: Oxford University Press, pp. 193–204.

Lieberson, S. (1997) 'The big broad issues in society and social history: application of a probabilistic perspective', in V. R. McKim and S. P. Turner (eds), *Causality in Crisis? Statistical Methods and the Search for Causal Knowledge in the Social Sciences*, Notre Dame, IN: University of Notre Dame Press, pp. 359–85.

Littlewood, W. (1999) 'Defining and developing autonomy in East Asian contexts', *Applied Linguistics*, 20(1): 71–94.

Locke, J. (1997) *An Essay Concerning Human Understanding*, London: Penguin.

Lovett, F. (2006) 'Rational choice theory and explanation', *Rationality and Society*, 18(2): 237–72.

Lynn, R. (1988) *Educational Achievement in Japan: Lessons for the West*, Armonk, NY: M. E. Sharpe.

Lyotard, J. B. (1984) *The Postmodern Condition: A Report on Knowledge*, Manchester: Manchester University Press.

MacDonald, P. K. (2003) 'Useful fiction or miracle maker: the competing epistemological foundations of rational choice theory', *American Political Science Review*, 97(4): 551–65.

Mackie, J. L. (1993) 'Causes and conditions', in E. Sosa and M. Tooley (eds), *Causation*, Oxford: Oxford University Press, pp. 33–55.

McKim, V. R. (1997) 'Introduction', in V. R. McKim and S. P. Turner (eds), *Causality in Crisis? Statistical Methods and the Search for Causal Knowledge in the Social Sciences*, Notre Dame, IN: University of Notre Dame Press, pp. 1–19.

McLaughlin, B. P. (1995) 'Varieties of supervenience', in E. E. Savellos and U. Yalçin (eds), *Supervenience: New Essays*, Cambridge: Cambridge University Press, pp. 16–59.

McLaughlin, B. P. (2005) 'Supervenience', in *Stanford Encyclopedia of Philosophy*; http://plato.stanford.edu/entries/supervenience (accessed 31 August 2007).

Marton, F., Dall'Alba, G., and Tse, L. K. (1996) 'Memorizing and understanding: the keys to the paradox?', in D. Watkins and J. B. Biggs (eds), *The Chinese Learner: Cultural, Psychological and Contextual Influences*, Hong Kong: Comparative Education Research Centre; Melbourne: Australian Council for Educational Research, pp. 69–83.

Maxwell, J. A. (1996) *Qualitative Research Design: An Interactive Approach*, Thousand Oaks, CA: Sage.

Maxwell, J. A. (2004) 'Causal explanation, qualitative research, and scientific inquiry in education', *Educational Researcher*, 33(2): 3–11.

Mayer, R. E., Tajika, H., and Stanley, C. (1991) 'Mathematical problem solving in Japan and the United States: a cultural comparison', *Journal of Educational Psychology*, 83(1): 69–72.

Maynard, A., and Chalmers, I. (eds) (1997) *Non-Random Reflections on Health Service Research*, London: BMJ.

Mellor, D. H. (1995) *The Facts of Causation*, Abingdon: Routledge.

Menzies, P. (2008) 'Counterfactual theories of causation', in *Stanford Encyclopedia of Philosophy*; http://plato.stanford.edu/entries/causation-counterfactual (accessed 31 August 2007).

Micklethwait, J., and Wooldridge, A. (1997) *The Witch Doctors*, London: Mandarin.

Miles, M. B., and Huberman, A. M. (1984) *Qualitative Data Analysis*, Beverly Hills, CA: Sage.

Milgram, S. (1974) *Obedience to Authority*, New York: Harper & Row.

Mill, J. S. (2006) *A System of Logic Ratiocinative and Inductive, Volume 7 Books I–III*, Indianapolis: Liberty Fund.

Milwain, C. (1998) *Assembling, Maintaining and Disseminating a Social and Educational Controlled Trials Register (SPECTR): A Collaborative Endeavour*, Oxford: UK Cochrane Centre.

Milwain, C., Chalmers, I., Macdonald, S., and Smith, P. (1999) *Cochrane Collaboration Methods Group Newsletter*, June; http://hiru.mcmaster.ca/cochrane/newslett/mgnews.htm (accessed 10 July 2000).

Mitroff, I. I. (1983) *The Subjective Side of Science: A Philosophical Inquiry into the Psychology of the Apollo Moon Scientists*, Seaside, CA: Intersystems.

Mok, I., Chik, P. M., Ko, P. Y., Kwan, T., Lo, M. L., Marton, F., Ng, D. F. P., Pang, M. F., Runesson, U., and Szeto, L. H. (2001) 'Solving the paradox of the Chinese learner', in D. A. Watkins and J. B. Biggs (eds), *Teaching the Chinese Learner: Psychological and Pedagogical Perspectives*, Hong Kong: Comparative Education Research Centre; Melbourne: Australian Council for Educational Research, pp. 161–79.

Morgan, M. S. (1997) 'Searching for causal relations in economic statistics: reflections from history', in V. R. McKim and S. P. Turner (eds), *Causality in Crisis? Statistical Methods and the Search for Causal Knowledge in the Social Sciences*, Notre Dame, IN: University of Notre Dame Press, pp. 47–80.

Morrison, K. R. B. (1993) *Planning and Accomplishing School-Centred Evaluation*, Dereham, Norfolk: Peter Francis.

Morrison, K. R. B. (1995) 'Habermas and the school curriculum: an evaluation and case study', Unpublished PhD thesis, University of Durham.

Morrison, K. R. B. (1998) *Management Theories for Educational Change*, London: Paul Chapman.

Morrison, K. R. B. (2001) 'Randomised controlled trials for evidence-based education: some problems in judging "what works"', *Evaluation and Research in Education*, 15(2): 69–83.

Morrison, K. R. B. (2006) 'Paradox lost: towards a robust test of the Chinese learner', *Hong Kong Education Journal*, 34(1): 1–30.

Morrison, K. R. B. (2008) 'Educational philosophy and the challenge of complexity theory', in M. Mason (ed.), *Complexity Theory and the Philosophy of Education*, Oxford: Wiley-Blackwell, pp. 16–31.

Morrison, K. R.B., and Ieong, O. N. A. (2007) 'Does repeating a year improve performance? The case of teaching English', *Educational Studies*, 33(3): 353–71.

Morrison, K. R. B., and Tang, F. H. (2002) 'Testing to destruction: a problem in a small state', *Assessment in Education*, 9(3): 289–317.

Morrison, K. R. B., Gott, R., and Ashman, A. (1989) 'A cascade model of curriculum innovation', *British Journal of In-Service Education*, 15(3): 159–69.

Mortimore, P., Sammons, P., Ecob, R., and Stoll, L. (1988) *School Matters: The Junior Years*, Wells: Open Books.

Müller, T. (2005) 'Probability theory and causation: a branching space–time analysis', *PhilSci Archive*; http://philsci-archive.pitt.edu/archive/00001737/01/prob_bst.pdf (accessed 24 October 2008).

Mullis, I. V. S., Martin, M. O., and Foy, P. (2003) *TIMMS 2003 International Mathematics Report*, Boston: TIMMS and PIRLS International Study Center, Lynch School of Education, Boston College.

Najmanovich, D. (2007) 'From paradigms to figures of thought', in F. Capra, A. Juarrero, P. Sotolongo and J. Van Uden (eds), *Reframing Complexity: Perspectives from the North and South*, Mansfield, MA: ISCE, pp. 91–105.

Nash, R. (1973) *Classrooms Observed*, London: Routledge & Kegan Paul.

Nash, R. (1999) 'Bourdieu, "habitus" and educational research: is it all worth the candle?', *British Journal of Sociology of Education*, 20(2): 175–87.

Nietzsche, F. (1973) *Beyond Good and Evil*, Harmondsworth: Penguin.

Noah H., and Eckstein, M. (1990) 'Trade-offs in examination policies: an international comparative perspective', in P. Broadfoot, R. Murphy and H. Torrance (eds), *Changing Educational Assessment: International Perspectives and Trends*, London: Routledge, pp. 84–97.

Norkus, Z. (2000) 'Max Weber's interpretative sociology and rational choice approach', *Rationality and Society*, 12(3): 259–82.

Novemsky, N., and Kronzon, S. (1999) 'How are base-rates used, when they are used: a comparison of additive and Bayesian models of base-rate use', *Journal of Behavioral Decision Making*, 12(1): 55–69.

Oakley, A. (1998) 'Experimentation in social science: the case of health promotion', *Social Science in Health*, 4(2): 73–89.

Oakley, A. (2000) *Experiments in Knowing: Gender and Method in the Social Sciences*, Cambridge: Polity.

OECD (Organization for Economic Co-operation and Development) (2004) *Learning for Tomorrow's World*, Paris: OECD.

OECD (Organization for Economic Co-operation and Development) (2007) *PISA 2006*, Paris: OECD.

Olssen, M. (2008) 'Foucault as complexity theorist: overcoming the problems of classical philosophical analysis', in M. Mason (ed.), *Complexity Theory and the Philosophy of Education*, Oxford: Wiley-Blackwell, pp. 91–111.

O'Neill, J. (1995) *The Poverty of Postmodernism*, London: Routledge.

Pawson, R., and Tilley, N. (1993) 'OXO, Tie, brand X and new improved evaluation', Paper presented to the British Sociological Association annual conference, University of Essex, cited in A. Clarke and R. Dawson (1999) *Evaluation Research*, London: Sage.

Pearson, K. (1892) *The Grammar of Science*, London: Black.

Pinker, S. (2007) *The Stuff of Thought*, London: Penguin.

Porter, T. M. (1986) *The Rise of Statistical Thinking 1820–1900*, Princeton, NJ: Princeton University Press.

Pratt, D. D., Kelly, M., and Wong, W. S. S. (1998) 'The social construction of Chinese models of teaching', *1998 AERC Proceedings*; http://www.edst.educ.ubc.ca/1998/98pratt.htm (accessed 14 May 2001).

Pratt, D. D., Kelly, M., and Wong, W. S. S. (1999) 'Chinese conceptions of "effective teaching" in Hong Kong: towards culturally sensitive evaluation of teaching', *International Journal of Lifelong Education*, 18(4): 241–58.

Reay, D. (2004) '"It's all becoming a habitus": beyond the habitual use of habitus in educational research', *British Journal of Sociology of Education*, 25(4): 431–44.

Reichenbach, H. (1956) *The Direction of Time*, Berkeley, CA: University of California Press.

Robitaille, D. F., and Garden, R. A. (1989) *The IEA Study of Mathematics II: Contexts and Outcomes of School Mathematics*, Oxford: Pergamon Press.

Rosenberg, M. (1968) *The Logic of Survey Analysis*, New York: Basic Books.

Rossi, P. H., and Freeman, H. E. (1993) *Evaluation: A Systematic Approach*, Beverly Hills, CA: Sage.

Rudduck, R. (1981) *Evaluation: A Consideration of Principles and Methods*, Manchester: University of Manchester Press.

Russell, B. (1913) 'On the notion of a cause', *Proceedings of the Aristotelian Society*, 13: 1–26.

Russell, B. (1948) *Human Knowledge*, New York: Simon & Schuster.

Ryan, A. (1970) *The Philosophy of the Social Sciences*, London: Macmillan.

Sacks, P. (1999) *Standardized Minds*, Cambridge, MA: Perseus Books.

Salili, F. (1996) 'Accepting personal responsibility for learning', in D. A. Watkins and J. B. Biggs (eds), *The Chinese Learner: Cultural, Psychological and Contextual Influences*, Hong Kong: Comparative Education Research Centre; Melbourne: Australian Council for Educational Research, pp. 85–105.

Salili, F., and Hau, K. T. (1994) 'The effect of teachers' feedback on Chinese students' perception of ability: a cultural and situational analysis', *Educationl Studies*, 20(2): 223–36.

Salili, F., Chiu, C., and Lai, S. (2001) 'The influence of culture and context on students' motivational orientation and performance', in F. Salili, C. Y. Chiu and Y. Y. Hong (eds), *Student Motivation: The Culture and Context of Learning*, New York: Kluwer Academic, pp. 221–47.

Salmon, W. C. (1984) *Scientific Explanation and the Causal Structure of the World*, Princeton, NJ: Princeton University Press.

Salmon, W. C. (1993a) 'Probabilistic causality', in E. Sosa and M. Tooley (eds), *Causation*, Oxford: Oxford University Press, pp. 137–54.

Salmon, W. C. (1993b) 'Causality: production and probability', in E. Sosa and M. Tooley (eds), *Causation*, Oxford: Oxford University Press, pp. 154–71.

Salmon, W. C. (1998) *Causality and Explanation*, Oxford: Oxford University Press.

Santayana, G. (1913) *Winds of Change: Studies in Contemporary Opinion*, New York: Charles Scribner's Sons; http://www.archive.org/stream/windsofdoctrine17771gut/17771.txt (accessed 28 October 2008).

Savellos, E. E., and Yalçin, U. D. (1995) 'Introduction', in E. E. Savellos and U. D. Yalçin (eds), *Supervenience: New Essays*, Cambridge: Cambridge University Press, pp. 1–15.

Sawyer, R. K. (2005) *Social Emergence: Society as Complex Systems*, New York: Cambridge University Press.

Sax, L. (2005) *Why Gender Matters: What Parents and Teachers Need to Know about the Emerging Science of Sex Differences*, New York: Doubleday.

Scheines, R. (1997) 'An introduction to causal inference', in V. R. McKim and S. P. Turner (eds), *Causality in Crisis? Statistical Methods and the Search for Causal Knowledge in the Social Sciences*, Notre Dame, IN: University of Notre Dame Press, pp. 185–99.

Schellenberg, E. G. (2004) 'Music lessons enhance IQ', *Psychological Science*, 15(8): 511–14.

Schneider, B., Carnoy, M., Kilpatrick, J., Schmidt, W. H., and Shavelson, R. J. (2007) *Estimating Causal Effects Using Experimental and Observational Designs*, Washington, DC: American Educational Research Association.

Scott, J. (2000) 'Rational choice theory', in G. Browning, A. Halcli and F. Webster (eds), *Understanding Contemporary Society: Theories of the Present*, London: Sage; http://privatewww.essex.ac.uk/~scottj/socscot7.htm (accessed 19 February 2008).

Scriven, M. (1993) 'Defects of the necessary condition analysis of causation', in E. Sosa and M. Tooley (eds), *Causation*, Oxford: Oxford University Press, pp. 33–59.

Sharpe, S. (1976) *Just Like a Girl*, Harmondsworth: Penguin.

Sharpe, S. (1994) *Just Like a Girl: How Girls Learn to Be Women – From the Seventies to the Nineties*, Harmondsworth: Penguin.

Sheldon, T., and Chalmers, I. (1994) 'The UK Cochrane Centre and the NHS Centre for Reviews and Dissemination: respective roles within the Information Systems Strategy of the NHS R&D Programme, coordination and principles underlying collaboration', *Health Economics*, 3(3): 201–3.

Shi, K., Wang, P., Wang W., Zuo, Y., Liu, D., Maehr, M. L., Mu, X., Linnenbrink, L., and Hruda, L. (2001) 'Goals and motivation of Chinese students – testing the Adaptive Learning model', in F. Salili, C. Y. Chiu and Y. Y. Hong (eds), *Student Motivation: The Culture and Context of Learning*, New York: Kluwer Academic, pp. 249–70.

Shilling, C. (2004) 'Physical capital and situated action: a new direction for corporeal sociology', *British Journal of Sociology of Education*, 25(4): 473–87.

Slavin, R. (1986) 'Best-evidence synthesis: an alternative to meta-analysis and traditional reviews', *Educational Researcher*, 15(9): 5–11.

Slavin, R. (2007) *Educational Research in an Age of Accountability*, Boston: Pearson Education.

Smithers, A., and Robinson, P. (2001) *Teachers Leaving*, Centre for Education and Employment Research, University of Liverpool; http://www.teachers.org.uk/resources/pdf/teachers_leaving.pdf (accessed 6 May 2008).

Somers, M. R. (1998) '"We're no angels": realism, rational choice, and reliability in social science', *American Journal of Sociology*, 104(3): 722–84.

Sosa, E., and Tooley, M. (1993) 'Introduction', in E. Sosa and M. Tooley (eds), *Causation*, Oxford: Oxford University Press, pp. 1–32.

South China Morning Post (2008) 'Jail for teapot worshipper', 8 March, p. E2.

Stevenson, H. W., and Lee, S. Y. (1996) 'The academic achievement of Chinese students', in M. H. Bond (ed.), *The Handbook of Chinese Psychology*, Hong Kong: Oxford University Press, pp. 124–42.

Stevenson, H. W., and Stigler, J. W. (1992) *The Learning Gap: Why our Schools Are Failing and What We Can Learn from Japanese and Chinese Education*, New York: Summit Books.

Stevenson, H. W., Lee, S. Y., Chen, C., Stigler, J. W., Hsu, C. C., and Kitamura, S. (1990) *Contexts of Achievement: Studies of Achievement: A Study of American, Chinese and Japanese Children*, Monographs of the Society for Research in Child Development, 55(1–2): 1–123.

Stewart, M. (2001) *The Coevolving Organization*, Oakham, Rutland: Decomplexity Associates; http://www.decomplexity.com/Coevolving%20Organization%20EU.pdf (accessed 27 August 2001).

Stigler, J. W., and Perry, M. (1990) 'Mathematics learning in Japanese, Chinese, and American classrooms', in J. W. Stigler, R. A. Shweder and G. Herdt (eds), *Cultural Psychology*, Cambridge: Cambridge University Press, pp. 329–53.

Suppes, P. (1970) *A Probabilistic Theory of Causality*, Amsterdam: North-Holland.

Suppes, P. (1984) 'Conflicting intuitions about causality', in P. French, T. E. Uehling and H. K. Wettstein (eds), *Midwest Studies in Philosophy*, 9: 405–24.

Tam, O. I., and Morrison, K. R. B. (2005) 'Undergraduate students in part-time employment in China', *Educational Studies*, 31(2): 169–80.

Thomas, W. I. (1928) *The Child in America*, New York: Knopf.

Turner, J. (1991) *The Structure of Sociological Theory*; http://choo.fis.utoronto.ca/FIS/Courses/LIS2149/RatChoice.html (accessed 19 February 2008).

Turner, S. P. (1997) '"Net effects": a short history, in V. R. McKim and S. P. Turner (eds), *Causality in Crisis? Statistical Methods and the Search for Causal Knowledge in the Social Sciences*, Notre Dame, IN: University of Notre Dame Press, pp. 23–45.

Tversky, A., and Kahneman, D. (1980) 'Causal schemas in judgments under uncertainty', in M. Fishbein (ed.), *Progress in Social Psychology*, Hillsdale, NJ: Erlbaum, pp. 49–72.

Tymms, P. B. (1996) 'Theories, models and simulations: school effectiveness at an impasse', in J. Gray, D. Reynolds, C. T. Fitz-Gibbon and D. Jesson (eds), *Merging Traditions: The Future of Research on School Effectiveness and School Improvement*, London: Cassell, pp. 121–35.

Tymms, P. B. (1999) *Baseline Assessment and Monitoring in Primary Schools*, London: David Fulton.

Vanberg, V. J. (2002) 'Rational choice vs. program-based behavior: alternative theoretical approaches and their relevance for the study of institutions', *Rationality and Society*, 14(1): 7–54.

Von Wright, G. H. (1993) 'On the logic and epistemology of the causal relation', in E. Sosa and M. Tooley (eds), *Causation*, Oxford: Oxford University Press, pp. 105–24.

Waldrop, M. M. (1992) *Complexity: The Emerging Science at the Edge of Order and Chaos*, Harmondsworth: Penguin.

Watkins, D. A., and Biggs, J. B. (eds) (2001) *Teaching the Chinese Learner: Psychological and Pedagogical Perspectives*, Hong Kong: Comparative Education Research Centre; Melbourne: Australian Council for Educational Research.

Wedeen, P., Winter, J., and Broadfoot, P. (2002) *Assessment: What's in it for Schools?*, London: RoutledgeFalmer.

Weiman, H. (2004) *Gender Differences in Cognitive Functioning*; http://homepages.luc.edu/~hweiman/GenderDiffs.html (accessed 16 June 2007).

Wickens, P. (1987) *The Nissan Enigma: Flexibility, Quality, Teamwork*. Basingstoke: Macmillan.

Wilkins, L. T. (1969) *Evaluation of Penal Measures*, New York: Random House.

Willis, P. (1977) *Learning to Labour: How Working Class Kids Get Working Class Jobs*, Farnborough: Saxon House.

Wong, N. Y. (1998) 'The gradual and sudden paths of Tibetan and Chan Buddhism: a pedagogical perspective', *Journal of Thought*, 33(2): 9–23.

Wong, N. Y. (2000) *Mathematics Education and Culture: The 'CHC' Learner Phenomenon*; http://www.math.admu.edu.ph/tsg22/wong.html (accessed 12 June 2000).

Wong, N. Y. (2004) 'The CHC learner's phenomenon: its implications for mathematics education', in L. Fan, N. Y. Wong, J. Cai and S. Li (eds), *How Chinese Learn Mathematics: Perspectives from Insiders*, Singapore: World Scientific, pp. 503–34.

Wong, N. Y., and Wong, W. Y. (2002) 'The "Confucian Heritage Culture's" learner's phenomenon', *Asian Psychologist*, 3(1): 78–82.

Woodhall, M. (1997) 'Human capital concepts', in A. H. Halsey, H. Lauder, P. Brown and A. S. Wells (eds), *Education: Culture, Economy, Society*, Oxford: Oxford University Press, pp. 219–23.

Woodward, J. (1997) 'Causal models, probabilities and invariance', in V. R. McKim and S. P. Turner (eds), *Causality in Crisis? Statistical Methods and the Search for Causal Knowledge in the Social Sciences*, Notre Dame, IN: University of Notre Dame Press, pp. 265–315.

Zafirovski, M. (1999) 'Unification of sociological theory by the rational choice model: conceiving the relationship between economics and society', *Sociology*, 33(3): 495–514.

Zhang, S. Y., and Carraquillo, A. L. (1995) 'Chinese parents' influence on academic performance', *New York State Association for Bilingual Education Journal*, 10(summer): 46–53.

Zimbardo, P. (2007) *The Lucifer Effect: How Good People Turn Evil*, London: Rider.

Index

Routledge Education

6th Edition

Research Methods in Education

Louis Cohen, Lawrence Manion and Keith Morrison

'*Research Methods in Education* contains much theoretical material, but this is supported by many practical examples and down-to-earth guidance. It is very clearly written, and demystifies the theory aspects of education research. The 200 pages of supplementary material is particularly practically focused, and is a substantial improvement on the previous edition of the book - if you already have a copy of the 5th edition, I would suggest you consider upgrading ... If you plan to undertake serious educational research in your discipline, Research Methods in Education is an invaluable addition to your bookshelf.'
- *Bioscience Education, The Higher Education Academy*

This fully updated sixth edition of the international bestseller *Research Methods in Education* covers the whole range of methods currently employed by educational research at all stages. It is divided into five main parts: the context of educational research; planning educational research; styles of educational research; strategies for data collection and researching; and data analysis. The book also contains references to a comprehensive dedicated website of accompanying materials.

The sixth edition includes new material on:

• complexity theory, ethics, sampling and sensitive educational research
• experimental research, questionnaire design and administration with practical guidance
• qualitative and quantitative data analysis, with practical examples
• internet based research.

Research Methods in Education is essential reading for the professional researcher and continues to be the standard text for students and lecturers in educational research.

To access the dedicated website of accompanying materials, please visit
www.routledge.com/textbooks/9780415368780

2007: 246x189: 656pp
Hb: 978-0-415-37410-1: **£90.00**
Pb: 978-0-415-36878-0: **£25.99**

www.routledge.com/education